Raven Blair Davis
presents

# Careers from the Kitchen Table

## 3RD EDITION

### NATIONAL HOME BUSINESS DIRECTORY

**BONUS** INCLUDES OVER 8 HOURS WORTH OF DOWNLOADABLE AUDIOS!

INSIDER SECRETS TO STARTING & RUNNING A SUCCESSFUL HOME-BASED BUSINESS, EVEN DURING A RECESSION

*Featuring Interviews With:*

LISA SASEVICH, GEORGE FRASER, MARTIN WALES, LYNN PIERCE, JOHN ASSARAF & STEPHEN PIERCE

PLUS Over 50 Inspiring Business Success Stories!

Careers from the Kitchen Table National Home Business Directory 3rd Edition

This publication is designed to provide accurate and authoritative information in regard to the subject matter covered. It is a compilation of ideas from numerous experts who have each contributed stories and information. As such, the views expressed in each section are of those who were interviewed or submitted information and not necessarily of the author/publisher. It is sold with the understanding that the author/publisher is not engaged in rendering professional services. If legal, accounting, medical, psychological, or any other expert assistance is required, the services of a competent professional person should be sought. Author/Publisher specifically disclaims any liability for the reader's use of any forms or advice provided in this book. It is not warranted as fit for any specific use or purpose, but is intended to give general information that is as current as possible as of the date of publication.

Interior formatting and design: Peggy Knudson
Cover Graphic Design: Darnell Brown

First Printing December 2012

ISBM 978-1-62407-936-8

Library of Congress Cataloguing-in-Publication Data
Blair Davis, Raven

Careers from the Kitchen Table National Home Business Directory 3rd Edition

# Dedication

*WOW* another year has come and gone and with it many changes, adversity's and challenges but without a doubt just enough blessings and opportunities.

I especially want to dedicate this edition to my Mom, Emily Blair. Mom was the catalyst for my making the decision to take control of my life and make it something worthwhile. She passed away this year, and I want to acknowledge that for without her, the radio show and this book would not have been created. Be sure to read my individual story to learn the details on how she played such an important part.

I also want to dedicate this book to those who still believe in their dreams and are determined to create a better lifestyle for them and their family despite setbacks or challenges they face. For the entrepreneurs and business professionals who are choosing to not settle for survival during these difficult economic times but instead are determined to "thrive."

A very special thank you to our incredible featured experts I was blessed to interview on my show that gave up time from their busy schedule to come on *Careers From The Kitchen Table* radio show and share their insider secrets, strategies and formulas for success freely with the listeners. Their selflessness has assisted hundreds of thousands worldwide who have tuned into the show the past three years and to the many contributing authors who helped make this book possible with their amazing stories they shared from their hearts. Thank you so much for being a blessing to us all.

Special heartfelt thanks also to those that have supported me every step of the way which includes my dear friends and mentors Alex Mandossian my #1 mentor, Khaliq Glover, Greg Norman. Regina Baker and my dear friend, my assistant, and program director Peggy Knudson as well as the many sponsors who supported this book and the Careers Show and Amazing Women of Power radio network.

Thank you for all the support, long hours and hard work you contributed to the creation and success of this book. This book could not have been possible without you.

Sincerely,

*Raven*

# ~ Notes ~

# Table of Contents

*Dedication* _____ *1*

*Introduction* _____ *7*

*Careers From the Kitchen Table Mission* _____ *9*

*Raven Grills the Guru's* _____ *13*

    Lisa Sasevich The Queen of Sales Conversion _____ 15

    Stephen Pierce Author, Speaker, Internet Wealth Advocate _____ 25

    Lynn Pierce The Success Architect _____ 39

    John Assaraf Motivational Speaker – Breakthrough Strategist ___ 43

    George Fraser CEO of FraserNet _____ 55

    Martin Wales Marketing Expert and Media Personality _____ 63

*Stories From The Kitchen Table* _____ *75*

    Beverly Basila _____ 76

    Nancy Lee Bentley _____ 80

    Avalaura Beharry _____ 85

    Raven Blair-Davis _____ 89

    Blair Boone _____ 95

    Joe Louis Burroughs _____ 99

    Mable Cannings _____ 102

    Carmen Cook _____ 106

    Lynn Crocker _____ 111

    Adil F. Dalal _____ 115

    Michelle DeBerge _____ 119

    Joseph DiChiara _____ 123

    Lorena Douglas _____ 126

    Victoria Douskos _____ 130

    Linda Doyle _____ 134

    Lorrie Crystal Eigles _____ 137

| | |
|---|---|
| Dr. Anne Marie Evers | 140 |
| Dan Evertsz | 145 |
| Debra Faris | 148 |
| Barclay Fisher | 153 |
| Kim Fuller | 155 |
| Claudette Gadsden-Hrobak | 158 |
| Linda Giles | 163 |
| Kingsley Grant | 167 |
| El Ha Gahn | 171 |
| Cathy Hansell | 175 |
| Carolyn Jones, M.A. | 179 |
| Faye Kitariev | 181 |
| Dr. Dorine Kramer | 185 |
| Gwen Lepard | 189 |
| Debbie Luxton | 193 |
| JoAnn Martin | 197 |
| Louisa Mastromarino | 199 |
| Consuelo Meux, Ph.D. | 203 |
| Michelle M. Miller | 207 |
| Mari Mitchell Porter | 211 |
| Carol Neu | 215 |
| Danise Peña | 217 |
| Ruby Renshaw | 221 |
| Sandhan | 225 |
| Alycia Schlesinger | 229 |
| Linda M. Schulman | 233 |
| Veronica Schultz | 237 |
| Cathy Sexton | 241 |
| Carrie Sharpshair | 245 |

Kimberly Sherry _____ 249

Ng "Khai" Siung _____ 253

Lesley Sive_____ 255

Vanora Spreen & Diane Koz _____ 259

Dona Storey _____ 263

Marilyn Taylor _____ 267

Elise Thompson_____ 271

Dr. Huesan Tran _____ 275

Bonny Valentine _____ 279

Amethyst Wyldfyre _____ 281

*Quick and Easy Recipes for the Busy Entrepreneur* _____ 287

*In The Kitchen with our Special Contributors* _____ 267

Kelly Poelker _____ 268

LyHidy_____ 274

Saskia Jennings_____ 276

Raven Blair Davis _____ 280

*About Raven, aka, The Talk ShowMaven*_____ 320

*Raven's Recommended Resources* _____ 325

*Thanks to the Incredible Team!*_____ 326

*Thanks to our Sponsors* _____ 327

*Raven's Recommended Businesses* _____ 332

~ Notes ~

# Introduction

Are you ready to turn your dream into a reality??????

Well ....congratulations on taking a step to make a difference in your life by starting your own home business. By purchasing *Careers from the Kitchen Table Home Business Directory, 3rd Edition* you've just proven to yourself that you can do exactly what this book was written to help people do, which is to take action on creating the lifestyle you want and more importantly deserve! So, thank you for investing in yourself and taking that first step to becoming a successful home based business owner.

*Say YES to success!*

As you read through the stories from our featured guests, do you see a pattern? We all know starting your own business, whether brick and mortar or run out of the comfort of your home, can be a real challenge.

Our driving force in providing to you the **"Careers From the Kitchen Table Home Business Directory"** each year is to empower, motivate and  encourage you to never give up on your business dream because as the late great Napoleon Hill say's if you can conceive it and believe it you can achieve it.

We hope you find the inspiration to go forward with your dreams while reading all of the AMAZING Stories From The Kitchen Table section and be sure to not only read the excerpts from my interviews with our thought leaders on the cover Lynn Pierce, John Assaraff, Lisa Sasevich, Martin Wales, George Fraser and Stephen Pierce.  Be sure to click the Radio/Microphone icon in the e-book or copy the link in the printed edition to hear the entire interview....they are Incredible and packed with invaluable information tips and strategies.

Now let's get things moving right along so you can start reading and take immediate action. Lots of gold nuggets inside these pages.

~ Notes ~

# Careers From the Kitchen Table Mission

Has and will always be to let people just like you know:

Whatever you do now in your job, or have a passion to do – it can be turned into a profitable and fulfilling business and you can do it without hype and empty promises

There is a ton of information out there to motivate and inspire you, and while we do that too we don't just stop there. Careers from the Kitchen Table offers you the missing link by also telling you what you NEED to be successful and giving you the opportunity to shine just like the big dogs do.

We only put authentic people in front of you who can keep it fresh, have a customer service oriented business and base not only their business, but their lives on ethical choices. This is something that will never change at Careers from the Kitchen Table – not even when the economy has bounced back and is up and running again (and it will be)

We are here to help you WAKE UP and create your own Plan B, instead of hoping, praying and relying on someone else to create it for you. As much as we may not want to think about it, the reality is thousands of people's Plan A, which they were certain, would always be there for them, and has been taken away in this downturned economy.
So, let's get proactive and create a Plan B that can easily be turned into your first choice should it become necessary.

Every business owner faces challenges and hardships and our guests are no different. They come to the show to talk about those challenges, but more importantly how they overcame them to reach the level of success they presently enjoy. They also share their "recipes for success" in the form of tips, ideas, advice, suggestions, and the things that worked for them and helped them become successful with the hope that even just one of our listeners will gain some help or guidance from their story.

Everybody has a story to share and each person's story is different.  Who knows, maybe next year your story will be featured. Love to have you in here in the near future so if you want to discuss the possibility of you sharing your successful business story please email me raven@careersfromthekitchentable.com I look forward to hearing you

The truth of the matter is, owning your own business isn't a free or easy ride full of roses and sunny skies all the time. It takes hard work, determination and dedication among other things, but hopefully with the help of the excerpts of guru interviews and stories included in this book, you'll see that not only is it possible to create the life and business you've always dreamed of, but others have been there before you and are willing to help you along the way and make your journey a little bit easier. The key is not just reading this book – you must TAKE ACTION and APPLY the things you learn to your own business, which is why we've included sections throughout the printed book for notes. Jot down the steps you want to take as you're reading through the interview excerpts and stories.

**My Hope for You**

As I finish this introduction (I know you're in a hurry to get to the good stuff, right?) I want you to know deep in your heart that if anything is meant to be it's up to YOU. Realize that YOU are the architect of your life and you can design it anyway you want. You CAN change your lifestyle and your dreams really CAN become a reality.

Change starts within YOU. You must be the one to decide to make a change in your life and then take the actions necessary to make those changes. Search your soul, your true passion, your purpose and figure out the *'what'* part of the equation. What were you put on this Earth to do? Where does your passion lay? Once you figure out your *'what'*, step away from worrying about the *'how'*. Figure out *'where'* to begin and the how will come on its own.

I'll leave you with this quote to think about before you dig into the interviews, stories, success tips, recipes and recommended resources.

*"An enterprising person is one who comes across a pile of scrap metal and sees the making of a wonderful sculpture. An enterprising person is one who drives through an old decrepit part of town and sees a new housing development. An enterprising person is one who sees opportunity in all areas of life."*

*Jim Rohn, America's Business Philosopher*

*Raven with Jim Rohn*

## ARE YOU READY TO GET STARTED? GREAT! LET'S GET COOKIN!

# MEET OUR GROUP OF INSPIRING MENTORS, MASTERS AND AUTHORS!

 Lisa Sasevich

 Stephen Pierce

 Lynn Pierce

 John Assaraf

 George Fraser

 Martin Wales

 Beverly Basila

 Avalaura Beharry

 Nancy Lee Bentley

 Blaire Boone

 Joe Burroughs

 Mable Cannings

 Carmen Cook

 Lynn Crocker

 Adil Dalal

 Michelle DeBerge

 Joseph DiChiara

 Lorena Douglas

 Victoria Douskos

 Linda Doyle

 Lorrie Crystal Eigles

 Dr. Anne Marie Evers

 Dan Everstz

 Debra Faris

 Barclay Fisher

 Kim Fuller

 Claudette Gadsden-Hrobak

 Linda Giles

 Kingsley Grant

 El Ha Gahn

Cathy
Hansell

Carolyn
Jones

Faye Kitariev

Dr. Dorine
Kramer

Gwen
Lepard

Debbie
Luxton

JoAnn
Martin

Louisa
Mastromarino

Consuelo
Meux

Michelle M
Miller

Marie Mitchell
Porter

Carol Neu

Danise Peña

Ruby
Renshaw

Sandhan

Alycia
Schlesinger

Linda M.
Schulman

Victoria
Schultz

Cathy Sexton

Carrie
Sharpshair

Kimberly
Sherry

Ng Khai
Siung

Lesley Sive

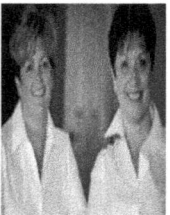
V. Spreen &
D. Koz

Doña Storey

Marilyn
Taylor

Elise
Thompson

Dr. Huesan
Tran

Bonny
Valentine

Amethyst
Wyldfyre

# Raven Grills the Guru's

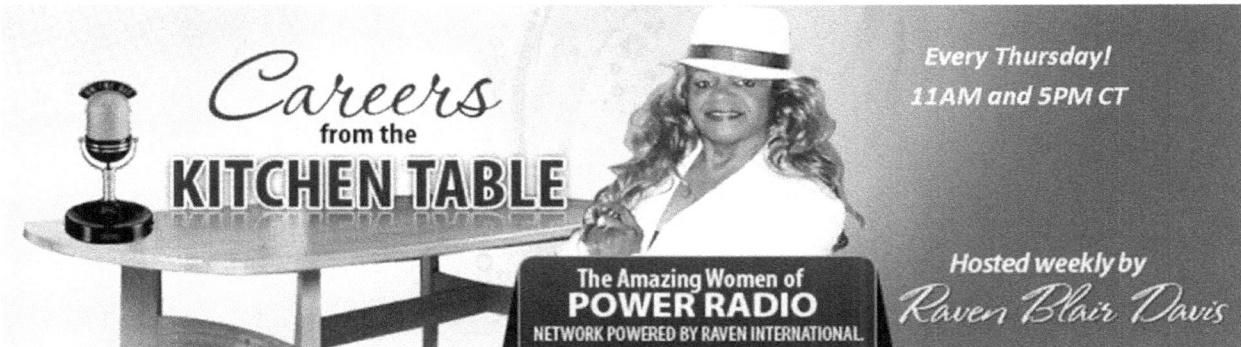

**ENJOY THESE EXCERPTS AND AUDIOS FROM PREVIOUS INTERVIEWS HEARD ON**

**1320 WARL, 1230 KLAV, CNN 650, CBS TALK 650**

**AND AMAZING WOMEN OF POWER NETWORK**

*Be sure to also visit* http://www.careersfromthekitchentable.com/audios *to get over eight hours of downloadable audio interviews!*

# ~ Notes ~

# Lisa Sasevich
# The Queen of Sales Conversion

Welcome to Careers from the kitchen Table. You know us we that show that teaches you how to cook without the cooking. Hi this is Raven Blair Davis, Raven aka, The talk Show Maven. We are so glad that you're back with us and look at that you bought a friend how cool is that. Hey if you missed the first part of the interview you got to go listen to it because we interviewed Keiko and she was all that and then some. Speaking of Keiko, she introduced me to this awesome lady that I am so excited to bring to you. I'm not going to tell her name yet. Now, I am too excited. First let me tell you that according to bestselling author Brian Tracy. Lisa Sasevich is one of the greatest discoveries in America today. Yes you heard her, Lisa Sasevich that is our gal. Robert Allen once went on to say, of course if you don't know Robert Allen, he is the author of multiple New York Times best sellers and he said this lady added a zero to my income. Now can you imagine? He already has a whole bunch of zeros right? Well he added more zeros to this income just by watching Lisa Sasevich. He says to watch that name and whatever you do be part of what she is doing, you are going to love her.

Lisa is known as the Queen of Sales conversion. Recently featured in success magazine and honored as one of America's top women mentoring leaders by WOW magazine. She teaches experts, who are making a difference, on how to get their message out and enjoy massive results without being "salesy". Don't you hate those "salesy" people? After 25 years, of winning top sales awards and training senior executive like Pfizer and Hewlett-Packard, she left corporate America and put her skills to the test as an entrepreneur. In just three short years, she created a multi-million dollar home based business. Get this lady's, with two toddlers in tow and don't say you cannot do it because I know that you can and she knows you can. So, I am so proud to introduce this lady. I going to tell you if you are tired of being the best kept secret in your field today is your chance to transform. If you love what you do but hate the sales part, you are in for a treat. So, if you're standing sit down and if you are sitting stand up. For sure because the undisputed expert on how to make big money doing what you love, the founder of the Invisible Close, Lisa Sasevich, the Queen of sales conversion. How are you doing?

**Lisa:** Raven you made me want to meet myself that was the best introduction I've ever had. Thank you.

**Raven:** Girl I was so thrilled when Keiko said that I have the 'hookup'. I was so glad because I've been on your tele-seminars and people have e-mailed me so many times saying you have to check her out because they know and I think I told you when we spoke, that I come from a

telemarketing sales background. They said as good as you are if you hookup with Lisa you girl are going to be really good. They said you're going to go from good to great.

**Lisa:** Awesome. Well I know you and I have been trying to do this for a long time because I love what you are doing and I had been dying to be on your show. I apologize for any background noise but as you know the only way you and I can match up our crazy schedules is to speak while I'm driving.

**Raven:** I know and I love that you took the time and agreed to do it while you're on the road and you are okay now. I am not going to have to worry about you. You can concentrate and do this right?

**Lisa:** I'm fine, I'm hands-free I got myself a fancy car. That lets me drive and talk at the same time.

**Raven:** All right, here is a disclaimer, don't try this at home.

**Lisa:** Don't try this at home.

**Raven:** You're the founder of The Invisible Close, and what is the Invisible close?

**Lisa:** The Invisible Close is a system, a mindset and all of the above to help those of you who are out there who love what you do but you hate the sales part. So you are looking for ways, to bring people to an on the spot decision without being pushy or "salesy" just like you said. So the invisible close system includes all kinds of ways that you can bring people to that decision in a way that feels great and authentic for both you and them. I have to tell you we must be talking about something powerful because God is raining down on me, with showers from above.

**Raven:** oh no! [laugh]

**Lisa:** Not only do we have driving but we have beautiful showers coming down on top of that. So if you have any trouble hearing me let me know.

**Raven:** Okay if you need to pull over, you let us know.

**Lisa:** Okay I'm feeling really good right now. It is really designed for entrepreneurs who are specifically heart centered entrepreneurs. As you heard me say, this is for people who love what they do and hate the sales part. It will work really for any service professional from lawyers, to healers, to shaman, to branding experts, and to doctors. I find that people who really find that they feel they've found water in the desert is all of those people who are just looking for a solution that feels good and gets the job done when it comes to attracting brand-new clients.

**Raven:** That's what it's all about, attracting new clients because you know a lot of times people think, okay I have these clients and they've been my clients for years they just keep bombarding those same client and you got to get new client. You have to get new ones.

**Lisa:** It's a combination Raven because yes you want to be taking your current clients to higher levels. The invisible close also includes how to make irresistible offers to increase the current business that you are doing with their current client base. We call that 'up sells' and 'cross sells'. So that is part of the equation. But let me tell you a little something and this is something I think most people overlook if you can grasp this one thing for a lot of people this could be the difference between breaking that six or seven figure ceiling that you have been staring at or standing right where you are. What that is...as you have heard, when you introduced me you said and a lot of people refer to me as a Queen of sales conversion. So a common question that I get is what is sales conversion in the first place? That is really an important question. Sales conversion is the number one, it is a ratio, sometimes is referred to as your closing ratio. It is the number of prospects from potential clients that you're talking to and how many of those become paying clients. What happens Raven; people spend a lot of money and attention trying to get new leads. You often hear people I have to get in front of more people, new leads. They don't take the time to gain expertise in how to convert those leads into playing clients. What happens, getting new leads is the most costly piece of your business it is the most time-consuming it takes the most energy and here is the bad news. If you are only getting new leads which are not converting them into paying clients, which was doing is... please don't shoot the messenger on this one... you are doing all the heavy lifting, all the hardest work for the next person in your category that comes along and did study sales conversion. They do know how to make an irresistible offer they do know how to bring someone to an on the spot decision. So let's say you are the feng shui expert of your town. Do you know what feng shui is?

**Raven:** Oh yes I love that. I have never heard anybody put into that scenario before. I like that Lisa.

**Lisa:** If you are feng shui expert for those who do not know it is the art of furniture placement in your home or business to improve energy flow. There are people that specialize in that. If you have been doing that 30 years and you are the expert and you give a great presentation and you convince 30 people that 'oh my goodness I need feng shui', but you do not do the invisible close and you do not make the irresistible offer. they all say thank you very much, they take your card and file it away right.

**Raven:** yes

**Lisa:** Well, you did a great job and this is what leaves you feeling like how come I have so many people that love me but they do not buy from me.

**Raven:** yes oh yes,

**Lisa:** You have had that experience right, we have all had that experience. They say, I love your work and I'm going to call you when? one day. Does that day ever come? No.

**Raven:** No.

**Lisa:** So what happens, the next guy, while you have done feng shui 30 years, this guy has been doing it for six months but he comes out and he makes a presentation. You already did all the hard work because you are the 30 year veteran and you convinced them that they need to but you did not make an offer. He gets out there for 10 minutes makes a mediocre presentation, nowhere near good as your presentation. Guess what, he makes an irresistible offer he knows how to use the invisible close and he ends up getting 60% of the room to converted into new clients and you are sitting wondering why is the new kid getting all the business. I still feel like the best kept secret and I've been doing this five times as long as him. That is the bad news if you do not pay attention to what we're talking about today.

**Raven:** What you laid out is so true, Lisa. I'm so excited about you being on; so many people are shying away from sales. I like to tell them, and I will like to get your thoughts on this, this is the time, if they have never sold they better learn how to if they want to stay ahead and survive during these difficult times.

**Lisa:** This has been obviously for many people the worst economy in the last couple of years, people have lost a lot and for a lot of people it is a really tough time. I have to tell you that the people who are using these practices this can be a time to shine; this can be a time of opportunity. I don't mean opportunity at the cost of someone else. I mean opportunity for you to get out there with your expertise, your blessing, that which you are uniquely designed for packaged it up in a way that it can get out and help people the way that you know you're supposed to help. Really everything I teach is in support of that. Raven my blessing, what I was put here for is really to help experts who are making a difference and get their message out. This is the area in which they tend to get so stuck. It is my blessing and my privilege to be able to give the tools that have people leap over this hurdle which are generally blocked and actually make money doing what they love.

**Raven:** Cha Ching. Cha Ching. Okay Lisa, let's talk about your background. How you became an expert in this area and then after that I would like to move in and talk about your irresistible offer because I know you have some things going on soon that we want to share with the listeners.

**Lisa:** Sure a couple of things. Number one, just to let you know where I came from to help those who are listening to see what we're talking about is something that you can use. Number two I would love to teach a couple of points if we have time about how your listeners can use the irresistible offer and start increasing their sales conversion today.

**Raven:** Starting today, wow!

**Lisa:** Yes this does not take a lot of time. It does not take a lot of money. It is so that you understand it, you get it and you implement it. Third of course I cannot hang up without making an irresistible offer so I have something for you to get people started today.

**Raven:** Fantastic

**Lisa:** So first off, my background briefly is I started in corporate. I was doing the double life and I know some of you are doing the double life and that is the one where you're making money from 9 to 5 doing something that you are so thrilled about and then on the nights and weekends you are doing the things that make the difference. You are raising funds, you are doing your blessings, you are helping people out or you are doing personal development. I was doing that. I was doing nights and weekends with what I love and trying to make money 9 to 5. Somewhere in my late 20s, I decided that I have to bridge these worlds. I want to be doing what I love and what I was made for all the time. Interestingly when I left corporate, I started with the company that was teaching women. Now you have to listen closely Raven.

**Raven:** Okay teaching women how to understand and appreciate men. So I was going out around the country leading seminars teaching women how to understand and appreciate men, to create partnership with the man in their life so that they can stay powerful and allow the men around them to stay powerful at the same time. So that was a big feat that was a big task. I got to talk to a lot of women all over the country. I wanted to share this because somebody who is listening may say, sure Lisa of course you, you may not know this but I took a million-dollar leap in the last three years. That's what I saying, the economy may be bad but if you use these techniques. I have hundreds and thousands of entrepreneurs who are using these techniques to sell and a "non-salesy" way to break the 6 to 7 figure mark even in this down economy. So this can be your time to shine. This can be your opportunity for all of you. The reason I want to tell you that is because there are some of you sitting there saying, You make money by helping because you are helping people make money. But I don't help people make money I am a veterinarian, I am a healer, I am a nutritionist. This is what I want to tell you, everything I've developed, I developed teaching women how to understand men. I developed it with, what we call in the industry, a soft offer. It's about health, nutrition, family, or communication. It is not about 'you giving me a dollar in our show you how to make 10'. So while my techniques work very well for what I do, I want all of you out there who are different practitioners who are not showing people how to make buck, you are helping them in other areas of your life. For people in your field it definitely can become the holy Grail when it comes to making money doing what you love. Making money doing what you love. There is no better feeling like that.

**Raven:** I used to not understand when people said you will know that you love what you're doing when you can't wait to jump out of your bed and do it. I really enjoyed that but then after a while Lisa it kind of died down to be honest with you. I am a keep it real person, I was not making the money that I wanted to make. When I started being more aggressive in a soft way, like you say and using what I knew for years such as getting on the phone and stop waiting for people coming to me. I learned the skills then that's when I say I'm definitely living my life and thanking God every day because there is nothing better, there really isn't. So someone plugging into you is just going to elevate their business and if you don't like the phone learn to like it.

**Lisa:** Let me tell you something we teach on how to close sales from the stage, how to get behind a telephone and how to close sales from tele-seminars. We get thousands of people on a tele-seminar.

**Raven:** oh good, so you mix it up so it's not just on the phone.

**Lisa:** We teach you how to do a one-on-one on the phone. How to use webinars, all in the different scenarios that you may be in. So, I want to give you some action points to your listeners. So that they can implement these things right away. Before I do, just in case there's somebody who's running short on time if anybody wants to start out and get a huge take on some things you can implement right away. I created something called a simple quick and easy ways to boost sales without spending a dime. Any of you listening today can pick that up as my gift at http://www.freesaletrainingfromLisa.com. FreesalestrainingfromLisa.com and I want to put that out because I know that once she get your hands on what I'm teaching you will see how easy it is but you're going to get hooked on converting sales. You're going to commit all of you listening to converting a higher percentage of people you're talking to into happy paying clients. Instead of always chasing to talk to more people but not converting them.

**Raven:** FreesalestrainingfromLisa.com

**Lisa:** FreesalestrainingfromLisa.com

**Raven:** Okay, thank you Lisa.

**Lisa:** Go there and grab the report. It's just a sample of something that you could get started with right away in that training one of the things we are going to show you in there, is how to use the irresistible offers.  The irresistible offers are what causes people to say yes on the spot and I want to give you guys a couple mistakes that I see people make so that you can avoid them and you can get started using your irresistible offers to get on the spot sales today. One of the biggest mistakes that I see Raven, is when people are not making an offer at all.  Just giving the value, which is a great thing to do but like the example that I showed you earlier if you don't make that offer you are setting up the next person your competitor to come in and you did all the hard work and they get the business. So the number one mistake of want you to go avoid I need make an offer.

**Raven:**  Make that offer.

**Lisa:**  You must have the hunger for what you have and then once they do you want them to make their move today. The other thing that I want to share with you is that when people first get started making an offer the other big mistake that they make is not putting a limiter on it. So I want everybody to write down two types of limiters.  It is very simple.  Time and quantity. Time would mean, for example hey I have a special deal and if you do coaching with me today you get five hours and you get a six hour free.  Another example, you get two massages and get a third one free.  Limited time means that's good for today only or that's good until Friday.  So what's limiting, to get people moving is the time. For example it's only good now after I step off the stage today. The quantity is how many.  You've heard it on the infamous infomercials the first X number of people, the first 17 people who call.  You even could be a physician or a doctor. You know the doctor could have a little extra time in his schedule this week, we have 8 appointments left, the people who call are going to get a free health analysis on top of the XYZ that they are coming for.  So if you add on a bonus and you limit the quantity of people can take advantage of it. Make sense?

**Raven:**  It definitely makes sense. Ok I knew about the time but I wasn't quite sure on how to transition in limiting the amount of people.  I know generally, when I put this one word into my offer and I say I'm looking for 'action takers'.  This is an action taker special price for you today only offer.  So how do you transition into the number of people?

**Lisa:**  Well it could be for example if you taking people, some people put them into small-group program or one-on-one situation.  The truth is you only have a limited amount of space.  I remember when I was looking for a life coach she only took 12 people a month and she already had nine people. She told me I got calls all day today and all day tomorrow to establish who my clients are going to be for the next six months. So I thought wow, she has all these calls today and all day tomorrow and three spots. This girl is good. So she said, you know I have three spots left and I also have this fast action scholarship, like you mentioned, access for you if you want to for today. So there is a posture that you need to take with this. Which I call, committed but not attached.

**Raven:** Committed but not attached.

**Lisa:** What that means is that you are committed that they make a decision. You know that serves them but you are not attached to what that decision is, yes or no. It doesn't matter as long as they make a decision. You know that you served them. The worst thing you can do is to make someone keep thinking about it. That is cluttering up there brain and cluttering up there life. So when you're on a call Raven and you're letting them know that you have a fast action takers pricing or however you structure it. You have to let people know. Look this is for you if you're ready, it's totally fine if you're not ready you can call back any time and it's totally worth it at the full investment. Right.

**Raven:** Yes right.

**Lisa:** Right so there's no pressure here. This is for you if you're ready and the words you want to use it, if you need time no problem is totally worth it at the full investment.

**Raven:** That is the soft way you are talking about. This way they do not feel, you are pushing them.

**Lisa:** You need to believe it; you need to stick to it. The words to use the way to lay it out so that you are creating tension but not pressure. Tension rises within someone; you need that for someone to buy for them to say yes. Pressure is the thing we want to avoid. We do not want to be pushing from the outside you said earlier you like to let people come to use you want to be pursued versus being a pursuer. So we can get everybody started doing that again at http://www.FreesalestrainingfromLisa.com. You're going to get a six day training series from me that every day is coming to give you something to try and I want everyone listening to be able to write me, e-mail us at lisaattheinvisibleclose.com and say wow I can't even believe if that was your free work, I can't even believe what must be in your paid course. You know Raven that we have a live event coming up in San Diego. I don't know how many listeners are in California we have people that come from all over the world but were getting together for three days in October and it is called impact and influence. We take all of this further, up sales, cross sales, one-on-one and how to get on the phone and close the high ticket sale. It's for someone that wants to come out and dive in deep. I just want to put it out there you can always check that out impactandinfluenceintensive.com. It's right around the corner, just coming right up in San Diego right by the airport on the water.

**Raven:** It's going to be nice. I am definitely going to be there, that is my intent. I want to give you a big hug and I want to be there and get that information.

**Lisa:** I love that, and the messengers are gathering Raven.

**Raven:** I want to be like Robin Allen get more zeros.

**Lisa:** That's right, in this world you never know. People have sat in my events right next to Robert Allen, Brian Tracy, John Assaraff, you name it. The Biggy's are using this work these days because it works its respectful and it is authentic. That is the combination that you know if you are heart centered entrepreneur this is what you looking for.

**Raven:** I am excited. You spend so much time with us and I want to give you the platform to share your final thoughts before we let you go. I have to bring you back when you have more time for sure.

**Lisa:** You got it. My thoughts for all of you are to be the client you want to attract. So if you are out there and people are telling you 'I love what you do let me think about it'. I want you to look into the mirror like Michael Jackson says right. That man in the mirror. Are you doing that? Oh my goodness, I need to get to the course but I need to think about it. I f you have people refunding you in your business, and you wonder why that has happened I want you to look into the mirror and check if you have refunded other people. I want you to be the client you want to attract. So if you want to attract clients that take immediate action and invest in themselves then my friend you have to start with yourself. You cannot expect, someone else to invest in themselves through you at a level greater than you invested in yourself.

**Raven:** Oh my goodness that was so strong. I hear mirrors cracking all around.

**Lisa:** It's my truth Raven and it has been the truth for me in my own business and I just hope that it got in to a couple of your wonderful angels that are listening.

**Raven:** Well it goes back to the old golden rule, whatever goes around comes around so if you're out there canceling and buying stuff and canceling for no authentic reason. Hey, you are going to get what you give.

**Lisa:** "Reap what you sow" It's been an honor. Thank you for all of you out there. If my work can get your work out a little further then I will sleep good tonight.

**Raven:** Hey, you know what everyone? If you did not write it down then right it down now. You want to go to FreesalestrainingfromLisa.com. We have been speaking with none other than the world renowned Queen of sales conversion herself. I'm talking about Lisa Sasevich. The founder of the invisible close.

**Raven:** Absolutely, isn't she all that, a bag of chips and then some? Thank you Keiko, for the hookup and thank you all for tuning in and you know what next week will be back with more from Careers From the Kitchen Table. Until then make sure you check out Lisa, I kid you not this is a really difficult time, were not claiming that but we are not burying our heads in the sand. You have to keep investing in yourself but you have to invest in the right things. It's all about to creating that sales conversion. It's all about knowing what to do and the right things to say in a soft-way.  Standing their ground without lowering prices, right Lisa. You got it. I could not have said it better my friend.

Listen to the full audio of this interview by clicking the Radio/Microphone!

Plus be sure to visit and subscribe to Raven's popular newsletter and freebie!
http://www.careersfromthekitchentable.com

~ Notes ~

# Stephen Pierce
# Author, Speaker, Internet Wealth Advocate

I have a fantastic guest for you tonight. I really do. His name? Stephen Pierce. Yes, the Stephen Pierce is here.

For many years, Stephen's name has been synonymous with success. Recognized as one of the world's leading internet marketers and business optimization strategists, Stephen wears several hats when it comes to his business, yes, he does. Not only is he the CEO of Stephen Pierce International, Inc., and is the mastermind behind DTA Alpha, he is a coach facilitator, and a certified, accelerated innovation trainer. He is also considered one of today's top authorities of creating rapid wealth using the internet, which we'll be talking about today. Stephen says, "Creating wealth is not just in what you do, it's in how you do it," and we're going to talk to him about that.

Now, whether Stephen is one-on-one coaching or speaking to a room of hundreds, he knows his stuff and he's serious about it. He wants to help the every-day person get out of the rut, whether he's coaching for a motor company or training the first-time internet entrepreneur, he's going to give it all he's got either way. Stephen is instinctively capable of devoting his efforts to design an optimized plan that will chart a path to success, and that's important, that's what you want to focus on, because so many of us, we just start a business and we have no road map to where we're going. And if we don't have a road map, we're going to continue going in circles and circles and circles, isn't that right, Stephen?

**Stephen:** Absolutely.

**Raven:** Welcome to the show, my friend, how are you?

**Stephen:** I'm doing extraordinary; it's good to be here. Thank you for the opportunity to come and join you and your audience.

**Raven:** Well, thank you. You know what, Stephen? I have to go back to what your quote was, you said, "Creating wealth is not just in what you do, it's on how you do it." Let's talk about that a little bit, share your thoughts on that.

**Stephen:** Well, it's about not just doing the right things, but it's about doing the right things the right way. And sometimes you can get caught up in doing the right things, but if you're not necessarily doing them the right way and you leave out something, like for example, if you're in the kitchen and you're baking a cake and you put the flour or the eggs, the sugar, or the vanilla,

whatever it is, everything in there but you leave out the baking soda, you know what? You're going to have a problem.

**Raven:** Yes, you are.

**Stephen:** We can get creative and maybe call it a big cookie or something but, you know, we know the desired outcome of it being a cake is not what you got and it wasn't because you weren't passionate, it wasn't because, you know, you weren't serious, it wasn't because you had bad intentions, you left something out. So, you know, you did the right things but you were doing them the wrong way.

So what we have to do, it kind of goes along the lines of, you know, people always ask you what do you think instead of asking you how do you think? And what you think is constantly rotating in how we think the different structures that navigate our thinking. So, I think it's important that we don't just focus on what it is we're doing, but we also focus it on how it is we're doing it, because that's going to unlock an unbelievable amount of success.

**Raven:** You are so right. You know what I liked about you? When I first heard the name Stephen Pierce, you had a very, very interesting story. I know you've had all this success and everything, but you really have true rags to riches story, Stephen, that's incredible. Would you share just a portion of your story with our listeners?

**Stephen:** Sure. You know, everybody, you know, in their life, they have the story of their life, they have that back story and those struggles and their trials and their tribulations. And many times we tend to think that it's only happening to us and that's not necessarily true. Everybody has that path that they traveled down and, you know, where they're tested and they either want to become weakened by the situation or they're going to be strengthened by the situation. And myself, you know, I didn't come from a broken home, my mom and dad were still together, and if anything, people probably said I broke the home.

But, you know, I was young, I didn't have a sense of my own identity at the time, I had a weak personality and I had a low self-esteem and I would just follow the person who seemed to have the strongest personality and the strongest self-esteem. And ultimately became a menace while I was in school, I got kicked out, left with a 10th grade education and running the streets. I ended up running around with the wrong people and I ended up in Greensboro, North Carolina, where I ended up getting shot. And I still remember that time. And I was in the Moses H. Cone Hospital and, you know, I had all these thoughts racing through my head.

But the interesting thing was that I blamed the entire world, it wasn't my fault, it was, "Look at what they've done to me." In other words, I was playing the victim, I gave all my power over to everybody else and I didn't want to take ownership of my life, and take responsibility for what it was I was doing. And it was like all these things were happening to me.

But then I had to mature, and that's important, before we reach mastery we have to reach maturity. So I had to reach the point of maturity and say, "You know what?

This is, you know, my fault, and I'm here, you know, not as a victim of my circumstances, but a creator of my circumstances, by the virtue of the choices that I made." But the other side to that was, you know, just as I created a series of bad choices that put me there, I can reverse that and create a series of better choices, good choices, higher choices, and put myself into a better place. And that's what I did.

And I learned an incredible lesson. I learnt that just because you decide in a moment to change your life and do something right or to walk the straight and narrow, doesn't mean in an instant everything materially, as far as what you see visually, is going to change.

So one of my biggest lessons was, you know, success happens gradually, then suddenly. You know? And that success happens over time, not overnight, like we would like for it to be. And where I learnt that is that when I decided to turn my life around and walk the straight and narrow was reading my Bible like crazy and I started reading all these books to renew my mind, it was at that point that I ended up filing bankruptcy and I ended up being homeless. You know, so it got worse before it got better.

But I didn't give up on that. I kept pressing forward and, you know, eventually I got introduced to the internet and using somebody else's computer and somebody else's internet connection, my first year on the internet I did over $500,000 in business and at that point in time, after I put my head back on after it was blown off by the results, I, you know, started to go full forward on this thing and not just create wealth for yourself, but travel around the world and share what's possible for other people.

**Raven:** Yeah, you have an amazing story, thank you for sharing it. And one thing that stood out in sharing your story with us is the fact that you, you know, you're being so authentic about this and so open and you're basically telling the listeners that just because you wanted to change right then, you're going to have to walk through the process, you're going to have to go through the journey, you're going to have to go through more challenges possibly, and more bumps in the road, but don't give up. I know you've heard, *Until Committed* poem to Goethe. How, when you stay committed, miraculously all kind of things start to happen, you don't even have to figure out how you're going to do it, just doors start opening and things start coming in your direction.

**Stephen:** Absolutely. And I believe that all of us are committed. The question is, what are you committed to?

**Raven:** Right.

**Stephen:** Are you just committed to doing and following through or you're committed to not doing it and following through, but either way, we're committed. You know, so we just need to check our commitments every single day to make sure that we're not committed to constantly being comfortable, but we're committed to being great. And regardless of what it is you're looking to achieve, you know, if you want to go in the gym and you want to get buffed and you want to get into shape, you can't just think about it, buy a bunch of magazines and books and supplements and a diet plan. You have to get into the gym, which means lifting weights, you're going to sweat, it's going to be a little bit painful, but you want to get stronger, you're going to grow, and you're going to reach the objective.

**Raven:** Got to work.

**Stephen:** But it doesn't just happen being passive thinking about it, you have to be proactive and go out there and get it.

**Raven:** You are so right. I've often heard people say, especially when you first start your business, you have to work it like you're working a job.

**Stephen:** Well, yeah, because there's this curve that I think all of us are on and it starts with probably when we just initially think about it, it's what I call, "less sweat, less equity," because we're not necessarily doing much, so we're not making much. And then we kind of go through this curve where there's more sweat, less equity, you start to do it, but you seem to be working harder, but not necessarily making the kind of money that you were expecting or getting the kind of results that you were expecting. And this is the point where most people bail out. It's like, "Gosh, I'm putting in all this work, but I'm not necessarily getting the results." So despite the evidence that they're making progress, they tend to bail out. But for those that hang in there, and instead of getting depressed and bailing out, they remain determined and persistent and they just make the modifications to keep moving forward, they've reached the point where there's more sweat and more equity, which means they're still kind of working hard, but now they're making more money or getting more of the results that they wanted.

And now they get to this point where they have this momentum and then they swing up to the point that we all want to be at, which is less sweat and more equity. And it's at that point where you're not working nearly as hard, but you're making tremendous amounts of money.

**Raven:** I love that, tremendous amounts! Sounds good to me, Stephen.

Well, let's jump into the questions that the listeners have sent in. What do you contribute your success to?

**Stephen:** Well, there are probably a lot of factors, kind of like a chef making a dish. You know, you have all these different spices and recipes, and the recipe, and it just comes out to be this one great dish. But if I were to narrow it down to some very specific things, I would say that it's, you know, being focused, being consistent, and being patient. And focus, I think, has three different dimensions to it. It's what to focus on, when to focus, and where to focus. Because many of us, we can know what to focus on, but sometimes we put ourselves into an environment where while we know what to focus on, it becomes hard to focus because of, you know, all the distractions in the environment. So, I mean, you break a man's focus, you pretty much break his life.

So we have to know, you know, what to focus on, when to focus, and where to focus and we have to be consistent at what it is we're doing because through consistency, we get the power of cumulative effects. It's not what we do one time or sporadically or erratically or when we feel like it, because certainly success or building anything extraordinary is not about the feeling, it's about the commitment.

And you have to be consistent with that commitment and it's something that we renew every day; we don't make the commitment on January 1st at one point in time when we're excited, it's a commitment that we renew every single day by choice, not by feeling.

**Raven:** Right.

**Stephen:** But by choice. And then we have to be patient. And I think that's one of the keys to the process, being patient to allow the process to work its thing. Just like when a woman gets pregnant, it's a nine-month process. Regardless of how advanced our society has become, its still nine months. It's not like an instant baby, you know? Even if you put popcorn in the microwave, you have like 30 seconds or so when the bag is spinning is around and nothing's popping. So while you may get it out in three, three-and-a-half minutes, there's still the process. Plant a garden, it's a process.

So what we have to do is we have to have an understanding of what the process looks like and the area that we want to succeed and be patient so that the investment that it is we're making, we can look to get that return on it.

So I think at the heart of it, those intangibles are the things that have contributed a lot to my success, being focused, consistent, and patient.

**Raven:** Focused, consistent, and patient. And you talked about a commitment again and I guess another thing that comes to mind, listening to you talk, Stephen, is the word passion, meaning you have to truly be passionate about what you're doing and the word persistent. How do you feel about those two words?

**Stephen:** Well, passion is that fuel. It's kind of like if you have an expensive automobile but there's no gas in the tank, it's not going to do much for you, you're going to look good, it's going to be a sexy looking car there, but it's just not going to move. And passion is that fuel in all of our tanks, so regardless of the vehicle you pick, regardless of your business, regardless of what it is you want to accomplish in life, if the passion isn't there, then you're not going to have that fuel that carries you every single day.  And I think that how we generate that passion is not because somebody gives it to us, because you heard some motivational speaker or you read some book, it's when we really connect with our life purpose, our mission, our meaning in life,

why we're here, what it is we're here to contribute,  the impact that we're looking to have on other people and ourselves, the value that we want to contribute to people and what that's going to ultimately mean, and we connect with that on an ongoing basis.  Many of us, we get so trapped and lost in the past with all these different regrets of the past, or we get lost and trapped with all these worries in the future or maybe we're in the present but we're overwhelmed with all the different things that we're supposed to be doing, that we're too busy and distracted mentally to even live our life or even to be passionate about something.

So it's a continuous process of paralysis where nothing is being done and frustration seems to be multiplying.  So what we have to do is we have to understand that we can't change the past, so we have to kind of let that be and we can't control the future.  We can influence it, but we can't control it, and how we influence the future is what we decide to do here and now.  So it's not about the regrets of the past, it's not about, you know, the worries of the future; it's about what we choose to do and be in this moment.

And I think when we choose something, it's not as much as much about what we're going to do, as it is a reflection of who we are and who we believe we can become.  And when we get in touch with that meaning in life, we have that passion and we're no longer living based on the ideas or egos of other people, it's about what we want to become, it's about what we feel as if we're here to do.  And at that point in time, nothing stands in our way.  So persistence becomes automatic.

**Raven:**  Oh, okay.  But it goes to how bad do you want it?

**Stephen:**  Yeah, because here's the thing.  Neither you, myself, or anybody else in this world, you can pick the person that may be your mentor up close or from a distance, it can be the Oprah Winfrey's of the world, the Will Smiths of the world, the Donald Trump's, the Bill Gate's, the Steve Jobs, or the Steve Pierce—it can be whomever it is.  None of us are more deserving of success than the next person.  And anybody that's listening to this or that's not listening to this; you're no more deserving of success than we are.

But the kicker is, is that life doesn't give us what we deserve, life gives us what we go claim.  And claiming is a proactive, daily process.  So we can't sit back and be passively thinking about and wishing about what it is we want.  We have to be out there proactively going to claim it and not deceive ourselves and con ourselves with this preparation process that kind of turns into procrastination.  What we have to do is we have to take action because it's not as much about, you know, knowing everything before we start, it's really about starting with what it is we already know, because action is our biggest teacher.  Nobody, no book, no video, no seminar, no coach, no mentor, nothing is going to teach you more than action itself. And you'll be surprised how much you begin to know when you start to take action.

**Raven:** That is huge what you said. I mean, it sounds like a small thing, but is huge, it's truly a big thing because so many people got wrapped up into *The Secret*, me included, and we get

wrapped up into the books and tapes and stuff, as you said, but the whole thing about it is, as you said, you have got to get past the procrastination and you have got to get in there, and I call it, Stephen, do the thing that has the power, because if you're not in the trenches and you're working hard and you're going at it full force, it's not going to happen.

**Stephen:** Right.

**Raven:** So you're so right. Why do you feel so many of us procrastinate? Is it the fear of success? Fear of failure? Fear of both?

**Stephen:** Well, it's the fear, I believe, of losing. I think people probably fear losing or failing more than they fear success itself. But the interesting thing is that, I think we're all born losers, and I don't say that as a negative, I say that as a positive. And everybody needs to listen closely. Either you lose the fear to live your life or you lose the freedom because of the fear. Either way, you're going to lose something. So choose what it is you want to lose.

And this whole thing about fearing the risk, there's always something at risk. Always. Every single time, there's no such thing as, oh, well, you don't want to take the risk, because the moment you don't take the risk to do something, to make your life better, to be able to contribute at a higher level or to pursue something that's going to make a better contribution to this world and to your family or improve the quality of life for you or your family, whatever, the moment you don't take that risk, then you risk not living the life that you ultimately want to live.

There's really no neutral ground. There's really no straddling the fence with all of this, so what we have to do is choose and pick our risks wisely and choose what it is we're going to lose. If we don't choose to lose the fear, then by default, we're going to lose the freedom to live our lives.

**Raven:** My goodness. There's some good stuff, Stephen. We're going to be talking today about assisting those people that truly want to get a business going, I mean, you know, this is the recession time, people are more open into trying to make some extra money.

**Stephen:** Right.

**Raven:** And I know you've got a lot of things that you want to share with them as far as starting the internet business. I know you talked many times and you have said, you know, you don't necessarily have to have a website to get going and you kind of shared a little bit of that in your story. Tell us more about that.

**Stephen:** Right. When it comes to making money on the internet or when it comes to making money with anything, the power of making the money is in the ability to market the products, and that ability is all about skill, and let's get one thing really clear. This whole thing about success, regardless of the level or the extent that you're thinking about achieving it, but let's just focus financially for now. Regardless of whatever that number is, it's not about talent, it's not about gifts, or this person has a special talent or this person has a special gift. Let me tell you something, every single person that achieves any level of financial success with their own two hands or assembling the right team, it comes down to two specific things, attitude and skills. And attitude is something that we all can control and practice every single day and skill is something that we can develop.

So it's not about, oh, they're more gifted than you. No, maybe they deliberately practice and drill and build their skills more than you. So if we know that we can control our attitude and we know that we can identify the skills that we currently have or the skills that are required to do something that we can build those skills, then there's no more excuse. It doesn't become what your potential or what your capabilities are, or your capacity is, it comes down to what are you willing to do to actually make it happen?

So I just want to make sure that we get that clear. And I think if you understand that this whole game is really about being resourceful, more so than it is what resources you have available to you. And by that, what I mean is, your success in going forward is not really dependent on, oh, you know, you don't have enough money or you don't have time. You have what it is you have and all we have is what we have and that's where we start.

So what we have to do is stop waiting for more resources to come in, if this happens or if that happens, and start being resourceful with what it is we have. For example, without a website, you can take stuff around your house that you're not even using any more and put it on eBay and sell it. And at that instant, you're on the internet and you're selling products and you're bringing in money. Some people do that just to bring in extra cash and then they end up turning it into a whole business. You can get rid of your junk on eBay, then you can go get rid of some of your family's junk, and then some of your friend's junk, and then you can just start going to yard sales and garage sales, and flea markets, buying up all this other stuff dirt cheap and then selling it on the internet.

Now, why does this work though, regardless of the economy? Because everybody's going to always be spending their money, regardless. Whether our economy is in a recession, a depression, or it's experiencing a growth period, people will continue to spend their money because the moment people stop spending their money collectively around this entire world, the entire world will become bankrupt. They may be more selective, but they want to go ahead and continue to spend their money. And with the internet and with the technology, we're no longer restricted and limited to, you know, local area codes or zip codes, or geography. We're now more so than like a US economy, it's an internet economy, because it allows us to tap into Australia, Asia, Canada, the UK, all these places around the world. So now your market becomes global in an instant. The moment you connect your computer to the internet and you start selling stuff, the entire world of the relevant people that will buy that, become your market. So without a website, you can put stuff on eBay as a starter, everybody has junk around their house that they're not using, my wife took 14 pairs of tennis shoes that I had that I wasn't wearing, they were a bunch of Nikes. Some were in better condition than the other, and sold every single pair on eBay.

**Raven:** Wow!

**Stephen:** And she took old video games, I mean, video games that you would think nobody would want because they're nowhere near the newest games for the newest consoles, but she sold all of those on eBay. I mean, I could run down an entire list of the crazy things that, you know, we have sold or that we've seen people sell on eBay. So with that, there's no excuse. Get rid of the stuff that you have in your house and in your garage that you're not using, lose the attachment, put it on eBay, and you will instantly start bringing in some money. Go to your family and friends; get their junk that they're not using. Maybe you cut a deal with them, and say, "Listen, whatever it is I sell, I'll give you 10 or 20% of that," now you got a deal, then from that, take a little bit of that money, go to pawn shops, go to antique stores, go to, like I was saying, garage sales and yard sales and flea markets, all these places where you can get stuff for pennies on the dollar and then put those things on eBay and before you know it, without a website of your own, you're starting to pull in money.

**Raven:** Absolutely. Wow, you gave the listeners some fantastic ideas. I actually knew a friend, she sold some books that she had around the house, Stephen, and she also made about $4-500 a week for a while doing that. On eBay!

**Stephen:** That's great. See, anybody can do it.

**Raven:** I know at the beginning, there had to be many challenges. What are some of the biggest challenges you faced and that you feel a lot of the listeners may face and what's the best way to get through them?

**Stephen:** Well, there's a disadvantage and there's an advantage. The disadvantage that I had was there no mentors, there were no models out there that I could follow at that time, so I was really learning through trial and error and feeling my way through.

So I think one of the biggest hurdles that I had, is that I had no freaking idea what to do. It's just that I knew I wanted to do this, but I wasn't going to let my ignorance of the process be an excuse for me not doing anything.

**Raven:** Right.

**Stephen:** So I was feeling my way through and just stumbled my way through and I matured and I grew and I figured a whole bunch of things out along the way.

Now, you know, everybody that's listening to this, hey, they can take that route if they want to, not suggest it, or they can follow models and blueprints that are already working and shortcut the process, eliminate a lot of the pain, the heartache, and the waste of time and costly mistakes that, you know, myself an other people have made and go right to the winning ideas and strategies and tactics and tools that are being used right now to help people make money on the internet. So don't allow yourself to go through unnecessary struggle, because there's now people like myself out here that strongly advocate using the internet to build wealth, which can give you blueprints to make a much faster and more painless process for yourself, if there's any pain at all. Because the not knowing can be, you know, painful. If you have people that work hard, and you can talk to them all day, they're not necessarily producing the results, but they're working hard, they're tired, it's like they're trying, they're trying, they're trying. What I'd like to say, have you ever seen somebody dribbling a basketball really fast that doesn't know how to dribble? I mean, if you see them, they are trying really hard, and it is pathetic and hilarious at the same time.

**Raven:** All over the place.

**Stephen:** All over the place, you know what I mean? And the reason it looks so bad is because they're trying to do something fast that they haven't learned how to do slow well. So they haven't built the skills but they want to build speed. So it's one thing to be effective, it's another thing to be efficient. If you want to be both, learn how to do it right and then pick up the speed. I say, you know, it's better to work smart first and then work hard and the reason why is, who wants to work hard doing a bunch of dumb stuff?

**Raven:** Really.

**Stephen:** Right? So understand how to execute it, and then, once you know how to do it, then you can pick up the pace. Then you can pick up the speed. But to work hard doing stuff the wrong way is just idiotic to me.

**Raven:** It is. And you know what happens? You end up getting frustrated, throwing your hands up, and saying, "The heck with it."

**Stephen:** Right. You know, just relax, slow down, take your time and learn how to do it right because many people, they miss opportunities, not because the opportunity didn't work, but because again, remember we talked about focus, consistency, and patience? They didn't have the patience to learn how to do it correctly and then execute it correctly and allow it to work.

**Raven:** Just to remind everyone, you're listening to 1320 WARL Am Radio, and we are talking to Stephen Pierce. Stephen, go ahead and give out your website for those people that want to pull it up and be browsing it while they're listening to the show right now.

**Stephen:** You can go over to MakeRealMoneyOnTheInternet.com. That's http://www.MakeRealMoneyOnTheInternet.com. In fact, if you go over there, you can get a copy of my 133-page book called *Make Real Money On The Internet*, and instead of paying the $19.95 book price, I will give it to you for free, all you have to do is pay shipping, which is under 5 bucks, and I'll just get the book sent out there to you. And literally, if you go through those 133 pages, you will know precisely what to do to start making money on the internet before you even finish reading the book.

**Raven:** How cool is that? How can someone get started with minimum investment and minimum risk, because people are holding on to what they got, Stephen, they're like, "Oh, no, I can't start an internet business!"

**Stephen:** And that's interesting, we talked a little bit about risk. What I would challenge people to do is to change their focus, and the reason why is because I would put people in two specific categories when it comes down to the level of achievement. And those that are underachievers, and by underachievers, I mean it's not that they can't really achieve at the highest level, it's that by virtue of their choices and their filters and their criteria, they put themselves in a position where they don't achieve much. And what I mean by that is, that the criteria that they use before they decide to do something, really throws them off. And they use three things mostly. Is it easy, is it convenient, and is it affordable? If it's not going to be easy, convenient or affordable, chances are they're not going to want to do it.

Now, I'm not saying, you know, those aren't important, but they're certainly not the first things you should be asking yourself, because if you look at anybody that's achieved, heck, forget about achieving at the highest level, achieving at some level, it's never really easy, it's certainly not convenient, and for many people, it's not even affordable.

But the question we need to really ask ourselves is, is it worth it? The moment we understand something is worth it, easy, convenient, and affordable is not something that we're considering, because we're going to find a way to make it happen because we understand it's worth it. Now, all of a sudden it comes down to the meaning, the motivation, the mission, why we're doing this, and when we know something's important, we're going to find a way.

So as far as minimum investment and minimum risk you get out of something, you know, what it is you put into it, for the most part. And what you may not put into it with financial equity, you may have to put into it with what's called sweat equity, which means, you know, your own personal labor. But whatever it is, you have to be willing to let something go. Because I believe that success and moving to that next level in life is not so much what you're willing to do as much as it is what you're willing to give up. Because everybody has 24 hours in a day, everybody has a certain amount of money that it is they're making. If they want to grow that, they want to expand that, they want to expand the impact of that. Well, you're going to have to trade something that you have in your life right now to move you to a place in life that you haven't been to before. So what you have to figure out is what hours are you willing to trade?

What money are you willing to trade?  Because if you're not willing to make the trade, then life isn't going to give it to you.  You know, that's just how it works, I don't make up this rule, that's just how it works.

**Raven:**  Right.

**Stephen:**  So you have to decide, if you want minimum investment of money and time, minimum at risk, then look for minimum return.  If you want to go forward, then let's not look at, you know, how we can minimize the investment of our time and our money and our risk, let's look at what it is we ultimately want.  It's called being unreasonable.  And what I mean by that is, many people are too reasonable in life in the sense that they tend to go for what it is they think they can get, as opposed to what they really want.

So forget about what you think you can get, what do you really, really, really, really want?  What is that ideal lifestyle looking like?  And then work backwards and ask yourself, what level of commitment do you need to have in every area of your life to make that happen and then you have to be willing to make a choice to do that and commit to that consistently.  And when you do that, whatever it is you want in this life is going to be available to you.

**Raven:**  Wow.  Final question is, do you feel, Stephen, I mean, really feel, that now's the time for the listeners to start their home business, even though we're in a recession?

**Stephen:**  Well, absolutely.  Interesting enough, if you look at history, in the Great Depression, many of you are probably familiar with the brand Estee Lauder.  Estee Lauder was started in the 1930's, in the heart of the Great Depression.  You have companies like Federal Express and Microsoft and Hyatt and tons of companies that were started either during the oil crises or the Eisenhower recession or companies that rose up out of the ashes of the dot-com busting, like Amazon and Dell Computers and eBay.

So it's in these times right now that some of our greatest opportunities financially start to emerge.  It's really about perspective.  What it is you're focusing on.  You can look at right now you and the economy and the country is drowning in a sea of debt or you can say, "Wait a second, we're drowning in a sea of opportunity, let me go ahead and grab an opportunity, latch onto that thing and maximize it for all it's worth."

And, you know, I know we're running out of time, so maybe on the show next week I'll talk about, you know, a particular way that I look at change and how we can actually use change that's happening right now.

**Raven:**  Okay, you know what?  That's exactly where we'll start.

**Stephen:**  All right!

**Raven:** For sure. So we're going to meet back next week, same time, same place, with Stephen Pierce, but don't go away because we have the second part of our show coming up real soon, Stephen's website is MakeRealMoneyOnTheInternet.com. Did I get it right, Stephen?

**Stephen:** That's right.

**Raven:** Okay.

**Stephen:** MakeRealMoneyOnTheInternet.com, get a copy of my free book shipped directly to your door.

**Raven:** Stephen, this has been great, we'll see you next week. Thank you so much again.

**Stephen:** Thank you.

Listen to the full audio of this interview by clicking the Radio/Microphone!

Plus be sure to visit and subscribe to Raven's popular newsletter and freebie!

http://www.careersfromthekitchentable.com

~ Notes ~

# Lynn Pierce
# The Success Architect

You're going to absolutely love her. Who am I talking about; I'm talking about none other than Lynn Pierce. She's known worldwide as the "Success Architect" and for the past 30 years she has taught thousands of entrepreneurs, home based business owners, speakers, authors, coaches, consultants and sales teams how to tremendously increase their income (by as much as 500%) while reducing the stress of the sales and negotiation process...and having more free time to have a great lifestyle with that additional income! She's all about you having the lifestyle you deserve and not working yourself to death.

Lynn is the host of "Success Blueprint Radio", co-author of more than 10 books and the author of, "Breakthrough to Success; 19 Keys to Mastering Every Area of Your Life". Lynn's new book, "The Soul of the Career Woman; How to Reclaim Your Life, Reawaken Your Soul Without Giving Up the Cash", Lynn is a great lady and diffidently someone you want to get to know follow and stay plugged into . She's so amazing and helped me so, so much and that's why I asked her to be my guest today. Hey I owe a lot to her thank you Lynn and welcome to the show

**Lynn Pierce:** Thank you Raven, I think this is the first time that I have had a round of applause from a radio show. What a great way to be introduced.

**Raven:** What is your background and how did you start to become successful?

**Lynn Pierce:** Since we are talking about sales would you like to talk about how I got started in my sales career?

**Lynn Pierce:** Most people that know me, think that I would be the most unlikely person 'ever' to be in any kind of sales. You have to picture this, in the middle of winter in Wisconsin. I am 22 years old sitting in my little brown pinto, so that tells you just how long ago that was. After just a few months in real estate, I already came to the sad realization, that I could not possibly do what they were telling me to do, for me to become successful. I could not go knocking on doors or what they called 'farming my area' to get listings because I was terrified that someone would answer the door and I would have to talk to them.

I was so shy, I was at risk of becoming a failure at what I really wanted to do, Yes, I did want to sell real estate at the time. So I would sit in my car, literally praying that no one would be home and that no one would answer the door. There was one moment that I was at this grey two-story house. That experience became a defining moment in my life, as I walked away from the door grateful that no one was there, this thought came into my mind that there is something wrong with this picture. I thought, "I want to be in real estate but I don't want to do this by any stretch of the imagination". That was when I stated to ask myself some better questions and as soon as did that everything shifted for me. Within that same week, I stated doing business in a way that works for who I am as a person rather than trying to fit myself in the box that everybody else told me I had to be in. From that point on, I did my business differently. I did it in a way that worked with my personality and that was when I just took off and I had a very successful 25 year career, in real estate all over the USA, including 6 years in Mexico. Within that period of time, I literally started in pretty much the same economic situation that we are having right now. So, I went through times that were bad and I went through times that were prosperous and back again. I created a system for myself that works. People can plug into and be yourself and find a way to communicate who you are and what your business has to offer. Why someone would want to do business with you. In a way that is completely comfortable and natural for whom you are.

**Raven:** Tell us about revenue of relationships...

**Lynn Pierce:** Well, that is really, really simple. The revenue of relationship is about how you bring forth your authentic power passion and persuasion to get everything you want and deliver everything that your prospects or clients want. So, it is a win-win and a simplistic way of looking at it but really it is about you embodying everything that you truly are. You are bringing your true self to the conversation. With your main objective to be, how can I serve the other person in the best way possible? Knowing that your purpose is to serve others, then you will be well taken care of.

**Raven:** How do you go about creating a great first impression?

**Lynn Pierce:** What could be the bad news is that you only have 3 seconds to make a good first impression. Depending upon your situation, if there is any way for that other person to see you or observe you before you are actually introduced that impression has already been made. So be aware of how you act, in your surroundings before you meet someone. The big key, is sincerity. When you greet your prospects make sure that you clearly give them the impression that you are happy to meet them. A lot of time if you are in your head and you are thinking about something else or you are thinking about the presentation that you are going to make or maybe you are stressed because you really need to make some money. And you are thinking about that, the look on your face is not one that says wow I am fully present and happy that you are here. So, it is something that you need to be continuously aware of and that means having a genuine smile on your face making full eye contact. Warm handshakes with everyone and if you are talking to a family that includes the children, make sure you shake their hands and acknowledge everyone. And don't forget to thank them for their time that they are spending with you. Because that is important to.

**Raven:** How can each and every listener that owns a business connect with people who are not like us personally? That is we do not have much in common with the customer. Is this impossible or possible?

**Lynn Pierce:** It is possible for you to learn how to connect with everybody. The reality is that there are four major personality styles and in the work that I do I break it down into how you can connect with each one of the personality styles. That is deeper information, but the important thing is that you can connect with anybody . Think about it like, you are at a cocktail party. You want to break the ice with small talk. Small talk means something that is not controversial. Small talk creates rapport by establishing friendly common ground and in a matter of minutes you can find a place to connect with anyone. At the same time that you are having small talk, that doesn't require a lot of brain power. You are also paying careful attention to their body language. Looking for indications of personality styles and if there is a couples or a group of people that are in charge. Look for who is in charge, and the power of the relationship. This type of conversion, is filler until you get seated or let's say you are meeting at a restaurant, Starbucks where everybody has what they want. So there are a couple of different things that you can talk to anybody about. The weather is one, if they drove to the meeting, how the drive was considering the way people move around these days. A question that you can ask anyone to start a conversation is like so, "Raven are you a Houston native? Have you always lived in Texas?" I can ask, Raven, how did you get involved in the radio business, that is really interesting. Or what is the best part of being a radio show talk Raven, or does your family live in the area? Or are you spread out all over the country? So those are things you can ask anybody and the most interesting thing is every personality style will answer them completely differently. So part of the talking people who want to get you money is that ability to get to yes without selling. Being able to have a conversation, that is customized to the personality of the person you are talking to.

**Raven:** Where can our listeners go to learn more about conversation styles?

**Lynn Pierce:** Go to http://www.lynnpierce.com and click on my blog. I posted an article yesterday. It talks about where I am doing a special live two part teleseminar. In the teleseminar I take people through a complete quick start system where I call it "Getting to yes without selling 2.0 in today's world", with all the different ways we communicate and connect with people. Also, on how to attract people who want to give you money. You can go to http://www.lynnpierce.com click on the blog and It will take you to the post where you can get more information.

**Raven:** Why is listening and not talking the true key to getting you to yes faster and more often?

**Lynn Pierce:** People want you to show interest and approval of them. And most people seldom have anyone show sincerity interest in what they do or who they are. Much less ask them what they think. If you have sincere interest you will find the prospect much more willing to talk because they don't necessarily have the opportunity to do so. That will give you all the information that you need to customize whatever you are going to present. To exactly to what it is they are looking for.

**Raven:** So what is the key to getting the information of what people really want even when they do not know what they want?

**Lynn Pierce:** Well, think back to the last time you had a really great dining experience. You remember if you asked the waiter for his suggestions and the waiter asked you questions, like what you feel like eating and I bet you that the next thing they did was in the particular category that you were most interested in. They told you what their favorite was and what the favorite dishes of other people are and why they liked it the best. You can apply the same thing to any business and that is a simple way of personalizing your product or your business opportunity for your prospects. It's the same way. You get the same results. I bet that you would also order desert from that waiter if he gave you a really good idea about your entrée and the chances are that he will get a much bigger tip and you will recommend him and the restaurant because of the personalized attention. It came from asking a few extra questions and really listening to what you the customer are saying.

**Raven:** How can our listeners starting a business or stuck in a slow business, show fear of asking for the money.

**Lynn Pierce:** Your ability to ask for money is all about your beliefs. It's right between your two ears. Everything around money. The money that you make. The money that you are requesting. The products that you sell. It is all about you beliefs and your beliefs about money control who you ask and how you ask and when you ask and how much you ask for. A big part of it, is related to how much money you feel comfortable deserving and earning. It's really important to look at your money beliefs, that's were all these issues start. You must feel like you are worth it. There are a few books to help you out. Og Mandino "The greatest salesmen in the world". George Clason, "The Richest Man in Babylon" are two spiritually based books that are all about being of service in sales. That will help you shift your beliefs around money, shift your beliefs around being in sales and what you deserved to be paid.

Lynn Pierce: Congratulations Raven on your success I am really excited for you.

**Raven:** Thank you Lynn, our listeners will really gain from the information you have shared.

Listen to the full audio of this interview by clicking the Radio/Microphone!

Plus be sure to visit and subscribe to Raven's popular newsletter and freebie!

http://www.careersfromthekitchentable.com

# John Assaraf
# Motivational Speaker – Breakthrough Strategist

Have you, like many, been asking yourself, "What's the most effective way of dealing with this recession and how am I to survive it? How am I to grow and even overcome it?"

Well, let me tell you, my friend, it's mind over matter, it really is. You see if we do more than we've done before, be more committed to our success than we were last year, stop buying into that hype and just claim, "Hey, I am not a victim of my circumstance, this recession is not even coming in my area." Be more of an extraordinary, savvy businesswoman or businessman, not just the ordinary. Step out of the box, do something different, get creative in your business. Go out there and get those customers, claim them, affirm that they are out there for you, attract them, you can do that. If you're truly ready to transform your business like I know you are, and you're looking for the winning formula for growing your business, achieving financial success so you can live not an ordinary life, but an extraordinary life! Then tonight you are indeed at the right place because we have the answer, yes, we do, to those questions and even more.

In fact, we have the author that wrote the book, *The Answer*. He's going to show you how to grow your business faster rather than slower, how cool is that? Who am I speaking of? Well, I'm going to give you a hint. You've seen him on *Oprah*, on *Ellen*, *Anderson Cooper 360*, *Donny Deutsch*, *Larry King*, and tonight, you're going to hear the straight talk from him himself. I'm talking about none other than the man that's got the answers, John Assaraf.

Before I bring John on, let me just share a little bit about him. He's a CEO of One Coach; he's an international best-selling author, lecturer, and entrepreneur with a passion for brain research in quantum physics. His expertise is helping entrepreneurs and small business owners achieve success in business and life. He's one of the distinguished thought leaders at the Marshall Goldsmith School of Management and has built wildly successful companies in real estate, internet software, and business coaching and consulting. John is one of the experts featured in the hit film—I watch this every single day, I kid you not—*The Secret*. And he has launched One Coach, business coach franchising company that helps entrepreneurs and professionals grow their small business revenue so they can achieve that financial freedom, live that extraordinary life that you, I, and all of us deserve.

**Raven:** Hi, John!

**John:** Hey there! What a great intro, thank you so much.

**Raven:** Well, you deserve it. How are you?

**John:** I'm doing just awesome.

**Raven:** Well, fantastic. I'm excited to have you here, the audience has been saying, "Okay! John's going to be here! John's going to be here!" They're ready for you.

**John:** Well, that's good!

**Raven:** So I got to ask you, because I've been listening to some of your interviews and I guess I've been plugged into the new John, but I didn't know that you were, at the age of 16, you were a street kid, getting into trouble, selling drugs.

**John:** Oh, I got into so much trouble as a kid. I was on the wrong train, going in the wrong direction and picking up speed.

**Raven:** Wow. Well, what was the deciding factor in saying enough is enough?

**John:** Well, you know, I grew up in a loving, caring home where I knew right from wrong and I wanted more in my life, but there was this, I guess there was this mindset that I had that if I wanted more I had to either take it from somebody or steal it from somebody, and that I wasn't smart enough or good enough to learn how to earn it. And so I had a challenge with my self-image, telling myself stories, now that I look back, that in order for me to have more, you had to have less. And I didn't know anything about myself. I didn't know anything about the universe, I didn't know anything about the law of attraction or about learning, you know, new skills and becoming more in order to have more.

And I was really blessed when I was 19, I met some individuals who started to teach me, to show me, that there is a better way, there is an actual easier way that you feel better about yourself and that you really can achieve whatever it is you choose to achieve, if and when you change from the inside out. And I just became fascinated with that.

**Raven:** You were right at 16 or 18 at that point?

**John:** Well, from the age of around 13 to about 17, I really just did a lot of not very nice things. And then I stopped that when I was 18 years old basically, and I knew that if I was to continue on that path that either jail or the morgue was really the only path that I was heading towards, and neither one was something I wanted to go towards.

**Raven:** Well, you were smart to have that wake-up call and to want much more of your life. And I know that this is a business show, but most of us are parents or grandparents, and so what would you tell the person that's listening right now, that say, "Wow, I'm dealing with a teenager like that," or you know, "his friends or her friends are like that." What would you say to them to get them on the right track, if they have a loved one or a child or a grandchild that's kind of in that path or at least hanging around people like that, John?

**John:** Well, you really can't say anything to them. And this is one of the discussions I have, you know, with parents all the time. Is think about when you were, you know, 13, 14, 15, 17. Did you want to listen to your parents? No.

And one of those things that we have to understand is, is asking ourselves different questions will give us better answers. And here's the question: Why is my child, nephew, niece, whatever the case is, behaving this way? And you remember the old saying that birds of a feather flock together?

**Raven:** Oh, yeah.

**John:** Well, the reason is because of their self-image. So guys or gals, we do what we do, we say what we say because of our own self-image and our own perception equals our projection. So when we have this self-image of ourselves that we're either good enough or not, smart enough or not, too white or too black or too Asian, whatever the case might be, whatever we have these beliefs, those beliefs about ourselves, whether they're true or not or irrelevant, will dictate our behaviors. It'll dictate who we hang around, it'll dictate what we think, and it'll dictate what we do.

And so as opposed to telling a kid or an adult, "You can do better, you're smarter than that, you shouldn't hang around with those kids," blah, blah, blah, blah, blah!

**Raven:** Yeah, yeah, yeah.

**John:** And so the question is, okay, so if I'm not supposed to do that, what should I do? And the answer is, show them a different environment. And the answer is, show them a movie, a book, a rapper, and I don't mean a wrapper like a candy wrapper, I mean like a, you know, people that they idol that broke free from what they were doing before. Show them that there's hope, show them a different way. Don't tell them. They don't want to be compared, I don't want to be compared, and you don't want to be compared.

And so we have to understand that it's not that they're not doing the best they can, they are based on what they believe to be true about themselves and their beliefs of what is true about themselves may not be accurate, but they're still their truth. And we will always act out and always project what we believe at a subconscious level to be true about ourselves and what's possible for us.

**Raven:** Wow.

**John:**  And the reason I say this is when I was younger, I had individuals who cared about me that showed me.  And not only did they show me, but then they taught me.

**Raven:**  And that's the difference, they didn't try to tell you.

**John:**  And that was the difference.  That was the difference.  And it's not enough.  You know, if you can have a child, because, you know, yeah, I want help, see, but it's virtually impossible to help a child or an adult that needs help that doesn't want it.

**Raven:**  Yeah.  You know, you have really brought up some good points here and again, I know, you know, this is not, jumping into our business questions, but all of us, you know, we have children and stuff and we care about them, and like you said, and it could be an adult that's troubled through things.  And a lot of times the difficult times, like the recession, can bring out the worst in people.  So this is a great time to watch the movie and to read books like *The Answer* and all these, I love these books with these different stories in them, you know, that talk about how an ordinary person became extraordinary, some of the challenges they went through and stuff.  I think we're just filled with great information, now we have no excuse.

**John:**  Well, and the information is wonderful, but information on its own is really a waste of time.

**Raven:**  Yeah, because you're just letting it go in one ear and out the other, so to speak.

**John:**  Yes, and it's not intentional.  You know, when we were in school, when they gave us new information, they drilled it into us through practice, drill, and rehearse, practice, drill and rehearse, practice, drill and more rehearse.  And then, you know, we memorized it and it became part of who we are.

Well, guess what?  When you're, let's say in business or you want to start a new career or start a business, well, there's so much new stuff to learn.  And we don't learn based on reading a book or a paragraph one time.  If you think about a Hollywood actor or actress, when he or she is given a new script, they have to learn that script thousands upon thousands of times, hundreds, if not thousands of hours of practice and rehearsing, until it becomes a part of them where they can act the play or the role.

If you are in business or you are looking for some new result in your life that encompass having to learn new things, the same rule applies, you have to somehow make that new information a part of who you are so that then you don't have to think about  you're never going to see an actor or actress on the screen who is practicing their role.  They are it!  They become the role!

**Raven:**  They're in it.  In the moment.

**John:**  And in becoming the role, they are able to express all of the emotions of the role so that we could sit there and look at them and cry or laugh or gasp.  Well, guess what?  We have to learn how to become so congruent with the new level of success that we want to achieve, that through repetition of thought, repetition of visualization, repetition of behaving that way, faking it till you make it, it becomes the new you.

**Raven:** You got to walk the walk and talk the talk.

**John:** Or even fake it till you make it!

**Raven:** Absolutely. Wow. Well, thanks for sharing that with us, that was a lot of valuable information and we appreciate it.

But let's talk about that book, *The Answer.*

**John:** Sure.

**Raven:** First of all, I love the cover.

**John:** Thank you.

**Raven:** Nice look and very attractive book, definitely the kind that you can just leave out on your coffee table, it looks so good so that when people come by, they can pick it up, I like that, John.

**John:** Thank you.

**Raven:** What inspired you to write this particular book?

**John:** A couple things. Number one is, after I was in the movie, *The Secret*, a lot of people, you know, really didn't understand *The Secret*, and thought it was hokey-pokey and that there wasn't any science behind it and that it was foo-foo esoterically stuff. And I've been very fascinated with science and I want to know the answers to things, so I'm not just okay with this—for example, somebody says, "You should visualize your success every day." I want to know why? I want to know how does it work, how to do it specifically, how long does it take, what guarantees do you have that it will work. I want to understand when somebody says visualize, how it works and why. I want to know when somebody says, "Use the law of attraction, have a positive attitude and you'll attract positive things in your life." Well, how to imagine that? Like where do you get the fact that it works.

So I did all the research for the last nine years and I wanted to share that research. But not only did I do the research, I've been in the world of business development and growth, building my own companies, for 29 years. Also been in the personal development and growth and I wanted to marry the best of what I've learned about building companies so that people can really have that American dream. You know, if you can earn the amount of income you want to earn and have a business for yourself, and then guess what? You're feeling great, you can do the things you want to do, you can buy the home and the retirement and the kids lifestyle and the charity that you want to contribute to. I think that everybody deserves that right.

But it's also for people who do the right things in the right order. And building a business is complex, it's not just, you know, do it in your pajamas every day on the weekends, you can make some money doing it in your pajamas every day on the weekends, but you have to do the right things in your pajamas every day on the weekends.

So the question is, where are you going to learn to do those right things? And I wanted to be part of the solution and my goal is to help millions of business owners around the world achieve financial freedom by learning the right things and then by making sure that they apply the things that they learn.

And so I wrote the book with my dear friend, Murray Smith, and then we started a company called One Coach, that helps small business owners learn what they need to learn, and keeps them accountable to doing what they should be doing.

**Raven:** So you guys just didn't leave it at giving them the information? Kind of going back to what you were talking about before, John. You gave them the other piece of the puzzle with your One Coach program.

**John:** When you think about information, right now, whoever is listening, they can stop right now, they can go onto Google, they can type in any question they want, and in the next 1 minute, they can have 100,000 answers for that question. But that's not enough. The question that I always ask people is: If it's not about the information, then what is it about? And the key for all highly successful people is application of the right information.

So what we've done with One Coach is we don't just give people the right information, but we've created a process and a system to keep people accountable to actually doing what they should be doing, taking day to day action, week by week action, the right type of action, and giving them the support that they need to be able to consistently move from one level to the next, or maybe from start up to their first 50,000, from 50,000 to the next, you know, 50,000, to 100, and then to 200, and 500, and a million.

And in doing that, we're creating an environment where business owners can thrive and get from one level of success to the next and not do it alone. And that was really one of the other keys, is you've got to do it by yourself, but you can't do it alone.

**Raven:** I like the fact that you spoke about holding them accountable, because that is a real key, isn't it?

**John:** Absolutely. I mean, if you think about it, why do most people go on diets or have New Year's resolutions, within a week or two or three, even though it's something they really, really, really, really wanted, they stop? It's not because they don't want to succeed, they're just conditioned to a certain way of thinking and behavior and they need a different process and a system to keep them accountable to new thoughts and new behaviors, and that's why we do what we do.

**Raven:** You brought up something a few minutes ago, you spoke about when you wrote the answer, it was because you really wanted to know more about visualizing, why should we visualize and how do you visualize? So let's go back to that a moment.

You hear you should visualize your success. First of all, how do you do that, John? And then what happens if we don't?

**John:** Well, if we understand why we want to visualize, there's a part of the brain that doesn't know the difference between something that you imagine and something that's real. And that's the subconscious part of the brain. And why is that important? Well, we know that the subconscious mind is responsible for 96-98% of our behaviors. So if we want to alter our behaviors, we can't alter our behaviors long term if we are not conditioned at the subconscious levels to behave and think a certain way or a different way.

And so part of the brain is responsible for choosing the goals or the dreams that you have, but it's not the part of the brain that's responsible for taking action. And so that's number one. So we have this, think about your brain like software in a computer, all right?

**Raven:** Okay.

**John:** And once there's a program or a software program, it does what the program stipulates. If you want a different result, it's not enough to just say, "I want a different result." You have to change the software inside the brain just like you would in the computer. Visualization is one of the ways to access the software of the brain. And a simple way to visualize, number one, is to write down, for example, exactly what it is that you want. A new vision for your business would go something like this: "I'm so grateful for the fact that my business is now generating $100,000 a year. And the clients are loving my product or service and referring their friends to me consistently, my staff or my team." So what you do is you create like a little script, like you would a Hollywood movie, but you write it in a positive and as if it's already happened perspective. So you don't do it in the past or in the future, you do it as if it's true and real right now. And then you take that written document and you visualize it every morning when you wake up for three or four minutes, as if it was real. And then you visualize it again just before you go to bed, as if it was real.

And why do we say before bed and when you just wake up? Well, that's when the part of the brain that's a little bit tired, that filter, is set aside and your brain is much more receptive to changing the software.

**Raven:** Oh, okay.

**John:** Okay? And when we visualize, we can both read and feel it, or once you've done it a few times, now you want to close your eyes and now you want to make believe, just like you did when you were a kid. And you pretend that that story is you and that's your life and that amount of money is coming in and the amount of money that you're giving to charity and the things you're doing to help other people, your family, and your friends. What is your retirement like, how much money is coming in, what are you doing with it, how are you walking, how are you talking?

And what you do in this is you are actually creating a new pattern in the brain, you're creating a new software pattern in the brain that through repetition, it becomes part of your fixed psyche or brain. Once this becomes part of this fixed side of yourself, your brain automatically takes it over, no differently than the fact that you don't have to think for a second about putting on makeup, you don't have to, if you've been trained, think for a second about getting dressed or brushing your teeth, or driving a stick shift. But at one point in your life, you did have to think about it, it did take coordinating your thoughts and your actions. But through repetition, you were able to convert those thoughts and those actions into an automatic pattern.

Well, when we start to think about automatic patterns that are at the next level of our success and we repeat those over and over and over again, we start to formulate that pattern in the brain and here's the beautiful part, and here's why affirmations done properly, work. Part of the brain's responsibility, not only is it to keep you alive, but it's also to make sure that it's simplifies tasks and it simplifies anything that is repeated over and over and over again into an automatic software program. And then it's running 24 hours a day, 7 days a week. And so there's a reason for a little bit of the madness, it's really us taking control of our brains and reprogramming it so that we are in control versus what was told to us by our parents or our teachers or our experiences or the TV.

**Raven:** You know what? I have actually in the past, I guess you could say three years, I've been reprogramming myself and getting really plugged in to books and audios and going to events. But also, applying each and everything I learned and I break it down one step at a time, conquer that and then move on. And I have completely changed over in the past couple years, it's unbelievable.

But what I found, John, is it gets easier and it gets more natural. You just start to attract all kind of things coming my way and I'm like, "Wow, I want to do this more!"

You spoke about how when you're looking at things and thinking about things before you go to bed, I find myself at times in bed just getting extremely creative, John, and I jump up and I'll write down some thoughts. And then the next morning, I'll get up and I'll grab that piece of paper that I wrote in my sleep, slept walked and wrote, and I started putting into action and it works.

**John:** And it does work. It absolutely does work.

**Raven:** And I found that very interesting, at first it was kind of like, wow! You know, because you think in your sleep and I'm literally writing down how I'm going to create income the next day. And I put it on my computer, I go back to bed, I jump up the next morning and I take the exact piece of paper, break it up into action steps, and it always amazes me, it ends up being a great day following it. And I'm like, "Wow, I should go to sleep more often, John."

**John:** Well, what happens is, actually when you're in that brainwave frequency, you're actually in a receptive frequency, okay? Where the universe is actually downloading information to you.

**Raven:** Wow, that's so interesting. Very interesting.

**John:** Yeah, we have five different brainwave frequencies, but most people are only in two of them.

**Raven:** What are the five?

**John:** There is beta brainwave frequency, which is what people are in right now.

**Raven:** Okay.

**John:** There's alpha, there's theta, there's delta, and gamma. Think of it this way; think about driving a stick shift car.

**Raven:** Okay.

**John:** You know how when you're in first gear, it revs up the engine and you can pick up speed really fast?

**Raven:** Um-hm.

**John:** What happens if you keep your foot on the gas?

**Raven:** It'll go crazy!

**John:** It'll burn the engine up.

**Raven:** Yeah.

**John:** Well, guess what we're doing?

**Raven:** We're doing the same thing?

**John:** We're staying in beta most of the time and we stress ourselves out.

**Raven:** Is that why we start feeling overwhelmed and then we give up?

**John:** Yes. Yes, yes, and yes. And so but what happens in a car? As soon as you drop the gear from gear one to gear two, the car actually goes faster, but the engine goes slower.

**Raven:** Oh, you can tell I don't drive a stick shift.

**John:** Okay. You can drive, what happens if you keep going and you keep moving it up to the next threshold, as soon as you go into the next gear, the engine actually works less and the tires still go faster. And so what happens is there are certain gears that we're learning are for thinking gears, certain gears we're learning are for doing gears, certain gears that we know of are receptive gears. No different than a radio station that receives and transmits information. That's what our brain is doing all the time.

The key is to learn how to move from one brainwave frequency to another and you have been what I call, unconsciously competent. So you weren't aware of what you were doing, yet you were doing the right thing.

**Raven:** Oh, okay, and I've heard people talk about that before.

**John:** Albert Einstein, you know, went into meditative states all the time. Edison used to sit in a chair, okay? With two steel balls in his hand and he, as he would fall asleep, he would be awakened by the balls dropping on the floor, then he would write down his best ideas.

**Raven:** Wow! That's fascinating, I love it!

**John:** All right? And so what you're doing is, you're doing the exact same thing and coming up with ideas to make money.

**Raven:** I know!

**John:** And you're

**Raven:** I'm so thrilled; I'm like, "Oh, let me go to sleep! So I can wake up and make some more money!"

Believe it or not, John, our time has run out, but you have agreed to come back and join us next week, so we want to thank you right now for giving us all this information. Today, John has been helping us get our mindset, understand why we think the way we think, and why we need to get into action and not just sit there, and visualize, and hope to attract, but you really do need to make the thing happen.

**John**: Absolutely. If anybody wants some free videos on how to grow their business, go to OneCoach.com.

**Raven:** Oh, you got to go to OneCoach.com. You know, I was looking at those videos the other day, the Business Growth video series?

**John:** Yep.

**Raven:** Love them. Go there, go to http://www.OneCoach.com, and then be back next week as we continue with John and we're going to really get into some business questions and get you those answers that you want, things like how you can find that right customer, I think John calls it the ideal customer. And we're going to talk a little bit more about how you, the business owner, can step out of the box and get creative! Go out there and make that thing happen and so you won't have to worry about the recession.

**John:** You're welcome. Thank you.

Listen to the full audio of this interview by clicking the Radio/Microphone!

Plus be sure to visit and subscribe to Raven's popular newsletter and freebie!

http://www.careersfromthekitchentable.com

# ~ Notes ~

# George Fraser
# CEO of FraserNet

Speaking of awesome interviews, I'm so excited to introduce you to our featured guest, oh, wow, before I bring him on, let me say this, you're going to want something to write with so you can take some copious notes and if you're standing, sit down, if you're sitting, stand up, because this man is amazing and I'm so thrilled to bring him to you. Let me tell you a little bit about him.

Well, first of all, *Upscale* magazine named him one of the top 50 power brokers in black America. *Black Enterprise* magazine calls him black America's number one networker on the covered issue of personal growth guru. Stephen Covey, he says he's a masterful teacher, TV host and journalist. And Tony Brown called him a visionary with the rare combination of leadership and management skills. He was featured in the New York *Times*, best-seller *Master of Networking*, along with Colin Powell, how cool is that?

Who am I talking about? Well, none other than George C. Fraser, chairman and CEO of FraserNet Inc. and one of the foremost authorities on networking and building effective relationships, as well as the publisher of the award-winning *Success Guide Worldwide, the Networking Guide to Black Resources*, and the founder of the annual Power Networking Conference that I get to go to June 9th.

Now, also, George is a popular speaker and author of inspiring talks on success principles, effective networking, wealth creation, business ethics, and this man just has so much going on. I mean, you know, people have on *CNN Wall Street*, his message and he is someone you definitely want to stay plugged in. So we're going to go ahead and are just a few minutes of our interview today, but I'm going to tell you how you can go back and hear the full, entire interview, because he had so much we couldn't squeeze it in in 10 minutes.

So without further ado, George Fraser. Hey, George! Welcome to Careers from the Kitchen Table.

**George:** Wow, you have energy! And you are incredible, Raven. Thank you so much for the work that you do and the contribution that you make to a greater community, we love you. Just keep doing what you're doing because you're extraordinarily good at it and it's an honor to be on your show.

**Raven:** Thank you so much, I appreciate that.

**Raven:** You're from Cleveland, I'm originally from Cleveland.

**George:** Yeah! God bless you, I thought you sounded intelligent.

**Raven:** Went to Shaw High School years ago, my friend.

**George:** That's what I'm talking about.

**Raven:** Now, you're still living in Cleveland?

**George:** Oh, absolutely, I'm not far from Shaw High School, I know Shaw High School and I've spoken at Shaw High School, it's a great school.

**Raven:** Wow! Okay. Cool, cool.

**George:** They just built a new one.

**Raven:** Oh, they did?

**George:** Yeah, they did. Tore it down and built a new one.

**Raven:** Yeah, well, the last time I was up there, looked like they needed to build a new one.

**George:** They did, yeah, absolutely.

**Raven:** So that's a good thing. Okay. I want to talk to you about networking and building relationships, and I know you're really big and you speak on this in the African-American community, so I'm going to ask you just kind of broaden that a little bit for all of our audience.

**George:** Sure.

**Raven:** How did you start, first of all, in being a business owner?

**George:** Started the business 25 years ago and started in my house, where most small businesses started. Steven Jobs started in his garage and, you know, our friend over at Microsoft, Bill Gates, started in his house. So, you know, most small businesses start with an idea in your home and then you expand and grow. So, yeah, you know, it was a bolt of lightning, I think, that hit me, because I had spent almost 20 years in the public and private sector in leadership positions with Proctor-Gamble for 13 years, I was the vice president of United Way for 3 years, and then an executive with Ford Motor Company for 2 years. So I spent a significant part of my early development learning the masses, learning the skills, both the soft skills and the hard skills, the marketing, branding, advertising promotional skills, leadership skills, on somebody else's time and that's what I recommend anyone to do if they want to start a business, learn on somebody else's time.

**Raven:** Yeah, get that self-development in, huh?

**George:** That's right, get it in, make, you know, make mistakes on somebody else's money. We're all going to make mistakes, make no mistake about it.

**Raven:** Can we go into mistakes and why they happen?

**George:** You can't even imagine how much of Proctor & Gamble's money I screwed up, you know, just making mistakes. It's not intentional, but just, you know, I made the wrong decisions. So learn on somebody else's time that would be my first piece of advice. Find something that you love, find something you're excited about, find a business that you might be interested in, and then find someone who's already in that business, all right? And then beg them for a job, even if you have to volunteer. You know, work for them and learn the business from the inside out. I mean, duh! I mean, why would you want to start on your own? I mean, if you want to own a barber shop, you know, learn how to cut hair. Cut hair for somebody who owns a barber shop. Learn how the business of barber shops. And I'm just over-simplifying here. And then go out and start your business.

**Raven:** Yeah. Well, you're right, and that's what we're, I appreciate you saying it, because that's what we always share with our listeners. You know, why you have a job is the perfect time to start a home-based business.

**George:** Absolutely.

**Raven:** Because you're not stressed out, you got a check coming in, and just cut down on some of that TV time and play time.

**George:** There you go. I mean, we watch, African-Americans in particular, watch 70 hours of television a week, that's 10 hours of television a day, can you imagine that? I can't even imagine that.

**Raven:** Wow.

**George:** Right? And, you know, here's what I know. The first eight hours that you work, I don't care what it is that you do, if you're working for somebody or if you're in business, the first eight hours is the subsistence, right? You can have a place to live and a car and something over your head and some clothes. That provides you subsistence. It's what you do after those eight hours is when you can have the extras, right?

So especially if you're in business. A business, you know, I worked 12 to 14 hours every single day of the week. There is no day of the week that I am not working on my business. Now, people, I say its work, but it's not work to me, I love it! There's nothing else I'd rather be doing on earth. I mean, I'd rather be doing what I'm doing than on a "vacation." Right? On vacation I'm bored to death. I'd rather be doing what I am doing, because I love it, right?

Now, it took me a while to develop the skills and to nurture the thoughts and the ideas and to garner the resources, both the hard resources, money, and the human resources, right? But at 42 I started my business. But there's nothing I'd rather be doing. And so it's that 12-14 hours that I work every single day, which I don't really call work, that has made me wealthy, quite frankly. Not 8 hours a day, not 6 hours a day, not 5 hours a day, not watching 10 hours of television a day, you ain't going to get there, I'm sorry. If that's what you want to do? Then do it, then just, you know, don't go into business, get a job for the government.

**Raven:** Yeah, or a hobby.

**George:** Yeah.

**Raven:** Yeah, because you're so right, you know, just hearing you say that, it made me think of, you know, when I first got into my radio business, I had to self-teach myself from the hospital while I was waiting for my mother to get well, and work a part-time job making $200 a week and that was at the age of 55.

**George:** Wow.

**Raven:** And seeing my mother in the hospital, I knew there were going to be medical expenses and I couldn't keep doing what I was doing, George, or I was going to keep getting what I was getting. And at that point, things had to change, not only for me, but for my entire family. So I had to, as they say, put the pedal to the metal.

**George:** That's right.

**Raven:** And I had to get the thing done. There's an old quote, or one of my favorite ones, you may have heard it, by a former hall of fame wide receiver, Jerry Rice that says, "I will do today what others won't so I can live the life tomorrow like others can't." And I keep that quote and it keeps me, it makes me, whenever I want to look at TV or go out and play because it's a beautiful sunny day and I want to go sit by the pool, I look at that and then I look at my list of things I need to do to get to the next point.

**George:** That's right.

**Raven:** Yeah.

**George:** That's right. So, you know, you have the right ideas and you have the right concept and you're going about it in the right kind of way. And, you know, my advice to people who are thinking about entrepreneurship, first and foremost, and we talked about this earlier, is prepare yourself. You know, get the education, get the training, you know, go to workshops, read, and get the experience, volunteer if you have to, you know, and get a personality transplant, right? I mean

You know, business is about relationships. Without relationships you have no business, without relationships you have no business being in business. In fact, the business we're all really in, is in the business of building relationships. The reason I'm doing this telephone interview in the middle of a conference that I'm getting ready to put on for 1,000 people in Atlanta, is because of a personal relationship, right? So it's about relationships.

So, a lot of people don't have the kind of personality that will enable them to do the selling, to do the marketing, to do the branding, to cultivate, nurture, and build relationships at work, at home, and in the community, which they can ultimately use and leverage to build their business. So you've got to prepare yourself, you've got to make sure that you have a high emotional quotient, not just a high IQ, and, you know, an emotional quotient, your EQ is the determining factor on your ability to cultivate, nurture, and to build relationships at work, at home, and in the community, and are you good at that? Because as a business owner, you're going to have to work with and through people or you're not going to develop any business, and you have to inspire those people and you have to, you know, provide aspirational and inspirational advice and counsel, you have to motivate them, you have to, they have to like you because people, you know, do, you know, work with people that they like.

So personality is a huge, important part of it and, you know, one of the places you can go and pick up personality tips and speaking tips and writing tips is Toast Masters. Every city in America has a Toast Masters. Go to a Dale Carnegie course, you know, learn sales techniques. Everybody needs to learn how to sell. Everybody should take a selling class, either in a college, or college, go to a community college or go to a private institution, and learn how to sell, because we're always selling. We're selling 24/7, right?

**Raven:** Oh, yeah.

**George:** We're either selling ourselves, selling our thoughts, ideas, selling our positions, selling our products, or selling our services, we are always selling. We're selling our children on doing the right thing. So there are techniques for that and there are strategies and there's a psychological tactics, and I don't mean that in a negative way, I just mean that if you're going to succeed in life, you better learn how to sell. If you're going to succeed in business, you better learn how to sell. If you're going to succeed in business, you better learn how to speak and write. If you're going to succeed in business, you better have a personality that is charismatic and attractive to people. So that's my first piece of advice, prepare yourself for business.

Secondly, build a network. Build a personal, operational, and strategic network, because you can't get there on your own. There's a beautiful Bible passage, John 5:30, "And Jesus said, 'I of my own self can do nothing.'" Now, this is Jesus. Jesus couldn't do it on his own, right? So why would you? Why would you think you could achieve anything significant, anything worth talking about on your own, my yourself, in a vacuum? You can't. You know, and I tell people all the time, at some point in time in your life, your relationships will mean more than your education. Right? Right? Introduce me to your five closest friends and that will tell me who you are, your network determines your net worth.

**Raven:** Your network. Absolutely.

**George:** Right?

**Raven:** Oh, yeah.

**George:** So build a net worth. Number three, save your money. Protect your assets. Bad credit and gratuitous spending will take you down. Delay your gratification, brothers and sisters. Invest in what you love and invest in what you know, and if you love it, but you don't know it, find someone who does and serve them eagerly. Okay? But you got to save your money, right?

**Raven:** Right.

**George:** If you save your money, your money will save you.

**Raven:** I love that.

**George:** My father taught me many years ago, if you only got a few dollars, you can only do a few things!

**Raven:** And you're right.

**George:** Save your money.

**Raven:** And your money will save you.

**George:** And your money will save you.

**Raven:** I love that! That is good.

**George:** Right?

**Raven:** That is so good.

**George:** Number four, look for a growing business sector, healthcare, information technology, education. You don't have to start a business from scratch; you can buy a darn business. Right? And we don't need any more funeral parlors, beauty salons, and barber shops.

**Raven:** Got enough.

**George:** We've got enough of those, right? Think outside of the box. We can do more than sing and dance, play football, baseball, or basketball, unless you can own a basketball team or a baseball team or a football team, then I'm down with that. Right? So look for growing business sectors, right?

We get so caught up in the grind of the businesses, the historical businesses of our past that we don't think outside of the box. Serious money is not being made in barber shops, I'm sorry. You know, it's just not. Or beauty salons, unless you're going to open a chain of 1,000 of them, that's different.

**Raven:** Right.

**George:** Right? Number five; align yourself with a strategic partner, somebody who can bring somebody to the table, right? A deal that you don't either have the capital, talent, or infrastructure, right? So align yourself with a strategic partner if you generate value, right? Nobody is going to take you off the playing field. So you can't have a strategic partner if you don't bring anything to the table. Let me say that differently. The Creator has made it possible and made sure that every single person on the face of the earth will eat at the table of life, okay? He will be invited to the table to eat, I promise you that. Certainly in America. You will be invited to the table to eat.

But if the only thing you do when you're invited to the table is eat and you don't bring anything to the table, you will not be invited back. So the question is: What are you bringing to the table? What are your marketable skills? You know, maybe you're really educated; maybe you got a PhD, so what? I don't care. Have you converted it into marketable skills? Right?

And the marketplace determines the value of those skills. And you take your education and your skills into the marketplace, add value, and then get an exchange for that value. If you're only making $10 an hour, you're only worth $10 an hour, I'm sorry. I don't care. Right? I don't care what you think or what you say; the marketplace determines how much you're worth. So what are your skills worth?

My skills are worth $15,000 an hour. That's what my skills are worth, that's what I charge for a one-hour speech. That's what the marketplace pays for me because I have created that value, that's what I bring to the marketplace. So you can have all the education you want, but have you converted it into a marketable skill that you can take out into the marketplace, add value, and then get an exchange for that value? What is that value? That's the question. How much you making, right? So whatever you're making is what the marketplace values. It doesn't value you at any more than that.

So if you want to increase your value, if you want to make $100 an hour, $75 an hour, $200 an hour, $1,000 an hour—what skills do you have to learn in order to do that? How do you increase your value? So that's a whole other lecture.

And then a final thing is leverage whatever assets you have in addition to your ability and skill, via political clout, and you can demand that companies address opportunities for minorities in all sectors of business. So you've got to leverage your assets, right? That you have in addition to your ability and skills. So what assets do you have and how do you leverage? Do you have political clout? Do you know important people? Do you know powerful people? Do you want to meet powerful people? If you want to meet powerful people, you have to be where important people are. You see? I tell people that all the time. If you want to meet important people, you have to be where important people are, because they ain't coming to you, you have to go to them.

**Raven:** You have to go get them, yep.

**George:** Right? So those are my six things that I would advise young entrepreneurs to think about before they step out here. Now, they can start in their home, no question about that, that's where, most small businesses start, they start with an idea in their home, right? But prepare yourself, build a network, save your money, look for a growing business sector, align yourself with a smart strategic partner, and then leverage whatever other assets you have.

It ain't more complicated than that.

**Raven:** Yeah. And what you outlined were very simple steps and I appreciate you breaking it down, too, enough to where people can know what each step means and the power behind it. One of the favorite ones that you tapped into that I like was when you talked about creating your value, your market value. Then that's important because a lot of the people that are listening to this show, they have already started their business.

Be sure to listen to the entire interview – click the radio/microphone below or visit the link.

Listen to the full audio of this interview by clicking the Radio/Microphone!

Plus be sure to visit and subscribe to Raven's popular newsletter and freebie!

http://www.careersfromthekitchentable.com

# Martin Wales
# Marketing Expert and Media Personality

All right let's move to our first guest because I'm excited that we have Martin Wales. He is a dynamic guy. We are going to bring him on in just a second. Let me tell you a little about Martin. Martin is a fabulous person. He has the 'voice' since he is a talk show host. Today he is coming to talk to you about how we can increase our customer base. How we can treat our customers' right and he has some giveaways to offer. Listen if you want more customers and clients get ready to hear from today's special guest expert. So if you're sitting stand up and if you are standing sit down. You do not want to miss this man. He is the founder of customercatcher.com where they help you get customers to a point where they beg him to stop. I love that...To where you beg him to stop. Martin is a media and publicity expert. He is featured in number one best sellers in like Guerrilla Marketing on the Front Lines book and The Success Secrets of the on-line Marketing superstars book. He is also in the book Walking with The Wise Entrepreneur along with co-author Suzie Orman, Robert Kiyosaki, and Harvey Eckard. There is so many to name, I can just go on and on. On top of being a respected author Martin is a columnist, talk radio show host, and TV personality he is the man. Martin, are you there yet?

**Martin:** I am absolutely here. Hello Raven. Hello Everyone.

**Raven:** Hey Martin. It is so great to have you here. It really is we are so excited. You have so much going on. I want to tell the listeners that they do not want to go anywhere. I know you have some goodies to give away later. Everyone gets something to write with you will want to take copious notes. You want to get the information from Martin near the end. While you are at it go grab your healthy coffee. If you want to know what I'm talking about go to http://www.sippinghealthycoffee.com. Now enough already let's get to Martin. Martin tell us a little bit about yourself, you know in the next minute. Catch us up on who you are where you came from and all that good stuff.

**Martin:** Why listen to Martin Wells who is Martin Wells? Well I am the executive producer of PayPal radio. I hosted radio for Microsoft. Like yourself talk radio is a great way to get in touch with people but where did I come from? I came from where you did, a career from the kitchen table. I was a high school teacher. I had no sales or marketing training. I did not have business training, journalism or radio broadcast training nothing like that. I left teaching at five years. I worked at personal development sales and ended up selling life insurance door-to-door. To make a long story short, within four years I was vice president of marketing for a $26 million dollar company with three divisions and a million dollar marketing budget. How do I get from where I was to there? Well I used publicity. I use my mouth, I talked and I got publicity. I became a consultant so now I was and for employment I worked from home, my home office. It is the way to do things. I don't think people care if you're in the home office anymore. So many people work from coffee shops. If they paid Starbucks rent the company would be richer rather than selling a five dollars cup of coffee. So, really what is it about me? Where did I get my expertise? It's from being out there. How do I get more customers when I didn't have any money? I had three new babies to feed. I was new to the industry. So starting from zero, I moved from something to even more something. Now I'm having a good time. So I had a lot of fun but also along the way I learned how to get customers without spending a lot of money. That is why we say at http://www.customercatcher.com, we help you get so many customers that you will beg us to stop. Because there are so many ways to do it.

**Raven:** Three babies. You were busy.

**Martin:** Babies came, one year at a time.

**Raven:** I love that. Saying "so many customers that you will beg you to stop". That is a unique selling proposition.

**Martin:** That is one way to get customers. Be different, have a unique look. Have that something that grabs people's attention. In fact I ran into something today. I always keep my eyes open all the time. I educate myself every day about marketing. I saw an ad today for coughs syrup. The ad said "we like sick days without the sick part". It suggests that people are using their sick days to take a day off not just because they have a cold or cough. So what can you say? From another caught syrup company there is another slogan "it tastes awful but it works". What can you say to attract people's attention despite speaking? The cheapest way to get customers. Just keep talking about your business and how it helps people.

**Raven:** Absolutely.

**Martin:** Introduce yourself, as "hi I am Martin Wales from customercatcher.com". I don't say hi I am martin Wales from Houston. It's great that you're from Houston but I can find that out later and go to a rodeo with you. In the meantime people listening want to know who are you and what you can do for me. So make sure you use your mouth. Talk to more people. If you're not meeting five or 10 people a day by e-mail, phone, blogs or at networking events then you are not working hard enough. That's right. A basketball coach of mine said to me if you're not fouling enough then you're not in the game. You want to get out there. I used to work with Tony Robinson of personal power. He said if you don't know who to talk to then throw a rock. Whomever it lands beside that is your next prospect so make sure you do that.

**Raven:** I love that.

**Martin:** Next is leveraging what you are doing now. Get more referrals. I get referrals from people who do not buy from me. So I talk to prospects who are excited, they liked it but in the end something happens. For example a budget isn't right at several hundred plus person company when they only have a 10 person company. Whatever the case may be. Yet they like you as a person and they like the concept but when the truth is out, the cards laid on the table it is just not a perfect fit right now. We don't force a sale, but we do say, who else do you know that will benefit from this. You have invested time and energy and effort educating the prospect getting them to like you and developing a friendship. It's a mistake to turn away when they say "it is not for me". They have hundreds of contacts. If they really like you they will refer you. So make sure you do that. Sell more to your existing clients. How often do you call back your existing clients? How often do you check in just to make sure everything is working okay, whatever it is. As soon as you make a sale make sure you follow up. Find out when the initial problems but keep falling back, not to sell but to check on them. You will stay at the top of their mind. For example, if they want to know who is the florist that they can use in the neighborhood your name will be at the top of their mind because you area a friend and not some pushy salesperson.

**Raven:** You gave some dynamic tips. I know one that I use for sure when I first bought out with my business... when I first had my woman of power radio show. I jumped on all the big guys and big gals conference calls. Because I knew they were going to have a lot of people. Just like you said Martin, I would join the call early and say "hi this is Raven Blare Davis from women power -- radio.com or Careers From the Kitchen Table.com "or whatever is the address of your website. That is one of those things that is, as you say a little thing but a big thing, because people are Goggling you while you say your name. I thought that was really awesome and all the tips that you have given are great. We have just about two minutes before break. If we have to come back and finish the answer to this we can. I'm going to ask you this really quickly. Should we focus our attention on one marketing a tactic at a time?

**Martin:** What you need to focus on is the strategy rather than the tactic. Strategies are focusing on a niche within the industry. For example, so rather than just selling car speakers you focus on selling European car speakers or American model speakers. That is something specific. Performance car tires or something like that. You have to have a strategy and then develop new tactic. What you need to do is to focus on strategy rather than the tactic.

**Raven:** ok, good point.

**Martin:** The strategy would be focusing on....something specific like performance car tires. So you have to have a strategy and then develop your tactic. We can cover more after the break. I will try to cover as much as I can now. Really what you want to do, is to focus on one. So once you have a strategy you want to focus on it. For example you focus on European car speaker systems. Okay that is my niche now I can do the tactic. Then ask when those people in the niche go? What forums do they go to and what blogs do the visit. Who is already the big blogger in the industry that I can create a relationship with. What events do they hang out at. For example, what if there are car shows, where everybody dries up and presents there model cars. They sits on a lawn chairs and everybody drives up to talk about the engine parts. I call it the hot dog theory of marketing. You know who makes the most money sometimes at the NFL games. It is the guy with the hot dog cart outside because someone else paid $2 million to get 70,000 people in a stadium. Somebody paid $250 million for the stadium. Somebody paid $500 million for the superstar quarterback. The hot dog stand man has a cash business. His customers then select their own hot dog preference and are doing most of the work; they select the ingredient to put on it. The guy has a cash business. He rolls the cart away and goes home for the night

**Raven:** Hold your thoughts. Right. What we're going do is take a quick commercial break. We'll pick up right when we come back. Sorry to interrupt you. Everyone you are listening to careers from the kitchen table. This show is all about teaching you how to cook without cooking with good old successful business tips. Yes, we will be back right after this commercial break..

**Raven:** Welcome back this is careers from the kitchen table teaching you how to cook without cooking. Yes indeed. My name is Raymond Blair Davis, Raven aka the talk show maven. We are back with Martin Wales. Martin is hot, hot. Martin we were talking about focusing our attention on one marketing tactic. I'm going to let you finish your point before we go on to the next question.

**Martin:** Well you need more than one tactic. I don't really like the battlefield theme but you know that you must have a strategy because you want to win the war even though you won't win every battle. Tactics are things like using e-mail with smart auto responders. So if you are working from home and you don't have a lot of resources you may not have people answering the phone live. What you can have is a giveaway offer. For example I'm on the radio today and I'm giving away a free video training and I will be giving away a complete copy of my book. I do that using the power of the Internet. It's not just about getting access to traffic on-line. It's about using the Internet to be more productive. You want me to give away a link right now?

**Raven:** Yes go ahead and give away a link and then we will move to the next question.

**Martin:** You can get a full and complete book called how to get more get more customers without spending a lot of money low-cost and no-cost marketing strategies. Simply go to http://www.customercatcher.com/freebook. You should know how to spell free, I'm thinking. Free book "B.o.o.k". Just like the librarian told you. So that allow us, if I'm speaking somewhere at an event and this is key here is about leverage. If I want to speak at an event, sure impress the 50 people in the room or the 2000 people in the auditorium whatever it is but give them something free. Let them sample you. Let them take you home. Just like a Costco or Sam's Club. They're going to sample you, people who sample from the buy from you. So give them a sample. You make it productive and that is a tactic. Do not rely on one single strain of marketing or prospects. If you had good fortune with very small newspaper classified ads. Don't use that strategy only. Why would you do that? That's like having a one legged table. You want a business that is like using a one legged table. You want a business that is supported by multiple streams of marketing and prospects. Referrals from your existing customers. Traffic on the Internet pay per click ads. Publicity is huge. I hope we talk about publicity if we have time. Free publicity getting on radio interviews. TV interviews, Internet radio and pod-casting as well as traditional broadcasting radio like right now at CNN. Make sure you have multiple streams of prospects coming in. Leave coupons on counters tops. Home parties things like that. Garage sales, as church social, and all those sorts of things we can sponsor tables. That doesn't mean that you're out there hawking big time, like standing on the table and saying buy these fish bowls. That is not what it's about. This is getting known so that people get to know you and ask you what do you do Raven.

**Raven:** You know the things that you're mentioning are so good. I'm saying to myself wow, there is no way I'm going to get all his inside secrets today he is going to have to come back. You know what we're going to try to squeeze into two more questions. One question you want to talk about publicity so let's move to that. Then give us a couple take action steps. You know this show is not about listening it is about taking a.c.t.i.o.n. We have about 3 minutes to wrap up both.

**Martin:** There are lots of ways to get free publicity without getting arrested, naked or dying.

**Raven:** Without getting naked? OK, go ahead.

**Martin:** That's it without getting naked. You know what they say. You are not famous until you have a stalker or you're naked on the Internet. But let's avoid that. You can get publicity in several different ways. One way is to publishing articles. Using articles.com is a free resource you can post articles and they are actually syndicate. Syndicate means that they have sent out. Next is to respond to great people like Raven will invite you to be on their radio show. Always try to get on radio. The number one thing is to make sure to give something away. Make sure there is a reason to contact you. Also there is a call to a.c.t.i.o.n.

**Raven:** Yes

**Martin:** Next use digital press releases. If you just use standard press releases, remember that they used to fax them out. Those radio stations and news room studios put them into the garbage right away. Now you can use digital press releases because they are links back to your website. You have links to live video and links to audio. This is the way to do it. Third, be the media. Raven you are walking talking living example of creating the media. Have your own talk radio show. We're on CNN for goodness sake. You cannot get more credibility than having CNN behind your name and slogan. Right, you can't beat it. So be on radio talk show host. That's what I teach, isn't how we met right? We both talked to each other about hosting our own radio show. http://www.Radiotalkshows.com is where I talk about this in more detail. It's a great ways to get customers. Let's only reason why I mentioned. Be the media. When you write an article you're the columnist. When you host a radio show you are the star, you're credible. When you are on television hosting a 1 to 2 minutes segment like I did on a TV network. You get calls from other media. Have you ever given notice to why the Washington Post columnists are interviewed on television and radio people are interviewed. Larry King is a radio guy on TV so is Howard stern if you can stand to watch him for 5 minutes. So be the media as well as get it into traditional media. Check out http://www.Prnewswire.com where you can get listed as an expert. They may have a fee for that even though they used to not. Lots of different places where you can get listed. Have your own blog. Get your opinion out there. Responsible blogs like the Huffington Post. Put your opinion out there with a live link in your signature file. That's were you say bye bye. Martin Wales http://www.customercatcher.com/free for your free video training. Always leave a footprint.

**Raven:** Oh you can take a deep breath now. You got a lot of information out there my man. Wow Martin. OK, give us a couple more take action steps.

**Martin:** An action step that you can take right now is going to your e-mail and add a signature file. Don't just put a quote. Quotes are nice but they did not make you money. Do you want to feel good or do you want to eat good. So, what you need to do is put into a signature file with a link to something else. Hi thanks for e-mailing me about something else by the way if you want a free 20 part video on how to get more customers go to customercatcher.com/free. So put in a affiliate link, a link to your blog if it is separate from your main website. Invite people to things that you are doing on-line at different sites, blogs that is an affiliate program. We teach people how to write books in 14 days. We provide that in the e-mail signature. Next thing you need to do is to mix it up. I'll give you a quick little bonus here you know how you have a vacation....

**Raven:** Martin, I have to ask you to hold on that let's take a quick break. We will come back and you can wrap up their thoughts then you can give them your information. Don't go anywhere your tune into careers from the kitchen table. Yes we are cooking but we may not be at the kitchen table right now. But we are cooking up in the studio right now. We'll be right back with our final comment from Martin Wales right after this commercial break.

**Raven:** Welcome back we are so glad you're here. We have Martin Wales is our first guest. You are tuned into Careers From the Kitchen Table brought to you by http://www.sippinghealthycoffee.com. Welcome Martin Wales we had just about one more minute. I don't want to think about you leaving here without giving people information on what you have to them the free gift and how they can get in contact with you. Then we are going to have you come back. How about that?

**Martin:** That will be wonderful. Always loved listening to you there the enthusiasm that you give is great like the website sippinghealthycoffee.com. I can smell it now. Where you get what we are talking about today, if you like to get free video-based training on-line. Do it when you want at a time that is convenient for you. To get more tips of how to get more customers. Go customercatcher.com/free. That is customercatcher.com / free, all lowercase f.r.e.e that's a good example. We talked about a free book offer you can get that at http://www.customercatcher.com/book. That is the whole entire version of my book that we hope to publish this year. Published in hardcover or soft-cover whatever it is going to be. Imagine 9535 copies of the book sold. Unlike you Raven I work from home I have over 9500 books sold. I would love to talk to you. If anyone would like to talk to me they can e-mail me at mw@customercatcher.com or Google Martin Wales and you will find me.

**Raven:** Alright my friend Martin you are fabulous. I just love you, thank you so much for coming on being a guest here at CNN 650 radio. I appreciate you. We will be talking soon my friend thank you much

**Martin:** My pleasure, God bless you take care.

Listen to the full audio of this interview by clicking the Radio/Microphone!

Plus be sure to visit and subscribe to Raven's popular newsletter and freebie!

http://www.careersfromthekitchentable.com

For more exclusive interviews like these be sure to join award winning talk show host and celebrity interviewer **Raven Blair Davis** each week for insider secrets, tips, strategies and formulas for success to help you grow your business faster rather than slower!

# *"Careers from the Kitchen Table"*

*Selected as one of the Top 100 Best Small Biz Podcast in 2011 by Small Business Trends.com*

## *America's Hottest Home Business Show*

**Hosted weekly by Celebrity Interviewer and Award Winning Talk Show Host Raven a.k.a.** *The Talk Show Maven*

*Visit* http://www.careersfromthekitchentable.com *and listen to years of archived audios from these experts, sign up for the free newsletter too!*

## Even more bonus audios
### *http://www.careersfromthekitchentable.com/audiobonus*

Former CNN/CBS radio personality, founder of AWOP Radio and celebrity interviewer Raven Blair Davis is looking for experts that may be interested in having their own radio show on her positive programming radio network. AWOP reaches up to 3.5 million listeners worldwide.

If it sounds like something you are interested in, let's schedule a time to talk so you can learn more about her award winning shows http://www.careersfromthekitchentable.com and http://www.womenpower-radio.com.

If you are a business owner and would like to air a 30 to 60 second commercial during Raven's show, call Raven via 800.431.0842. All commercials remain in each interview for a minimum of 6 months to a year. You will also receive a MP3 recording.

# *Raven International presents*
# *World's Leading Positive Programming Network 24/7!*

**AWOP** is under the umbrella of **"Raven International Media Productions"** as: *"Amazing Women of Power Talk 24.7 Network Radio."* The network consists of Raven's award winning talk shows: "Women Power Radio" and "Careers from the Kitchen Table," as well as her Celebrity Rave Reviews Talk show, plus over 30 other Amazing talk show host shows ranging from empowerment, round table discussions, health, law of attraction, business finance, spirituality, family programing, as well as an *Amazing Men Of Power* line up of shows on Fridays.

## The Amazing Women AND Men of Power Radio Network Schedule:

Sunday – Spiritual Family and Children Programming

Monday – Empowerment, Inspiration and Motivational Programming

Tuesday – More Empowerment, Inspiration and Motivational Programming

Wednesday – Health, Beauty, Metaphysical and Law of Attraction Programming

Thursday – Finance, Business Careers & Job Programming

Friday – The Amazing Men of Power & Music Lineup

Saturday – All Shore Encore – the best from the week's programming

We love social media too!  Connect with us on FACEBOOK by clicking **here**.
http://www.facebook.com/AmazingWomenofPower

To listen to the network LIVE – CLICK HERE or visit http://www.awoptalk247.com

Former CNN/CBS radio personality and celebrity interviewer Raven Blair Davis is looking for experts that may be interested in having their own radio show on her positive programming radio network.  AWOP reaches up to 3.5 million listeners worldwide.

For more exclusive interviews visit http://www.CareersFromtheKitchenTable.com or tune in live every Thursday and Saturday at Noon Eastern time.

# Want to have "your" own radio show and interview your favorite thought leader, author or celebrity?

Now you can get my easy to follow step-by-step formula for creating and launching your radio show and land that dream interview!  You'll get exact steps to go from zero to launching your first show in less than six weeks!

*Discover the real secrets to:*
- *Just how easy it really is to create and launch your show without having to buy expensive equipment*
- *How being a talk show host can be a great platform for you and your business*
- *What type of format is best for you and how long your show really should be*
- *The easiest way to create content for your show that will keep your listeners coming back for more*
- *How to get the guest of your dreams without paying them anything*
- *The fastest, easiest and simplest way to attract and build a worldwide audience*
- *When you should do a free vs. paid internet radio show or podcast*

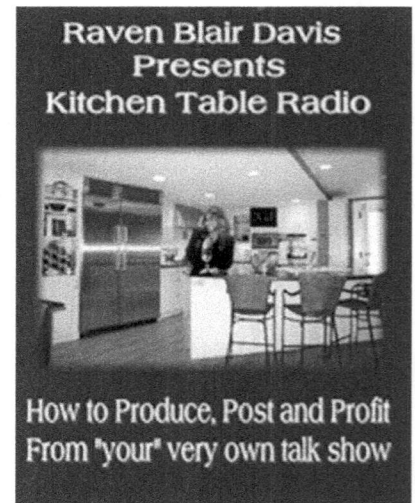

Raven Blair Davis Presents Kitchen Table Radio

How to Produce, Post and Profit From "your" very own talk show

**Bonus Audio:**  *Powerful You* founder Sue Urda interviews Raven on why one should do radio.  http://raven.audioacrobat.com/download/ee27c6a6-9968-bbd6-c6d9-f0df6db510b6.mp3

# Why be interviewed or mentored by Raven?
## See what others have to say...

*I have appeared on more than 800 radio interview shows in the past 20 years, and my time with Raven Blair Davis on her show <u>"Careers from the Kitchen Table"</u> was one of the most enjoyable ever.*

*She is a rare combination of dynamic, spontaneous and fun, as well as thoroughly prepared, deeply insightful and a great listener who responds with great follow-up questions as well as her own experiences in a way that moves the conversation forward without stealing the focus. I would highly recommend being on her show to anyone who is serious about getting your message out to more people—and enjoying the process at the same time.*

Jack Canfield
America's #1 Success Coach
www.JackCanfield.com

# KITCHEN TABLE RADIO

### INSIDER SECRETS TO PRODUCING, POSTING AND PROFITING
### FROM YOUR OWN TALK SHOW

## Unleash the power of your voice! Order yours today!
### http://www.kitchentableradio.com

## FREE CONSULTATION

Call or email Raven today to schedule your no cost, no obligation 15 minute consultation!

Email: Raven@Womenpower-Radio.com
Call 800-431-0842

OR Visit http://www.kitchentableradio.com now!

# ~ Notes ~

# *Stories from the*

# *Kitchen Table*

Enjoy these engaging stories from Entrepreneurs, Solopreneurs, and Founders of Non-Profit organizations as they share their challenges and how they've come to where they are today!

## ~ Notes ~

# Beverly Basila

*"Happiness cannot be traveled to, owned, earned, worn, or consumed.  Happiness is the spiritual experience of living every minute with love, grace, and gratitude."*
*Denis Waitley*

## Gluten Sensitivity: Beverly's Journey From Sickness To *Success!*

Beverly's journey from sickness to success has truly been a fascinating and memorable one.  Her healing started with a prayer request that was heard and answered by God.  It was this prayer that saved Beverly's health and became her life's testimony of faith and healing.

For many decades Beverly struggled with ill health.  She spent years searching for answers and kept persevering until she found them. The more she tried to get well, the harder and more complicated the process became.  In her own strength, healing was not completely achievable, but in God's strength it happened overnight.  Although the healing came quickly at first, it was the beginning of a long and interesting road.  Beverly was soon to learn that God wanted her on a journey to wellness through faith and perseverance.  He would start the process and lead her, but then she would have to continue it by stepping out in courage and faith in order to complete God's plan for her life.

Eventually Beverly learned that Gluten Sensitivity was the cause of many of her health problems.  Beverly had become so sick that she was unable to travel for eighteen years.  However, six months after getting off of gluten, her health dramatically improved and she was on a flight to the West Coast to start her training as a Holistic Wellness Consultant.  Beverly immediately proceeded to take a total of seven consecutive trips within a two-year timeframe to continue her training with some of the leading experts in the holistic health industry.

Before her health turnaround, Beverly had debilitating fatigue that was starting to interfere heavily with her life; but after getting off of gluten and the other associated food intolerances that contributed to her ill health, Beverly's newfound energy allowed her to regain her vivacious zest- for- life attitude. She went on to read over 500 books within a four- year time period, as she has always had a passion for being a lifelong learner in order to enhance her life, as well as the lives of others.

After Beverly experienced the dramatic healing that occurred in her own life, she realized that she had to share this message of knowledge, healing, and hope with the world. A new mission and passionate vision arose in Beverly and she was determined to fulfill it! Beverly knew God was leading her into what would be the most enlightening and fulfilling time of her life as she started her own business step- by- step with His guidance and blessings.

Beverly's mother has played an important part throughout Beverly's life by role- modeling the traits which Beverly values the most in her professional life, as well as in her personal life. These traits include honesty, integrity, respect, professionalism, compassion, dedication, perseverance, teamwork, a positive attitude, authenticity, unwavering faith in God, and overflowing love & joy. Beverly says that her mother and eldest brother played a key role throughout her journey and that she is truly appreciative of their unwavering support and assistance. This aided in propelling Beverly into pursuing her God- given mission of making a positive impact on this world by inspiring and empowering others to live healthier, happier, and more fulfilled lives.

*Beverly Basila*

*Recipe for* SUCCESS!

1. Be Authentic

2. Share Your Gifts

3. Have An Attitude Of Gratitude

4. Encourage & Empower Others

5. Stay In Faith and Expect God's Best

6. Commit To Being A Lifelong Learner

7. Believe In Yourself and Follow Your Dreams

# *About Beverly Basila*

Beverly Basila, H.H.C., H.L.C., N.W.E., C.G.P. is a Certified Holistic Wellness Consultant in Miami, Florida. Her mission is helping to spread the message of knowledge, healing, and hope to all who are in need. Beverly's special areas of interest within her business are Gluten Sensitivity, Celiac Disease, Delayed Onset Food Intolerances, and the GAPS Protocol (Gut & Psychology Syndrome). Beverly is trained by several health institutes on the East & West Coast and is a current member of twelve organizations which include The Holistic Chamber of Commerce, The Celiac Disease Foundation, Gluten Free South Florida, The Institute for Functional Medicine, The Weston A. Price Foundation, and PATH (Positive Alternative Therapies in Healthcare).

Currently, Beverly is lecturing and is available upon request for speaking engagements. She has been invited to be interviewed on radio, video, & magazines, and to speak on her personal experiences as a Holistic Wellness Consultant at various conferences. Beverly is passionate and enthusiastic in her mission of helping others as she knows first- hand how much holistic lifestyle living can positively impact and change a person's life for the better.

Beverly is grateful for the brilliance and kindness of the various experts which she has been exposed to throughout her journey. Some of these memorable professionals have included the following: Paul Chek, H.H.P., Dr. Natasha Campbell- McBride, M.D., Kevin Brown, C.P.T., Dr. Tom O' Bryan, D.C., Dr. William Sears, M.D., Dr. Peter Green, M.D., Dr. Kenneth Fine, M.D., Dr. Leonard Smith, M.D., Dr. Daniel Amen, M.D., Dr. David Brownstein, M.D., Dr. Mark Hyman, M.D., Shelley Case, R.D., Dr. Aajonus Vonderplanitz, Ph.D., Sally Fallon, M.A., and Dr. Daniel Kalish, D.C.

During the present time, Beverly is in the midst of writing a book titled "From Sickness to Success ~ ~ God's Way". She hopes her story will help others as she shares how she went from decades of sickness and searching for answers into a transition of healing and success with God at the forefront of her journey. Beverly is constantly in pursuit of knowledge and healing so that she may share her God- given insight with others in order to help aid in their healing process as well.

Beverly Basila, H.H.C., H.L.C., N.W.E., C.G.P.
BeverlySmiles@aol.com
Holistic Wellness Consultant
www.BeverlysHolisticWellness.com

~ Notes ~

# Nancy Lee Bentley

*"Everything Circles in Season and Bears Fruit in its Time"*
*Anonymous*

## *Succeeding Inside Out*

Nancy Lee Bentley's "full circle" success journey with food started early, at age 5, making mud pies in the sandbox. Curiously, five decades later, she would find herself "stuck in the mud", "down but not out" at a pivotal, key turning point in her prolific, food communications career.

Born on a self-sufficient, family farm in the Finger Lakes, she gained an early appreciation for good food, a profound reverence for nature and the larger circle of life, as she spent after schools doing chores and learning how to cook. Her talent and zest for writing surfaced while working on the high school newspaper, culminating in a completely intuitive decision to pursue a combined food, nutrition and communications degree at Cornell.

Then with spoon in one hand and mouse in the other, she cooked and wrote her way through a bevy of food-related jobs, including her first -- the Junior Acct Exec position created for her by NY's largest PR firm -- followed by Madison avenue food photography stylist, test kitchen home economist, *True Story* home service editor. She started doing freelance writing projects, only to find that she loathed the hypocrisy of promoting processed, corporate foods.

Before long she felt compelled to get involved in consumer activism. Organizing the first Food Day, spearheaded by Robert Redford in 1972, set the stage for a lifetime of championing healthy food-related causes: organizing NY's first organic conference, speaking out about GMO's, starting a food co-op network with the Ozark Mountain Daredevils, while juggling foodservice jobs, raising her two small children and plowing their garden with a mule.

On her 33rd birthday, she was blessed with a hugely expanded "food circle" vision about evolving the conscious, healthy food system we really need, throwing her more intensively into her own healing and spiritual work and laying the "soil-to-spirit bridge" foundations for her current integrative body, mind, heart and soul work.

Success as natural foods marketing consultant came as she helped organize the first Organic Trade and certification programs was praised for her pioneering "Windows of Opportunity" organic/specialty produce report by the USDA, developed wheat-free recipes for Cher as a food allergy marketer, and baked Prince's purple-flower birthday cake, while catering for Aveda's illustrious founder in Minneapolis.

Ironically, her most profound insights have come, not from her successes, but from her knock downs. After co-authoring Dr. Mercola's TOTAL HEALTH Program, writing about global food politics landed her in hot water. The carefully planned launch of her self-published Truly Cultured was botched when the book was mysteriously "missbound" at the printers, taking her "out of circulation" and into a dark, almost four-year stall.  Nothing was going right.

Yet, all this adversity forced Nancy to re-view, painfully face and take responsibility for her own creation.  Out of this agony, her own authentic story and integrative "Recircling for Real" work has emerged. Now she helps women clients stop spinning their wheels, uncover their hidden blocks and start finding their own way to "Remembering" who they are.

*Nancy Lee Bentley*

*Recipe for* SUCCESS!

1. Select and lightly grease one gigantic slow cooker or casserole for your "Create Your Own" Reality and Life

2. Be very choosy in selecting only the juiciest, ripest goals for What You Want to create. Add a cup of raw honesty and carefully peel back the layers to expose and precisely define what success means to YOU

3. Make dough with what you know, but carefully add ingredients tailored and seasoned just for that perfect customer

4. Ensure proper structure and rising by inspiring and building your own support team, virtual or real. Don't overbeat yourself! Focus on what you do best

5. When the temperature starts to rise, keep stirring and stretching yourself, looking, listening and learning –for new ingredients, ideas and candid advice from others to fine tune your recipe

6. Just like good yeast dough, you'll probably get punched down several times, Know that Everything Circles and Cycles. It's part of the proofing. But it will produce superb, delicious results as long as you take a breath, keep focused on your vision and keep going

7. What's Your Authentic "Ingredient"? You are Unique, there's no one else like you. Remember Who You Are. What you can share of yourself and your own experiences can profoundly benefit and serve other sisters on their own journey.

## *About Nancy Lee Bentley*

Nancy Lee Bentley is a dynamic Wholistic Health Expert, New Thought Leader, Speaker, Author and Coach with a Full Circle "Body, Mind, Heart and Soul" approach to Food and Health. Author of *Truly Cultured* , this Celebrity Expert's been interviewed on all the major networks, not only because she's done just about everything you can do with food, but because she's a real, in-the-trenches pioneer who's helped lay the foundations for organic and natural foods, local food systems and holistic health in this country , the world, today.

In her "soup to nuts" career as Healthy Foods Chef, Custom Nutrition Specialist, Natural Foods Marketer, and Minister of Healing, Nancy Lee has also provided plenty of celebrity food support ---developing wheat-free recipes for Cher, baking Prince's purple-topped birthday cake, catering for Aveda founder, Horst Rechelbacher, and co-authoring *Dr. Mercola's TOTAL HEALTH Program.*

While she's been honored by Earl Nightingale, the USDA, 2000 Notable American women, The Messenger Network and top-rated Self Growth.com, Nancy Lee Bentley is most fulfilled empowering her clients and readers to stop spinning their wheels with recurring eating, weight, finance, relationships and spiritual problems , start finding their own way, "Recircling For Real" and Remembering Who They Are.

Nancy Lee Bentley, Wholistic Health Expert
Nancy@TrulyCultured.com
Full Circle Service Center LLC
www.TrulyCultured.com

# Avalaura Beharry

*"If your dreams do not scare you, they are not big enough."*
*Ellen Johnson Sirleaf*

## *Dreams. Determination. Destiny.*

Avalaura has dreamed big since she was a child.  As a child, she loved imagining her future and engaging in spiritual activities.  She knew she would do something great.

As an undergraduate, Avalaura studied psychology at Howard University.  This experience allowed her to use her leadership gifts, ability to discern the truth in situations and offer wise counsel.

After working for a couple of years, Avalaura returned to Howard to pursue her masters in social work.  A hectic two years of graduate school, internships, planning a wedding, and frenetic living took its toll on her; she was drained and forced to slow down.  This was the beginning of her spiritual awakening.  Her faith and relationship with God pulled her through this time of personal exploration and learning her purpose.  She reevaluated her life and her beliefs and realized that she was not only a leader, teacher and counselor, but a gifted healer destined to use her gifts in a major way.  For over two years, she worked in social work.  She was unfulfilled and frustrated.

It became so unbearable that after a spiritual retreat, she prayed for help.  She returned to work, only to learn that she had been fired.  Having never been fired before, she was devastated, yet relieved.  The seeds for Avalaura's Healing Center had been planted.  She embraced her passion and was ready to pursue her dreams.

She studied the healing arts and was certified in Reiki, Spiritual Counseling, Life Coaching, Hypnotherapy and Aromatherapy.  In November 2005, she opened Avalaura's Healing Center, a healing and wellness center in College Park, MD. Although she loved teaching workshops, doing speaking engagements and helping people overcome their problems, Avalaura began to feel restless.

She knew she was not living up to her potential and it was time for a change.  She needed a teacher, a spiritual advisor.  She studied yoga in India and thought she would meet her teacher there. She didn't. However, she loved India and began practicing daily meditation and yoga.

While meditating, she heard a familiar person's name. She trusted her intuition and contacted the man who would change her life forever. Unbeknownst to her, he was the one who would teach her everything about spirituality and healing. He comes from a long line of Spiritual healers in Africa. Amongst all of his students, he chose Avalaura to share all of his wisdom. He introduced her to the world of Marabout, where healing physical, mental, financial and spiritual conditions, legal problems, negativity, relationship problems, witchcraft, and more are all possible by evoking the highest spiritual powers. This was the work she was born to do. This was what she dreamed of as a child.

She is one of the few people in the United States to be gifted with this sacred knowledge and ability. With the addition of Dream Interpretation and Marabout Spiritual Healing to her Healing repertoire, she now helps people all over the world to heal and overcome obstacles and live their dreams.

*Avalaura Beharry*

*Recipe for* SUCCESS!

1. Make God the center of your life. Realize that nothing is possible without God and through God you can overcome anything. Develop spiritual practices that feed your spirit and strengthen your relationship with your Creator.

2. Trust your intuition and pay attention to your dreams. Both offer powerful guidance that will help you stay on your path.

3. Dream Big! Living and fulfilling your dreams is possible if you are disciplined, committed and willing to do the work to achieve them.

4. Take the time to learn who you are, your passions and your unique purpose for being.

5. Don't be afraid of change and living outside of your comfort zone. This is how you grow.

6. Seek help; you cannot be successful by working alone. Find good teachers, advisers and experts to mentor and guide your interests.

7. Healing, growing and changing is a process. Be patient. Know that things do not happen overnight. If you remain faithful and trust the process, you will succeed.

## *About Avalaura Beharry*

Avalaura Gaither Beharry, also known as the Spiritual Sage, is a Healer, Counselor and Spiritual Teacher who is the founder and owner of Avalaura's Healing Center, a holistic wellness center in College Park, MD. She combines her formal education, intuitive wisdom and life experiences to help people in the DC area and around the world to heal and transform their lives.

Her goal is to assist, inspire and empower individuals to discover their true selves and divine potential to live the lives they were born to live. Using various healing modalities including Marabout spiritual healing, Spiritual counseling, Life Coaching, Reiki, Dream Interpretation and more, she specializes in helping people overcome hidden obstacles, remove spiritual blockages and solve problems previously thought to be insurmountable.

Many of her clients are women who feel lost, unbalanced, unfulfilled and in search of change, purpose and direction. They love her grounded, passionate approach, sage advice and guidance. She provides one on one, in-person and phone/Skype sessions, and offers workshops and speaking engagements on dream interpretation, Reiki certification, crystal healing, spirituality, living your purpose and manifesting your dreams.

Avalaura is a Licensed Graduate Social Worker who holds a Bachelor's Degree in Psychology and a Master's Degree in Social Work from Howard University in Washington, DC. Additionally, she is a trained Reiki Master/Teacher, Certified Life Coach and Spiritual Counselor, Hypnotherapist, Holistic Aromatherapist and Yoga Instructor.

Born and raised in Connecticut, Avalaura is the eldest of three children, born to parents who are first generation college graduates. She has been married for 10 years to her spiritual partner and confidant, real estate entrepreneur, Anthony Beharry.

Avalaura Beharry
avalaura@avalaura.com
Avalaura's Healing Center
http://www.avalaura.com

# Raven Blair-Davis

*"I will do today what others won't, so that I can live my life tomorrow like others can't."*
*Jerry Rice*

## *The Power of Inspiration*

I personally know that the power of inspiration can change lives – it has totally transformed mine! My story is an example of how harnessing this power can help you achieve your goals and visions, way beyond your wildest dreams.

As a child, my parents wanted the best for me. However, my upbringing was very strict and having goals or dreams were not encouraged often. Little did I know that the strict ways in which I was brought up would later become the culprit for my life's obstacles, and the lack of positive support from my parents would later trigger a lot of self-doubt, low self-esteem, and little hope in accomplishing my dreams. As I became an adult, I grew accustomed to settling for what I had in life. I began to believe that whatever I had was exactly what I deserved...and nothing more.

But somehow I often found myself wondering, Why not me? Why can't I have more? I began to read books like *Think and Grow Rich*, by Napoleon Hill, *The Game of Life and How to Play It*, by Florence Skoval Shin, and *Unstoppable* by Cynthia Kersey. I really enjoyed the inspirational stories Cynthia told of people who at one time had very little in life who, because of their strong will and determination, were now best-selling authors, extraordinary athletes, business owners, and some were even of the rich and famous. I begin to buy more books and soon had my own library. I added CDs and DVDs, all containing incredible stories that inspired me. I attended seminars to learn from famous luminaries from all over the world, and I began to hope again. I started dreaming again only this time I was having some very lofty dreams. It felt absolutely wonderful! But after about four years had passed, I noticed I had not seen much progress or change. I was still living day-to-day, and other than learning from some dynamic people, I had not seen much of a difference in our lives. Frustration and disappointment set in.

**In my darkest hour, a light shined.....my journey begins!**

In February 2006, my mother went into the hospital for surgery. We thought she would be home in a week or so, but it turned into six months. During the first three weeks, I sat and watched my mother lying helplessly in the Intensive Care Unit. I wondered if she had done what she wanted to do with her life and if she had any regrets.

Surprisingly, I came to realize that these were the very same questions I had about my own life. I realized I hadn't done what I wanted to do with my life, nor did I know my true passion. I had been so busy doing things for everyone else that I didn't have a clue about my own true purpose, passion, or vision. This was the day that God put on my heart that it was now my time to shine – my time to give to others, to make a difference, and to change lives.

A few weeks later, right there in the hospital waiting room, I started sketching out the format for a radio show created to inspire, empower and uplift women like myself. Women Power Talk Radio was created.

Now, this was not an easy task, and I had to overcome many obstacles. I had little time and few resources, and I had never tried claiming my own power before. I felt shaky and insecure about my abilities. But I knew this time I couldn't give up. I stayed focused even though it was extremely difficult. I set a launch date for my first show, got the tools I required, lined up my guest, and two months later Women Power Talk Radio aired! (http://www.womenpower-radio.com) What an unbelievable feeling that was – I did it!

Today I can truly say that I've never been happier or more fulfilled. My radio show has expanded into a network with three radio programs, and my career as a talk show personality continues moving in new and exciting directions.

**Use Inspiration to Change Your Life: Five Essential Keys**

**1. Know that your dreams are worth the effort.**

And you are worth your dreams! Do whatever it takes to turn your dreams into reality. Be true to your vision and claim your power.

Being on the radio was a dream I had in my early teens, but somehow along the way I had given up on it, mainly because of fear. I was afraid I would fail the FCC test that was required. Now, here I was at age fifty-five, and my long lost dream of being on the radio had not only surfaced but was a living reality. And there was no FCC license required to have an Internet radio show or podcast!

I made a wish list of all the people I had admired throughout the years who I'd love to interview on my show. I wanted my listeners to hear their stories, learn their success strategies and formulas, and how they overcame their challenges. I wanted to be a modern day Napoleon Hill! I immediately began to send out email requests and make phone calls, sharing my story and asking if they would be willing to share their knowledge in order to empower others. One by one, without ever asking me how many listeners I had, they accepted my invitation. Yes, some of my very favorite authors and speakers – like Cynthia Kersey, Lisa Kitter, and Rene Reid Yarnell – agreed to be guests on my show! I've also had the incredible opportunity to interview acclaimed actress Jayne Kennedy, as well as former President Clinton's diarist Janis F. Kearney and Claudette Robinson, the "First Lady of Motown."

## 2. Ask and you shall receive.

Make a list of what you require and who could assist you. Don't try to do it all yourself. Have the courage to ask others for their support. You'll be amazed at how many people will willingly share their time and talents.

In my case, I asked family members, friends, and complete strangers, "Who do you know that would be open to being a guest on my show?" I needed a professional looking Web site, and I had no extra money to invest so I bartered to get the necessary tools and resources.

One day I was sharing some of my challenges with my friend Lisa, and I asked for her assistance in getting the word out about Women Power (http://www.womenpower-radio.com). She agreed to put a little blurb about me in her newsletter that would attract advertisers. A couple of days after our conversation I acquired over a dozen advertisers for my show, and since then I've had no problem consistently bringing on new advertisers and sponsors.

## 3. Ask yourself, *"How badly do I want this?"*

What commitments and sacrifices are you willing to make so that you can accomplish your dreams? What inspires you that will keep you going during the tough times? Remember, if you are lacking inspiration right now, a vision of being of service to others in your own, unique way can totally inspire you. Find opportunities to assist other people, and watch your business grow in abundance.

I often wondered how was I going to keep my show going, but I knew deep inside that I had a taste of what accomplishing goals and dreams felt like, and I wanted it bad enough that I was willing to do whatever it took, even if it meant I had to get up three hours early and go to bed three hours late. I had a burning desire, and I knew I had to keep going.

## 4. Success is a combination of "inspiration" and "perspiration."

Developing a winning action plan is truly one of the big keys to success. When I start my day with a definite purpose, the outcome is fantastic! Each night I plan the next day's activities to insure that it will be a productive day. One of the things at the top of my list is to reach out to three personal contacts a day. I do that to build deeper relationships, joint ventures, and gain more referrals. My first choice is to pick up the phone and call them, but if I am pressed for time I will at least send them an email wishing them a very blessed and prosperous day.

**5. "This too shall pass."**

When life throws you a curve ball (and you will come up against some big challenges), remember that you are in control of your life. Circumstances can be hard, money can be scarce, and times can be tough, but it's how you handle these circumstances and your drive to overcome obstacles that will ultimately make the real difference. Trials and tribulations build character, so embrace them when they come and be confident and strong. Never lose faith, and never give up!

Sometimes just as you think you've seen the worst, something else happens that brings you to your knees, praying once again for strength and endurance. At one point, my husband and I were going through some difficult financial times, and we got a letter from our mortgage company saying we were fourteen days from foreclosure. That's when I begin to get really creative. I was determined that we were not going to lose our home.
I decided to launch my new broadcasting course sooner than I'd planned, and to get the money we needed I would pre-sell the course. I began to get ready for it mentally. I watched the movie *The Secret* twice a day; I listened to my favorite audios of teleseminar secrets by Alex Mandossian, I called my support team of friends and mentors, and we simply spoke it into existence.

One day the phone rang. It was a friend of mine who had just returned from a conference in another country. She mentioned that the speaker spoke about how beneficial it would be for the people in attendance who aspired to be speakers should strongly consider a radio show or podcast.

She said she immediately thought of me. Without even thinking, I told her she had perfect timing because I was launching a course designed to have her show up and running in six weeks. She was excited and told me she had met three other people who desired their own show too. All four of them signed up, and after that, others appeared. Another dream came true despite the curve ball I was thrown!

Always be true to your inspiration, call upon the unstoppable power within you, never give up, and be inspired by others who have achieved their dreams. The power of inspiration will transform your life!

Raven Blair Davis – "The Talk Show Maven"
Founder & Host www.WomenPower-Radio.com    www.careersfromthekitchentable.com
www.facebook.com/kitchentablecareers    www.twitter.com/workathomeradio

## Recipe for SUCCESS!

1.  Start each morning by listening to messages that inspire or empowers you to go that extra mile...no matter what!

2.  Set your intentions each day to stay committed and laser focus to reach your financial goals. Do not get distracted or quit.

3.  Always think of what you can do differently than others in your industry and stand out above the crowd.

4.  Use the power of your voice to grow your business faster (use the telephone to prospect, podcasting, create audio-books, teleseminars)

5.  Develop a team to assist you and delegate. Free yourself up to work on your business not in your business. Do Not Try To Do It All Yourself!

6.  Speak it, Claim it, Achieve it and be UNSTPOPPABLE in your pursuit.

7.  Check emails twice daily and voice mail and stay in income producing mode 80% of the day.

*Raven and her Mother Emily*

*I credit my mother with so much of my success - here's a poem she has written that shows you why:*

## *Many Dreams*

As distant as it may seem, life is full of many dreams.  And if destiny had its way, we would look forward to a bright new day.

There would be no more sorrow, there would be no more pain, and no more misgivings that we could not explain.

So we dream of what we might have been, to bring us to a
perfect end.

But someone is watching us from above and that someone fills our hearts with glorious love and what we find in him is so true.  A big wide world, that's all brand new......field with gratitude, loves and delights laughter and sunshine...what a wonderful sight!

Life is full of many dreams and this is the dream I dreamed tonight.

Oh how sweet tomorrow will be a brand new world for you and me.

*Poet: Emily M. Blair*

## *More About the Compiling Author - Raven Blair Davis*

### *America's Leading Authority on Leveraging the Power of Your Voice!*

Raven Blair Davis, aka "The Talk Show Maven" is a women who, after many years of searching for her purpose, is fulfilling her lifelong dream.  That dream, twenty years in the making, was realized April 23, 2006 when she broadcast her first radio show right from her own kitchen table.

Born and raised in Cleveland, Ohio Raven currently resides in Houston, Texas where she is not only fulfilling her own purpose in life, but she's on a mission to inspire others to do the same, by giving them the opportunity to shine in what they do.

She's a pro when it comes to interviewing thought leaders, celebrities, power business owners and ordinary people with extraordinary stories. Here are just some of the people Raven has had the pleasure of interviewing on her shows:

Hip-Hop & Business Mogul, Russell Simmons
Talk Show Host Montel Williams
Jack Canfield America's #1 Success Coach
Cookie Man & Literacy Advocate, Wally Amos
Intl Motivational Speaker Les Brown

Lisa Nichols of The Secret
Alex Mandossian, Marketing Guru
Actress Fran Dresher
The View's Sherri Shepherd
Singer Florence LaRue of the 5th Dimension

# Blair Boone

*" "In the depths of winter I finally learned there was in me an invincible summer" -Albert Camus*

## *Our lives are not our own*

Blair was a singer and scholar.  At least, that is how he self-identified.  So, how was it that after successfully completing an Honorary Bachelor's degree in Voice Performance and Master's degree in French Literature from Syracuse University that he found himself deeply entrenched in the NYC rat-race working a corporate job he wanted to escape?  Like many who migrated to NYC looking to pursue their dreams, reality struck and student loan debt it seemed was the only thing destined to take center stage.

After spending over a decade redefining himself as client relationship manager in a corporate environment, Blair was dealt a personal loss that would reset the trajectory of his professional ambitions. His mentor and friend of over two decades, Mary Trueman had passed away at the age of 92.  And as anyone who has suffered a deep loss of someone dear, one understands that the number of years of the individual does not help to soften the blow felt by the heart.

Blair was introduced and began taking voice lessons with Ms. Trueman who he fondly nicknamed the "Truemanator" due to her unrelentingly demand for excellence.  Originally from the UK, she spoke French and German with native fluency and held the equivalent of Masters' degrees in Vocal Pedagogy and Piano Accompaniment from The Royal Academy of Music in London making her a titan in her young pupil's eyes.  He was in awe.  Ironically, this English titan who stood all of five feet tall became the person he held in the highest esteem.

Although, Blair's professional contact with Ms. Trueman ceased after he graduated high school and left for Syracuse University, he continued to work with her during the summer breaks privately.  Ms. Trueman and Blair never stopped speaking to each other every week since they first became acquainted when he was fourteen.  They spent countless hours together discussing music, poetry and life.  Their twenty-two year relationship as student, teacher, and subsequently the very best of friends inspired him endlessly so upon receiving word of her death, Blair's dormant artistic passions were reignited.  But, with a demanding corporate job in full swing, this did not happen overnight. With the skillsets he developed from working in client relationship management for several firms, Blair founded a nonprofit arts organization, The Art Song Preservation Society (ASPS) in memory of his beloved mentor, and even dedicated a vocal arts competition in her name.

Through the significant loss of cherished loved ones, Blair has come to realize that our lives are not our own.  As the film Cloud Atlas so eloquently summarizes, "from womb to tomb, we are bound to others, past and present, and every day with our actions, we birth our futures."

With ASPS, he has been able to make contact with some of the most accomplished professionals in classical singing including but not limited to, Dalton Baldwin, Corradina Capporello, Thomas Grubb, Dr. Carol Kimball, and Thomas Muraco. These remarkable individuals all recognized the value and legitimacy of his mission and graciously accepted invitations to join the ASPS Advisory Board mirroring the generosity that Mary Trueman showed Blair throughout the years.

At ASPS, Blair is able to match singers with professional mentors recalling the advice that was given to him by Ms. Trueman: "Act now! While you have the advantage of time on your side; waiting around only opens the door to loss of opportunity as it begins to pass. Plus ultra (Go further beyond)!"

*Blair Boone*

## Recipe for SUCCESS!

1. Truth is everlasting – honesty is the best policy so act ethically from start to finish.

2. From your deepest pain, make your most beautiful songs – rise to the occasion in the face of adversity!

3. Nothing ventured, nothing gained - You're not going to win big unless you risk big!

4. Ghandi once said, An eye for an eye will make the whole world blind" so don't fight fire with fire, instead rise above the fight.

5. Find something to laugh at every day. Having a sense of humor is the key to good relationships and maintaining perspective

6. Follow your passions and the means to support yourself will come, but if making money is your sole goal then life's true abundance will never materialize.

7. "Happiness is when what you think, what you say, and what you do are in harmony" (Ghandi)

# *About Blair Boone*

A native of Texas, Blair began his study of voice and piano in Houston before moving to pursue his Bachelor's in Voice Performance (honors) and Master's in French Literature at Syracuse University. During his academic tenure he was nominated for and received many awards such as Syracuse University's prestigious Remembrance Scholar Award in 1995 (named for the 35 students killed in the bombing of Pan Am Flight 103 Dec. 21, 1988 over Lockerbie, Scotland), and The SU Graduate Teaching Fellowship in French in 1996. He also studied voice and piano at the Strasbourg Conservatory of Music in Strasbourg, France. After graduating and moving to New York City, Blair began teaching French and coaching singers in French diction. During that time, he also transitioned into an executive role and accumulated nearly 10 years of project management and client relationship management experience serving most recently as the director of client relationship management at a document processing services firm in NY. He has managed a number of strategic relationships at major firms, publishing and advertising companies, including Yahoo!, MetroSource Publishing and CIBT, Inc. Blair is a member of NATS, NYSTA and CMS. He is also a published film and music critic having interviewed a wide range of artists from Grammy-nominated jazz pianist Fred Hersch to Grammy Award-winning Haitian-American singer and producer Wyclef Jean. He founded The Art Song Preservation Society of NY because of his concern and deep interest in promoting this declining area of classical vocal literature. Blair has studied voice with Mary Trueman (Rice University), JoElyn Walkefied-Wright (Syracuse University), and Elem Eley (Westminster Choir College), and has also studied piano accompaniment with Mary Trueman, and with Edward Nemirovsky in NYC. He is currently nearing the completion of a second Master's degree in Vocal Pedagogy at Westminster Choir College in Princeton.

Blair Boone
ASPSNY@gmail.com
The Art Song Preservation Society of New York, Inc.
http://www.ArtSongPreservationSocietyNY.com

# Joe Louis Burroughs

*"Knowledge as a mere ornament may bring a certain amount of self-satisfaction to all who possess it, but it is useless to all others until it is put into action"*
*The Law of Success, Napoleon Hill*

## From the Battle Field to the Kitchen Table

Joe was motivated to start a business by a client who was heading to war in 2003. This client had $41,000 in debt and the wrong kind of life insurance with not enough protection over paying for it. A Primerica Representative set with the client and doubled his protection for half the cost. The representative then took the savings and with other resources eliminated his debt in 18 months. His wife was relieved and they were able to buy a home and established a substantial savings. The client completed three combat tours and since retired from the U.S Marine Corps. The client I'm speaking of is Joe.

Joe joined Primerica in 2005 after hearing about a business opportunity from a Primerica Representative. At that time in his life, he was working as a US Marine and was searching for a chance to improve his family's quality of life.

Primerica allowed him to be his own boss, work as many or as little hours as he chose and enjoy an unlimited income potential — all while helping families become debt free and financially independent.

For me, the Primerica Opportunity was dreams come true. Today, my organization continues to grow and I'm on my way to fulfilling my goals and dreams. Primerica has changed my life! Please contact me for more information on the Primerica Opportunity and how you can receive a free, personalized Primerica Financial Needs Analysis.

## Joe Louis Burroughs

### Recipe for SUCCESS!

1.  Consume your own product first and Lead from the front - Never ask anyone to do what you are not willing to do

2.  Be coachable and accountable - When the student is ready the teacher will appear

3.  Be the most positive - No one likes a complainer

4.  Get your partner involve in your business - 2 is not addition its multiplication

5.  Build other Leaders and duplicate success - Leadership without a successor is failure

6.  Self-improve always learn - You are your greatest asset. Build a better you.

7.  Take massive action NOW!  "Why put off today what tomorrow may not allow"

# *About Joe Louis Burroughs*

Joe Louis Burroughs II, was born in Savannah, Georgia achieved a bachelors in Mechanical Engineering Technology and achieved Master of Science Degree in Management. Joe was commissioned as a Marine Officer 1989.

Joe retired a Bronze Star recipient after honorably leading Marines for 20year with three combat tours. His entrepreneur endeavors started in 2005 when he was discovered by a Primerica Regional Vice President who saw greatness in him. Joe joined the company and rest is history. His business accomplishments include becoming a full service agent 2005 a promotion to Regional Leader in Primerica the last step before becoming a Regional Vice President. He came into Primerica because he saw that he can make a million dollars in a short period of time. A $10,000 Jacket winner became the #2 and #3 agent in State of Colorado for production 2007. Numerous happy clients and produced leaders that have been number#1 licensed agent in the State of California and a $10k Jacket winner (who accomplished it in 2.5days a record). Joe will help 2000 families in a years' time to realize their financial goals and dreams. He is also the co-founder and President of ROA 4G Business Group, LLC the marketing arm of the talk 2000 initiative and crusade.

He is married to the former Dian Pratt College sweet heart, 3 beautiful teenage girls Tehya, Kayla (twins 14) and Marissa (17). He loves the Lord, Freedom and Opportunity

Joe Louis Burroughs
ROA 4G Business Group, LLC
www.investinyoutalkradio.com

# ~ Notes ~

# Mable Cannings

*"Success is to be measured not so much by the position that one has reached in life as by the obstacles which he has overcome while trying to succeed."*
**Booker T. Washington**

## *From Adversity to Passion*

According to Mrs. Mable (Harris) Cannings, "that although she is grateful now, she was the one that teachers pushed into competing in Spelling Bee Competitions and presenting the Occasion during scheduled school programs while in elementary and middle school." She confesses, "they must have seen something in her that she didn't see herself."

Although the daughter of a High School Valedictorian and entrepreneur, she still had not discovered who she was and felt socially awkward at times. As a result of early childhood obesity she suffered from low self-esteem and found herself compromising her legacy of excellence in order to be accepted by others. She said, "Those mistakes made as a teenager would soon cost her dearly". Mable graduated from high school and by the time she went off to college she had two children in tow.

One day while working on her father's vending truck route they drove through a housing project where she noticed two teenage pregnant girls sitting on the stoop looking very dejected and hopeless. She said, it was in that moment that she vowed not to become another statistic and to do something with her life. She went on to graduate with two degrees in Political Science and Urban Studies from the University of TX at Arlington and began a career as a Public Administrator.

Up until Oprah Winfrey hit the world stage, Mable says she really didn't have a role model other than Congresswoman Barbara Jordan who she loved to hear speak eloquently. It was during Mable's professional work as a Program Director for a minority business technical assistance program, that she discovered her love for small business and the opportunity to be creative and to make a difference. That connection to her past work with her father was a riveting dejavu' experience that provided the impetus for her to step out into her first business as a grant writer. She later opened her own small PR firm where she organized special events and marketing projects for non-profit organizations.

Ms. Cannings began to feel a call on her life to impact women and devised a plan to launch a movement to bring awareness to the plight of women and would brand her dream as the Conference for the Empowerment of Women. Ms. Cannings was able to promote the empowerment of women so successfully that she was featured on the cover of the Dallas Weekly and garnered massive media sponsors that would trigger the first Black Empowerment Conference for Women at the World Trade Center, Trade show and business Expo and spin off Magazine, the DFW Empowerment Report, which she published and produced. She ran this conference from the World Trade Center in Dallas for several years.

After returning to Nacogdoches TX in 1995, Ms. Cannings started and operated a retail travel and tour business where she handled corporate accounts for multiple businesses, individuals and school districts. She later purchased her own buses and escorted groups around the world.

She was drafted into the Women's Hall of Fame for Professional Women in 2003. After a devastating personal loss in 2006, Ms. Cannings closed her business and began writing and publishing. Her first published book **"The Heart and Soul of Business": One Woman's Journey** was released in late 2009 which earned her "Bestselling Christian Book" which catapulted her profile to a national level. She was featured on ABC and through numerous print media. Her passion to help other women became a driving force.

In 2012 she felt that it was time to take her business to the next level. After several months of planning, in June 2012, Ms. Cannings rolled out her new radio show, "Unleash Your Potential Radio" and launched a new Weekly Motivational Monday's Newsletter and monthly breakfast for women which was also featured on the local ABC affiliate. Ms. Cannings continues to work with aspiring business owners, non-profit organizations and coaches other women to be successful. Her next project will be to launch a television show embracing her powerful personal empowerment concepts.

*Mable Cannings*

*Recipe for* SUCCESS!

1. Know who you are

2. Know who you are and the purpose for which you're on the planet

3. Seek God, and learn everything you can bout the vision

4. Translate this knowledge into a written Plan of Action

5. Guard against Fear and Procrastination and other limiting beliefs

6. Connect with Eagles e.g. other successful people who can help to support you and help you to get airborne

7. Leap. Be willing to take the risk to succeed. Keep your flight plan handy and never stop! (Your Bible)

# *About Mable Cannings*

Mable Cannings, wife, mother, Entrepreneur, Author, Speaker, Radio Talk Show Host of "Unleashing Your Potential" and Motivational Mondays. As an Entrepreneur for 30 years, Ms. Cannings distinguished herself as the CEO of Cannings Group International and of MC Tours & Travel. In 2004, the City of Nacogdoches Women's Commission on Families inducted Ms. Cannings into the Woman's Hall of Fame. She is the recipient of numerous awards and recognitions, including being recognized in Washington D.C. by the Secretary of Labor for the Outstanding Volunteer of the Year. Ms. Cannings say's "she's most proud on her work as the founder of The Conference for the Empowerment of Women." She's a frequent speaker on high school and colleges campuses to challenge students to stay in school to achieve their personal and academic greatness. Ms. Cannings is a motivational speaker, keynote and seminar presenter to help women to discover their spiritual and economic path; she also writes and publishes books, e-books and empowerment journals to inspire others to reach "Outrageous Success" personal and business.

Mable Cannings
Mable@UnleashYourPotentialRadio.com
Mable Cannings Intl

~ Notes ~

# Carmen Cook

*"Set your goals high and don't stop till you get there."*
**Bo Jackson**

## From Fearful To Confident Entrepreneur

Carmen Cook nurtures her close personal relationships, is clear on who she is and what she stands for. Her current prosperous lifestyle and the way she conducts business require no external justification because of her professionalism and Integrity.

Let me share here this amazing woman.

Carmen was an entrepreneur at the early age of 6 years old in her native east coastal town in Puerto Rico. She was so resourceful and made the best out of bad situations. Several hurricanes came through her community every year. Afterwards she would go out and scan the shore line gathering old iron pieces that washed ashore.

She stashed her findings under the house. A local man came around in a old truck buying iron scraps. Every time she sold her iron scraps she would make a few dollars. Hurricanes were profitable for little Carmencita.

She moved to New York City at age 9 with family and lived on the lower east side Manhattan, at 327 East Houston Street. When she was in her mid-teens she once again got involved in business with Amway.

She was handed a suitcase full of products, hostess gifts, a broom and a mop to show at the home parties and off she went on weekends. She made money.

Her entrepreneurial spirit carried her into adulthood. Even after she became a registered nurse and joined the Army Reserves, she learned to make jewelry and made extra money from that new found skill.

In 1997 she became intrigued by the rumors that you can make money from the internet, bought her first computer and fell in love with the internet.

She also had a love for travel to exotic lands and in June 2002 traveled to Ghana West Africa to meet a child she sponsored there through World Vision. The visit to that country impacted her such that, a year later she founded the 501c3 America For Ghana Foundation.

Her commitment to help needy people in rural communities was unwavering. She began recruiting nurses, doctors and dentists and escorted them to Ghana to provide free medical care and took an abundance of supplies during the short term missions.

As Carmen became more and more knowledgeable about the internet, she began to make money from home business opportunities. Now that she has retired from the Army and her nursing career in general, she thrives helping other people profit from online business opportunities.

Her first book, The Serious Business Owner's Guide To Creating Customers For Life, she freely gives at http://www.300Comments.com.

Her core values are God first, family second, business and everything else, third. Her mission: To empower women through her online business ventures easily and consistently via education and teamwork.

Carmen loves people and the Law of attraction. She's living the life of her dreams and loves making a living from the internet, her products and joint ventures.  She recommends stay focused on your wants because your wants will take you to your dreams.

*Carmen Cook*

*Recipe for* SUCCESS!

1.  Follow your life-long passion. If you have been dreaming about starting your own business, choose something that you love. But make sure there's also a market for it! Success is not the key to happiness. Happiness is the key to success. If you love what you are doing, you will be successful. Albert Schweitzer (Nobel Peace Prize Winner 1952)

2.  Work on your business not in it. Once you have found your passion, start with a clear business plan and a well worked out business strategy. A business plan is an essential roadmap for your business success. A strategy helps you focus on long-term results. Drive thy business or it will drive thee. Benjamin Franklin (writer, inventor and one of the founding fathers of the United States)

3.  Define clear business goals. Know what is that you want to achieve at the end of the day, week, month and year. Define clear goals, track everything and monitor the results. Man is a goal seeking animal. His life only has meaning if he is reaching out and striving for his goals. Aristotle (Greek philosopher)

4.  Be a leader to yourself.
    Leaders have to learn to lead themselves to greatness through discipline, consistency, and taking action. Leaders reprogram their subconscious and focus on "I can", "I will", "I must".

5.  Take action. You must learn to be a decisive decision maker. Start by being honest with yourself, be a better listener and develop the skill to be an effective communicator. Growing confidence and mental toughness will assist you in taking the right actions at the right time every time until it becomes a way of life.

6.  Make your wants non-negotiable. Your wants are different from your dream. Want happens before a dream; today, next week, next year. Breakdown your dream into wants. Nurture your wants.

7.  Focus, focus, focus. Chet Holmes once said "It's better doing 12 things 4,000 times than doing 4,000 things once". If you want to get results, you need to focus your time and money on one thing. Without focus you're lost.

## About Carmen Cook

Carmen Cook is a fun loving woman born in the beautiful island of Puerto Rico. Her entrepreneurial heart lead her to experience many industry business models from direct selling to online businesses. She served in the military in the Army nurse Corps both in the Reserves and active duty. She was initially commissioned as a Second Lieutenant and retired 22 years later as a Major.

Carmen is married for over 40 years, has a son and daughter and two grandchildren. She is happily living in Central Florida running her home business and actively participating in the Toast Masters International club.

Carmen Cook
CarmenCookOnline@Gmail.com
Victory House Publishing

# Lynn Crocker

*"Anyone who has never made a mistake has never tried anything new"*
*Albert Einstein*

## *Stressed Out Ad Exec Finds Fulfillment as Life Coach*

When Lynn found herself madly running up and down the hall of where she worked trying to shake the stress and pressure of her job, she knew it was time for her to find something else to do.

Lynn's career in Advertising started soon after she graduated from college. She went to work for a well-known ad agency in the San Francisco Bay Area. Over the years, her career took her to gradually higher-level positions at ad agencies in Ft. Lauderdale, Miami, Atlanta and back to the Bay Area.

As Lynn's responsibilities increased so did the pressure. She describes herself as sensitive, empathetic, and kind. Three traits that did not serve her well in the cut-throat arena of agency work.

Seeking others like herself, she transitioned into the world of non-profit communications. While she found a meeting of the hearts with her co-workers the workload was double. The lean budgets of non-profits often require that staff people wear many hats and put in long hours.

Lynn did not mind working hard for a good cause, but after seven years in non-profit marketing communications she was beginning to lose her passion for the functions of her job. For her, writing press releases was a drag, cow towing to network news media was a chore, and overseeing the creation of brochures, annual reports, and campaign materials had lost its luster.

Plus, struggling to maintain a work life balance, she left the office every day at 5:30. But after her evening jog and dinner, she more often than not found herself in front of her computer trying to make a dent in her ever expanding "to-do" list.

Finding herself in crisis in the hallway outside her office caused Lynn to do some deep thinking.

It didn't take long for her to recognize that her favorite parts of each day were the times when a co-worker would present herself or himself in Lynn's doorway and ask "you got a minute?"

The role of "listener" was not a usual for Lynn. All of her life others have felt comfortable talking with her about the most fearful and intimate parts of their emotional experiences.

At the non-profit, Lynn was lovingly referred to as "upstairs HR" and had developed a reputation as an attentive, empathetic listener who didn't give opinions or judge but rather asked good questions and seemed to draw people towards their own answers.

The more Lynn pondered, the more she realized that THIS was what she was most proud of at the end of every day. Sure the well-crafted press release and attention getting brochure were important, but she was most excited by seeing people awaken into their own power.

It wasn't long before Lynn made the commitment to Life Coaching as my career.

Taking the plunge and leaving her Director-level position (and its salary) was scary, but Lynn felt that she did not have a choice. She knew that assisting others with understanding that their power comes from within and helping them unlock the answers and direction within them, was her calling.

These days Lynn enjoys the comfort of coaching others on how to create the life of their dreams from her own couch while having plenty of time to live the positively engaged and integrated life of HER dreams.

*Lynn Crocker*

*Recipe for* SUCCESS!

1. Be grateful for what you have

2. Visualize your desired outcome

3. Fill your head with positive information

4. Keep your body healthy

5. Emulate a role model

6. Don't procrastinate – It takes much more energy to think about not doing something than to do it

7. Create a structure for your day

8. Give yourself time to play and dream

## About Lynn Crocker

I am a certified Life Coach through Coach Training Alliance, an International Coaching Federation credentialed program. I have assisted countless individuals along their paths. Through my training I honed my listening skills and developed my natural intuitive abilities to assist my clients with finding the keys to unlocking their desires and creating the life of their dreams.

I am constantly learning about myself and striving to grow and evolve into a progressively happier and more content, centered, satisfied, alive, and engaged person. I am fortunate to have had people in my life who played the role of an empathetic, compassionate, and unbiased listening partners thereby assisting me with identifying and embarking on my next step. It was my desire to be this type of resource for others, that led me pursue Life Coaching as a career.

As a Life Coach I provide a safe environment for personal exploration, act as a sounding board for new ideas, and support my clients through big decisions and seemingly insurmountable goals. I do this through structured conversations and targeted questions designed to help my clients break through mental obstacles, move beyond the safety of what they know, and expand their thinking process. My clients find that having a supportive Life Coach by their side helps them navigate through this exciting but challenging time. My areas of focus are self-discovery and personal growth.

For me, Life Coaching is a calling. I am extremely grateful that my passions, skills, and talents have led me to engage in this personally fulfilling and rewarding career.


Lynn Crocker
Lynn@lynncrockercoaching.com
Lynn Crocker Coaching
www.lynncrockercoaching.com

# Adil F. Dalal

*"You can't solve a problem with the same mind that created it."*
*Albert Einstein*

## *The Great Metamorphosis*

Adil is a strong believer in his motto "You are more than you can ever imagine!" and is passionate about his mission to optimize human potential.  Adil grew up in Mumbai, India and when he was only 15 years old, Adil read the autobiography of Lee Iacocca and he knew that he wanted to live in USA.  Since Adil's Dad had retired, he could not afford to send Adil to USA for further studies.  Thus, Adil worked extremely hard to achieve his dream, stood first in the University in Automotive Engineering and got adequate scholarships to come to the USA.

He had to overcome several obstacles and on December 31, 1991 he finally landed in Michigan for his MSE in Mechanical Engineering.  Adil, again had to work extremely hard and life as a student in USA taught him many lessons but the values he was brought up with guided him throughout his career.  He soon became a Research Assistant and was also awarded a Graduate Research Fellowship at Western Michigan University.  The week Adil graduated he got a great job in a Medical organization and rose up the ladder quickly from an engineer to an executive while completing his second Master's degree in Engineering Management.

But he still felt something was missing and was not happy with the rat-race.  He spent several years in self-inquiry and as a result underwent a true metamorphosis.  He became an entrepreneur and started his own company, Pinnacle Process Solutions, Intl®, and helped several corporations eliminate waste from their organization using his expertise in Lean technology.  He soon realized that many organizations were not using lean tools correctly and moreover, were not maximizing the potential of their best assets, their employees.

He developed iLean® technology and helped individuals and corporations through his consulting, coaching and his workshops achieve their maximum potential.  He is a big advocate of eliminating stress from the workplace as he realized that stress is not only a leading cause of several health issues but also has a major impact on corporate productivity and on employee engagement. He has recently developed software called "Pinnacle Performance Zone™" which helps people self-regulate their stress within 10 minutes a day and also allows them to realize their true potential.

Adil expertise in his field has made his company mature from a sole proprietorship to a global company with clients in Africa, Asia, Canada, Europe, Mexico and Latin America. Adil is a renowned keynote speaker, volunteers as the Chair for the Human Development & Leadership Division of ASQ has authored The 12 Pillars of Project Excellence, and co-authored ASQ Lean handbook. He is also the host of his new radio show, See2B™: Visualize Your Potential.

Adil lives with his family in Austin, TX, is currently pursuing his PhD degree in Psychology and working on his third book, The Power of Visualization™. He could not have achieved this success without his metamorphosis from a productive "corporate being" to a great "human being".

## Adil F. Dalal

### Recipe for SUCCESS!

1. Know Your Strengths (and Opportunities) Self-awareness is always the best first step to success in any endeavor of your choice.

2. Focus on Your Strengths. Soar with your strengths instead of trying to focus on your opportunities.

3. Create a Personal Vision Statement. Aim for the Stars defining a long term vision is very critical to your success. The key is to aim for the stars as even if you miss, you will at least land on the moon.

4. Select a profession which you truly enjoy. When you enjoy what you do, you never have to work at it — it comes naturally; you avoid work, stress and have fun! Also, let Your Passion for your work show.

5. Invest in Yourself. Continuously upgrade your abilities. It is important to keep challenging your brain cells. If you are not learning, your brain cells are literally dying.

6. Focus on Good Thoughts, Good Words, and Good Deeds. No matter what the challenges in life; have a life filled with good thoughts, good words and good deeds.

7. Live a Legacy, Leave a Legacy™ Try to live a life which leaves everything you touch enhanced. Make your own legacy.

## *About Adil Dalal*

Adil Dalal is the CEO of Pinnacle Process Solutions, Intl®, LLC and the Chair of Human Development & Leadership division of ASQ. He is a keynote speaker, an executive coach and an internationally recognized expert and a thought leader in lean manufacturing and in project leadership. Adil is the author of "The 12 Pillars of Project Excellence", ASQ Lean Handbook and upcoming book, The Power of Visualization(TM). He is well known for pioneering several key advances in technical fields like Science of Simplicity™, Lean Project Leadership™ and in human capital enhancement like iLean® technology, Power of Visualization™ and Permanent Breakthrough Transformation™.

Adil's mission is to focus on enhancing the value of the 'appreciating assets' and optimizing the human potential in addition to developing the necessary technical skills for ensuring the long term success of individuals and corporations.

Adil is currently a PhD student and holds the following degrees: MSE in Engineering Management, MSE in Mechanical Engineering, BSE in Automotive Engineering. Additionally, he holds the following certifications: Certified Project Manager (PMP), Certified Quality Engineer (CQE), Certified Lean Bronze Professional (LBC) and Board Certified Executive Coach.

Adil F. Dalal
Pinnacle Process Solutions, Intl., LLC
www.pinnacleprocess.com

# Michelle DeBerge

*"Our deepest fear is not that we are inadequate. Our deepest fear is that we are powerful beyond measure. It is our light, not our darkness that most frightens us. We ask ourselves, Who am I to be brilliant, gorgeous, talented, fabulous? Actually, who are you not to be? You are a child of God. Your playing small does not serve the world. There is nothing enlightened about shrinking so that other people won't feel insecure around you. We are all meant to shine, as children do. We were born to make manifest the glory of God that is within us. It's not just in some of us; it's in everyone. And as we let our own light shine, we unconsciously give other people permission to do the same. As we are liberated from our own fear, our presence automatically liberates others."*
*Marianne Williamson*

## *The Learning Curve*

Michelle DeBerge graduated from The Coaches Training Institute while she was doing homeless outreach and working with mentally ill offenders. She found personal growth work very important and studied with some of the top workshop leaders and also graduated a yearlong women's leadership program.

Michelle then went through a life-changing event that caused her to reconsider her life. She decided to leave her job and open her coaching practice. She assumed that she would be busy right away because she new so many people from her past job.

She was very wrong. After waiting for a few weeks and not having any clients she began to worry. She did not have any experience running her own home-based business. She needed systems to manage her time, create content and market her services.

Michelle was passionate about helping people create the lives of their dreams. So she began a newsletter with only 5 people on her list. Every month Michelle would introduce her readers to someone that was changing the world and following their passion. She filled her newsletter with hope, possibility and real struggles that were overcome. Soon her list began to grow.

Michelle used FaceBook to promote her message, posting her newsletter, blog and her personal growth struggles and achievements. She began to interact with people all over the world. She made sure to answer every email, message or note so that she began to create

119

community with her readers.

She learned how to run a business and began to fill her practice with clients. Soon she had the opportunity to contribute chapters to different books featuring some of her favorite personal growth experts and her speaking career began.

Michelle knew when she started her business that she wanted to create a life with a successful practice that she enjoyed, and have more personal freedom. So she designed her business to fit her lifestyle. She now lives part time in northern California and part time in Cabo San Lucas, Mexico. She coaches her clients over the phone so that she can travel more and conduct her business remotely.

Michelle soon began to teach women executives how to have a better work/life balance since most of them spent more time working and less time living. With tools and strategies that she uses in her own life, she teaches her clients how to have more personal freedom, be more productive at work and have a more enjoyable life.

It took Michelle four years to create a successful business, but the hard work paid off. She had faced a huge learning curve when she began because she did not know how to run a business. Yet she always asked for help, took the classes she needed and asked other home business owners to mentor her as she learned.

Today Michelle enjoys her life as she travels, coaches, speaks and writes. A believer in continuing her education, she takes time to still attend workshops, seminars and conventions where she can learn new systems, tools and ways of making her business even better.

## Michelle DeBerge

*Recipe for* SUCCESS!

1. Always invest in yourself and your education.

2. Ask for help and support from experts in your field.

3. Break your goal down to smaller pieces and do one at a time.

4. Schedule time for both work and play.

5. Believe in your dream and work towards it.

6. If it doesn't work right away, keep trying.

7. Pick something that you are passionate about.

## *About Michelle DeBerge*

Michelle DeBerge is a professionally trained life coach, motivational speaker and author. She specializes in helping clients tap into their passions, clear their roadblocks and design lives of their dreams. Michelle has been recognized for her work both locally and nationally.

Michelle began to create the life of her dreams over five years ago after a life-changing incident. Using the tools she had, being a life coach, the law of attraction and a lot of personal growth work, she transformed her life. Her passion is helping others do the same.

Michelle spent years as a case manager for mentally ill offenders and was one of the founders of a team that created a Mental Health Court in Marin California. This court has become a model that is being used across the country. This model has reduced the recidivism in the jail system and has allowed the inmates to receive the medical treatment needed for their illness.

She professionally trained to be a life coach at The Coaches Training Institute and is a graduate of a yearlong women's leadership program. She has been locally and nationally recognized for her work.

Michelle believes that if you are following your passion that anything is possible. Tapping into the magic of manifestation is a powerful tool.

Michelle DeBerge
michelledeberge@me.com
Michelle DeBerge Life Coach
http://www.MichelleDeBerge.com

# Joseph DiChiara

*"I haven't had the time is a Dangerous sentence"*
*Napoleon Hill*

## *Cash Flow Now*

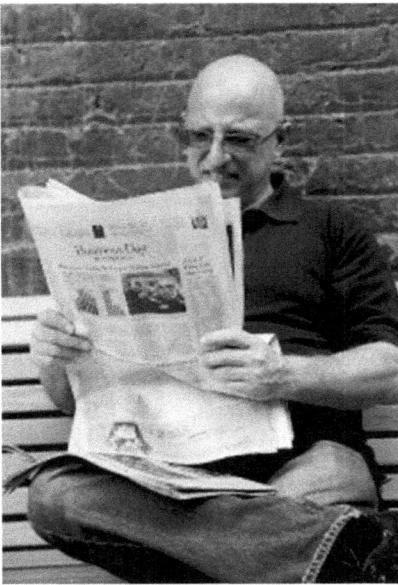

ICE CREAM! Joe's 1st successful business was an Ice Cream Truck. The summer before his senior year in Oswego he decided that he could make more money working for him and rented an Ice Cream truck. I wasn't surprised because Joey was always hustling. He had paper routes, sold flowers on street corners and always seemed to find ways to keep himself busy and make money at the same time.

When he was a teenager he created this baseball game that he played with dice. He had everything down to a science and even kept score, standings and stats. At one point he even thought about selling the game but we had no idea how to go about something like that.

So Joe went on to graduate with a degree in Accounting and became a CPA a few years later. "Living the dream" he got married, had 3 kids and bought a house in Hicksville, NY.

Early on though, thinking he was well on his way to success he found himself unemployed with a small family to support. With no jobs available Joe did what any respectable entrepreneur would do-he started a cleaning and maintenance business. Little Anthony's Cleaning Service named after his son. That business was eventually sold as Joe started selling insurance and financial products for John Hancock, eventually making his way back to the CPA profession. Joe excelled at every position in accounting always had some business on the side. He was always a few years ahead of the curve when it came to technology and how to use it in business. Before anyone was "paperless" Joe started this scanning business. The technology was new and the buggy but he felt that this was the future. Unfortunately the scanning business was dropped because of a dispute with the manufacturer.

Joe started and sold several accounting practices over the years. One practice was devoted to QuickBooks training and grew into a nice little small business that he was able to package and sell to a local accountant.

In 2004 Joe started Pro Bookkeepers Inc. which is a licensed remote bookkeeping system serving start-ups and Micro Businesses all over the US.

During June of 2010 while taking the Napoleon Hill course The Law of Success Joe's DiChiara's Entrepreneur Success System was born. It happened exactly the way Napoleon Hill describes it in his book Think and Grow Rich. Joe say's "It hit me like a bolt of lightning, I knew that what I wanted to do with the rest of my life is teach Success Principles to entrepreneurs all over the world"

As a regular contributor to www.micromentor.org as a volunteer business mentor and the Micro Finance organization www.KIVA.org Joe is making a difference in people's lives all over the world.

*Joseph DiChiara*

*Recipe for* SUCCESS!

1. A Definite Chief Aim-Know EXACTLY where you are going with your business.

2. Employ the Master Mind concept-Work with like-minded people

3. Do your Homework

4. There is NO substitute for WORK

5. Be Purpose Driven not Money Driven

6. Utilize Self Discipline to incorporate good habits

7. Maintain real time accurate books and records

# *About Joseph DiChiara*

Joe loves the concept of taking an idea and turning it into a business model that generates cash flow. He doesn't know why but it's as simple as that. The result of a good business model is positive cash flow and he is absolutely convinced that the only reason that anyone is in business is to create positive cash flow.

He believe that most dreams are achievable, no matter how big or how far out of reach it may seem now. If a person is passionate about their cause and has the right motivation Joe believes that he can help create a solid business model that can create positive cash flow.

Joe utilizes the 30 years of CPA experience and watching thousands of business owners painfully trying succeed, only to barley provide a modest living for them and their family.

Joe has found that the simple Principles laid out by Andrew Carnegie in 1908 can create the foundation entrepreneurs need to realize the American Dream and The Pursuit of Happiness and POSITIVE CASH FLOW.

Joseph DiChiara
Info@joedichiara.biz
Entrepreneur Success System
www.JoeDichiara.biz

# ~ Notes ~

# Lorena Douglas

*"It's time to start the life you have imagined."*
**Henry James**

## *Purpose Driven*

Lorena journey begin as a single mom with three children after spending 2 years struggling with leaving her secure job and a weekly pay check.   Finally in 1985 she stepped out on faith with God by her side.   She steps into entrepreneurship (crazy as people though she was). Without consulting anyone she made this decision and knew that if she had the determination and faith in God she could get thru this.

Lorena Is known as a catalyst for sparking that light inside of you, and wake the sleeping giant within you. She provides Life experiences, wisdom, and a listening ear, to help you to  overcome obstacles you may face in your journey and empowers you to overcome obstacles in life, achieve and clarify your goals, to take action and optimize self- balance to realize your possibilities, your purpose, goals and dreams.

She owned and operated Lorena's Nail Boutique and expanded to Lorena's Day Spa 1985-2001. But success was not easy she worked long hours while giving up a lot of a regular life.  She was dedicated and believing in her purpose and faith walk.

In the year 2000 Lorena life journey changed with the loss of her mother and through divorce, several unhealthy relationships and other areas in life.

She found herself stuck and was pressed to find a way to work through these issues, to a place of wholeness both mentally and emotionally.  She made a decision to seek the Bible for understanding the complexities that life brings. She relocated and remarried in the process while realizing the power of self-growth, uncompromising faith and possibilities.   Through 'the process' she founded Purpose Driven Life Coaching and Production a podcast talk show. Hosted by Lorena called Destiny Driven Radio was created As well as Gods message to the heart free conference bible study.

Lorena's life experiences have always been giving back to her community. Lorena believes that everyone has a purpose and destiny in life. While it may not always be Easy, making a commitment to unravel life's mysteries can be challenging and fulfilling even Through the struggle.

Lorena realized that her true purpose and passion was in her natural abilities as a gift, when she completed The Fowler Wainwright International (FWI) certification as a certified life coach certified Behavioral modification coach as well as a business owner for over 15 years and life experiences.

*Lorena Douglas*

*Recipe for* SUCCESS!

1. Put God first: Let go, let God lead you through your journey one step at a time walking on faith.

2. Define your life: what do you want the rest of your life to be about. if you can see it you can achieve it.

3. Reflect on the challenges: used your learned skills. Use those same qualities to grow your business.

4. Align yourself with like-minded individuals, mentors, continuing education, reading, join networking groups

5. STAY FOCUSED! Start while you are still employed and Get professional help.

6. Write out a Strategic Plan and Business Plan You need an agenda for daily success. Create contacts

7. Never give up no matter how hard it gets, the very time you quit is the very time you will have succeeded.

# *About Lorena Douglas*

Radio Host/CEO Manager and Certified Life Purpose/Behavioral Modification /Professional Coach who combines knowledge, interpersonal skills, self-motivation and resource enhance work productivity and employee and customer satisfaction.

Project Planning • Marketing and Fundraising• Certified Life Coaching • Employee Development and Intervention Strategies• Individual Coaching • Process Improvement Initiatives• Customer Service• Trainer/Facilitator.

Life Coach Rena D. Is known as a catalyst for sparking that light inside of you, and wake the sleeping giant within you. She provides Life experiences, wisdom, and a listening ear, to help you overcome obstacles you may face in today economic times. Life Coach Rena D. can assist you with dedicated support, and empower you to overcome obstacles in life, achieve and clarify your goals, take action and optimize self- balance to realize your possibilities, your purpose, goals and dreams.

Lorena's life experiences have always been giving back to her community. She continues to pursuit knowledge with the dedication in helping others.  A self-motivated professional and Entrepreneur. She effectively owned and operated Lorena's Day Spa, and was a Regional Account Executive, for Star Nail Products. She also serviced on varies committees, and ADM Bargaining Committee. She was feature in 1998 in a National Nail Magazine "Moving up, Moving out" As well as newspaper articles, and receiving an merit award, for demonstrating a commitment to professionalism. In achieving these awards as well being a single parent of 3 children along the way. Lorena continues to lead herself on the path of discovery and higher learning to help others and encourage them to acquire and improve lifelong goals. Using leading edge, proven FWI Institute Coaching structure skills, and life experiences

Lorena Douglas
Rena@destinydrivenradio.com
Density Driven Radio
www.destinydrivenradio.com

# ~ Notes ~

# Victoria Douskos

*"Doing what you love is the cornerstone of having abundance in your life."*
*Dr. Wayne Dyer*

## From Shy and Afraid to Empowered and Loving

Victoria grew up extremely shy and afraid. Her life growing up was marked with difficult challenges, much drama and constant upset.

She was desperate for answers and she knew the answer had to come from within her. She began after many years of struggling to search for answers. She began to read and met people who were more at peace. She got on the path of self-awareness and started to unwind the truths of who she really was. She started to journal. Victoria has healed herself of illnesses, been through a difficult divorce and has moved across the country a few times.

She learned a lot about energy and how it affects us. She became aware of herself and others. She came to many moments of realization which helped shift her out of her blocks. She sees now that everything in her life brought her to this place where she is stronger and more empowered to help other women and men see themselves clearly.

Victoria has come a long way in finding her voice and finding what makes her happy. She is anxious to share these gifts with others. It's all centered around loving yourself and releasing the past and the pain. She understands what the pain is about and she has learned to see it clearly. Once she was able to see the core issues surrounding the pain she saw that it had no power over her anymore.

She has come around from a shy passive unhappy girl to an empowered woman who is following and living her passion. She started her own business, started networking, reading and learning about marketing. She knows now what is needed to get a business going and is able to educate others on how to get started.

Victoria stepped out and took a chance on starting her own radio show and speaking from the heart.

It all starts with your passion. When you love what you are doing and you have the knowledge, it flows from your heart and soul with ease.

Victoria is a testimony to perseverance and strength in the face of struggle, emotional and physical pain and life challenges.   She knows the recipes to finding your bliss.

*Victoria Douskos*

*Recipe for* SUCCESS!

1.  Know what you want, think from the end.

2.  Are you living your passion, are you incorporating your passion into your business.  Are you living your truth?

3.  Start to imagine what that would look and feel like

4.  Set goals to work toward that dream

5.  Take care of your mind body and soul.

6.   Be grateful for all of your abundance, blessings in your life daily, it will attract more of the same.

7.  Learn forgiveness. Love when it is radiating from you will attract abundance and more love. It is the most powerful healing energy.

# *About Victoria Douskos*

Victoria Douskos RN, CCWC.  With over 20 yrs. experience in the healthcare industry, Victoria is a Registered Nurse, Certified Corporate Wellness Coach, Empowerment coach and she has over 10 years' experience as a Energy Healer.  She is also a program manager and executive producer of her own 30 minute weekly radio show on http://www.amazingwomenofpower.com/radio. The show is called Findyourblissradio.com.

Victoria has a great passion for helping people see the truth of who they are so they can live their lives with passion and purpose and in their BLISS.

She has lived through many difficult challenges in her life and in the process wanted to understand the core issues. She has journaled for years and so all of her breakthroughs have become part of her ability to help others heal themselves. Victoria is able to help people clear their blocks, and see who they are, so they can let go of everything that is holding them back from living their truth. She is nonjudgmental, compassionate, and loving.

Victoria offers tools for people to see clearly that they are not their beliefs, thoughts and behaviors.  Happiness begins from within.

Victoria Douskos
The Healer Within

~ Notes ~

# Linda Doyle

*"Life isn't about waiting for the storm to pass, but learning to dance in the rain"*
*unknown*

## *Inner Diva*

On the Grand opening day of Femme Addiction Studios of Fitness Linda lost a job of 17 years. Losing her job meant losing half of the family income with no notice, no unemployment and 7 mouths to feed, if that was not enough her husband was laid off of work within three weeks. The studio was not intended to replace one salary let alone two. So what do you do? Wait for the storm to pass or learn to dance in the rain? Well since Femme Addiction was intended to be a Pole Dance studio, Linda decided learning to dance would be the best answer.

Linda is the mother of four amazing children ranging in age from 14 to 27 and a 6 year old grandson. She has always been a full time mom and a full time employee and has always had the desire to do more. That nagging feeling that something is missing and what happened to me feeling has been hanging around for too long. So she decided to open a pole dancing studio. Fitness has always been part of her life and this was a different kind of a workout. This was an empowering, fun, challenging and sexy workout. She never thought that opening a women's fitness studio would cost her a career of 17 years, but moving forward and never looking back was the best choice she could have made.

When her studio opened women of all ages, shapes and sizes were ready to experience the sport of pole dancing along with the other cutting edge fitness classes she offered. Linda was amazed at the number of women who had that same feeling of something missing. The feeling for being mom and wife and somewhere along the way losing their sexy side both inside and out. She believes that the sexiest thing on a woman is confidence and that is something that will shine through no matter your shape or size. Living in an era of models that carry an unhealthy image, clothing that is revealing along with songs and movies that portray female sexuality in a negative way makes it hard for the average women to have self-confidence.

Linda learned in a short amount of time that what she offered women who came to her studio for pole dancing, chair dancing or cutting edge fitness was so much more than she ever thought possible. She found that women wanted to get back in touch with their inner beauty, their inner diva, that they wanted this for themselves. It was not about doing it someone else, but doing it to feel amazing in their own skin. They came to her for that motivation, encouragement and friendship. Linda has grown a business that includes ceo's and entrepreneurs as well as full time moms. She helps women get into the best possible shape of their live no matter their age or location.

What she offers at her studio and online is so much more than a typical gym membership, what Linda offers is a lifestyle of becoming Fit, Fabulous and Sexy. She invites you to come taste the addiction!!!

*Linda Doyle*

*Recipe for* SUCCESS!

1. Get in shape for YOU!!!
2. Schedule your workouts!!
3. Set small measurable goals!!
4. Increase the amount of water you drink!
5. Decrease portion size!!
6. Stop and look at how far you have come!
7. Stop waiting....Do it NOW!!!

## *About Linda Doyle*

Linda has taken her desire to live a healthy lifestyle and made it into a fun and empowering experience for everyone she meets. She coaches her clients in person and online via live workout sessions. She offers a half day "Sexy and I Know It" program to jump start weight loss and goal setting. She understands that we all need help and motivation to become the best possible women we can be and when we become fit everything in life is FABULOUS!!!

Linda Doyle
femmeaddiction@yahoo.com
Femme Addiction Studios of Fitness
www.femmeaddiction.com

# Lorrie Crystal Eigles

*"Tell me, what is it you plan to do with your one wild and precious life?"*
*Mary Oliver*

## *A Winding Road to Happiness*

Lorrie began life as a quiet little artist and a big reader. She blossomed when getting a BA degree in American Studies, Sociology and Art and through meeting students and professors who were interesting, kindred spirits. Her fascination in learning about people resulted in getting an MSED degree in Counseling.

Over the years Lorrie felt she was on a career roller coaster ride. She developed excellent career counseling, training, group facilitation and writing skills in a variety of positions within healthcare, higher education, small business, government and corporate settings. While she built a strong reputation for high quality work and caring relationships, she always felt that there was something more that she was meant to do.

As a Vice President and Outplacement Consultant for an international human resource consulting firm, she provided career transition coaching and training to hundreds of ego-crushed people who had been downsized from their companies. After several years she felt burned out. The stress had affected her to the point where she met with the company CEO and resigned without knowing what was next in her career, which was a frightening yet necessary step to take.

Recognized as a "Coach's Coach" who is authentic, creative, smart and enthusiastic, she quickly realized that starting her own business was the only way she could provide the highly individualized coaching that she loved to give her clients. While she felt as though she was about to jump off a cliff, on August 1, 1998 she took the leap and "Authentic Communication" was born! It was a true expression of Lorrie's gifts and commitments. The business has two income streams: creating and selling art that she loves and coaching clients to have the lives of their dreams. This frightening leap turned out to be one of the most important and best decisions of her life.

Business came slowly as she further built her name in the community through networking and giving presentations.  Then Lorrie heard about life coaching and knew that she wanted to expand the scope of her coaching business.  Graduating from the "Life Coaching from Falling Awake Training School" and then becoming certified through the International Coach Federation (ICF), Lorrie is at last doing the work she was meant to do.  Educating the public about what life coaching is and how it can benefit them has been challenging.  Yet she's excited to be a thinking partner and to guide clients to become the best they can be.  Her growing business, based primarily on referrals, has served hundreds of clients and is a testament to the great work she's done since founding her business 14 years ago.  Through her coaching she lives her life purpose:  To empower people to be true to themselves!

*Lorrie Crystal Eigles*

*Recipe for* SUCCESS!

1.  Set clear intentions at the beginning of each day about what you want to have happen.

2.  Be fully present with and listen carefully to your clients since they can tell when you're multi-tasking and not giving them your full attention

3.  Select a business where you're doing work that you love that will see you through all the ups and downs of building your business.

4.  Schedule time each week, if not each day, to do things (small, medium or large) that "feed your soul."

5.  Be authentic, who you really are, with all the people you have contact with (no matter what level they're at); this will distinguish you from others in your field.

6.  Realize it can take a year or more in a new business before becoming financially successful.

7.  Plan to take time to eat healthy and exercise; this will keep you energized when you're going in many directions with your business and life!

# *About Lorrie Crystal Eigles*

As a Certified Life and Retirement Coach and Visual Artist, Lorrie guides people to live happier and more effective lives. Her clients are motivated and moving forward in their lives. Through her warmth, acceptance and deep listening, Lorrie provides a safe, confidential space. In this environment, people see exciting new possibilities for themselves. She facilitates the coaching process for those wanting life enrichment, experiencing life transition, approaching retirement, and people who are creative: artistic or creative problem-solvers. Her clients design their "retirement" (next chapter of life), improve personal and work relationships, find and/or create fulfilling work or start businesses, balance busy lives and much more. They are business, non-profit and education executives, managers, professionals and small business owners in a wide range of industries.

Lorrie is a thinking partner who helps her clients clarify who they truly are, what they most desire in their lives and what their gifts/talents, passions and contributions are. She supports them in reaching their dreams and goals.

Her BA and MSED degrees are from Southern Illinois University--Edwardsville (SIU-E). She is a Professional Certified Coach (PCC) through the ICF, a Board Certified Coach (BCC) and a Licensed Professional Counselor (LPC). As an Award winning Visual Artist, Lorrie understands her clients' creative process.

Lorrie Crystal Eigles
Lorrie@myauthenticlifecoaching.com
Authentic Communications

# ~ Notes ~

# Dr. Anne Marie Evers

*"Ask and you shall receive; knock and the door shall be opened; seek and ye shall find."*
**The Bible**

## *From a Poor PK to Successful Entrepreneur*

Dr. Anne Marie Evers was born a poor preacher's daughter. Times were tough and when the congregation was struggling to feed their own families, there was not much left to tithe the preacher. At times their main food consisted of dandelion salads, soup, stews, etc.

She remembers thinking "Why are so we poor? Why do we always have to wear second-hand clothes? Why am I hungry? Why doesn't my dad get a real job so I don't have to work?" I'm just a kid!

At the age of 10 she helped out all she could. She had a paper route and job, before going to school cleaning dog kennels receiving twenty-five cents per hour to help pay for food.

A great deal of resentment towards her father and his choice of career was building up in her. She was bullied verbally by kids in her class and called names like, "Fatso, Stupid, Dumb, Poor and even Religious Goulash," (whatever that was). She thought she would never amount to anything and felt inferior to others.

Later she married her first husband and continued living in a verbal abusive atmosphere. He was a controller and later became an alcoholic. But this young lady had a spark of HOPE that kept surfacing.

Then she learned about the power of Affirmations, forgiveness, positive thinking and more. She started using Affirmations and created some Exercises and Affirmation Tools for herself that really worked! She decided to share them with others and wrote her first Affirmation book in 1988, now it is in its 8th edition!

Then her son was born with severely crooked feet, and needed expensive surgery. They were also struggling with lack of money and she decided to do something about it. So she started saying with great belief, faith and hope to her son, "David you will walk." She told others he would walk even though they scoffed at her telling her to be realistic. However, she kept on and a miracle happened. She got connected with the Shriners and they did the surgery and after care treatment and her statement came true. He did walk and is walking perfectly today, many years later!

She did many forgiveness exercises and released that pent-up, negative energy and anger for her father and others. Whenever a negative thought would surface in her mind, she would use one of her Affirmation Tools saying 'Delete, Delete, that's untrue," and she would immediately fill the space she had just created with a positive sentence.

Now she is PRESIDENT/CEO of her company, Affirmations International Publishing; Best-Selling Author; Coach; International Motivational Speaker; Minister; Doctor of Divinity; Radio/Internet Talk Show Host and more. She used her 'co-called failures as' extra-ordinary fertilizer' for her many wonderful successes. She affirmed (ordered) up her present husband and they were married in 2008. More Affirmation success! He built her an Angel Chapel in the backyard.

She says in her books 'Affirmations When Properly Done Always Work!'

## Dr. Anne Marie Evers

### Recipe for SUCCESS!

1. Use the unique and wondrous talents and gifts you have been given to help others and to make the world a better place for all.

2. You are who you are. Start from there and improve what you wish to improve upon and never give up.

3. Always treat others as you would like to be treated and that is with love, respect and consideration.

4. Do what you believe in and Stand up Big!

5. When you fall in love with what you do, you never have to work again.

6. Use your 'so-called' failures as 'extra-ordinary' fertilizer for your many successes.

7. It all starts with believing, respecting and loving self, remembering you are totally capable and wonderful!

# *About Dr. Anne Marie Evers*

Dr. Anne Marie Evers was a legal secretary, Real Estate Broker/Owner of Sumas Realty; Commercial Realtor in Canada. She was Director of Public Relations for a large Land Company in Seattle, WA and had her Stock Issuers' License selling Stocks and Bonds. She was Owner/Operator of several Restaurants with her first husband.

She is currently

- Best-Selling' author of many books/e-books on the power of Affirmation
- Ordained Minister
- Doctor of Divinity
- CEO Affirmations International Publishing Company
- Hosted over 600 Radio/Internet Talk Shows Coast to Coast and worldwide on the Web
- Co-author of Wake Up & Live the Life You Love in Spirit with Dr. Deepak Chopra, Dr. Wayne Dyer & Others
- International Motivational Speaker
- Columnist, Freelance Writer
- Workshop and Seminar Facilitator
- Creator/Reader of the Cards of Life – www.cardsoflife.com.

She enjoys a busy practice as Affirmation Coach teaching people the power of properly done Affirmations. She has created and taught 3 Anti-violence Children's' Affirmation Programs in both Canada and U.S.

She is a member of the Canadian Guidance and Counseling Association and trained at the Counselor Training Institute in Vancouver, Canada. She has Certificates in Child Psychology 212, Therapeutic Touch, Professional Development and others.

Anne Marie was awarded Honorary Doctor of Philosophy by Moffett University for her lifetime achievements and dedication in uplifting, educating and empowering people worldwide. Her significant contribution to the world of self-realization, psychology and personal development optimize the human spirit of service and speak to the oneness and potential for good available for all people.

Two of her brand new books just released are Affirmation Toolbox, by popular demand and many requests with over 150 different Affirmation Tools for most life challenges. And Affirmation Beauty Book – Ladies here is the book you have all been waiting for! Both available www.amazon.com Happy Affirming!

Dr. Anne Marie Evers
annemarieevers@shaw.ca
Affirmations International Publishing Co
http://www.annemarieevers.com/damevers

# Dan Evertsz

*"Successful People Will Do What Average People Won't"*
*Author Unknown*

## How the Parent of a College Bound Student Turned it Into a Business

Eight years ago, Dan's little girl was graduating from a private high school with a 3.4 GPA. Ashlee had just completed the application and acceptance process for college. She decided to attend Howard University. Dan was relieved and full of joy that the grueling college admission process was over. A year earlier, Dan was under the false impression that process was the same as when he entered college some thirty years earlier. As Dan reflected through the last years' experience, he was thankful and relieved it was over. What did he just go through? What do you mean; I should apply to at least ten schools? I applied to only four schools and was accepted to all. Dan had a 3.0 GPA and damn proud of it. Leadership, Community service, Internships, and Employment. What the heck is all of this? Dan's daughter was courted by George Washington University who was asking all these questions. Dan decided to visit their website and discovered they are charging $50,000.00 per year! He thinks to himself, the cost of my college education was less than Five Thousand Dollar per year. Are they crazy, I can't afford this. Let's look elsewhere, what the heck is going on?

After twenty seven years as a successful Mortgage Banker, Dan was burned out and looking for a new path. After traveling to Chicago to attend an overpriced two day workshop titled, "New Business Opportunities for Entrepreneurs", Dan had no interest in any of the business opportunities presented. He felt misled and ripped off. The majority of business opportunities were internet business based (Dan and knew technology was new and challenging), his mind wandered and kept focusing on the check he had written to Howard University for Ashlee's first semester. The yearly cost of attendance at Howard University was over Twenty Five Thousand Dollars. Dan awakens from his day dream as the next speaker (The mystery guest speaker Mr. X) comes on stage.

The first word out of his mouth was, "How many in the audience have ever heard of a College Planner?" No one raised their hand. Next question, "How many of your clients had to pay full

145

price for their kid's to go to college? He got Dan's attention. Long story short, Mr. X provided award letter examples of many six figure families that received financial aid and merit scholarships ( Free Gift Money) ranging from Twenty Thousand Dollars to Fifty Thousand Dollars. How was this possible?

Fast forward eight years to present, Dan reflects on his decision to invest $20,000.00 to join Mr. X's College Planner/Financial Aid coaching program. His company (Bay Area College Planning Specialist) has helped hundreds of middle class families' successful navigate the admissions and funding college process.

*Dan Evertsz*

*Recipe for* SUCCESS!

1. Go for your dreams and stay away from dream stealers.

2. Eliminate negative people from your life.

3. A great idea means nothing unless you move forward and try.

4. Read and research successful people in your industry. (Why did others fail)

5. You don't have to be perfect before you start your business venture (business cards, website, office, etc.)

6. Your business model should be focused on customer service and helping others

7. Successful companies always put the needs of the customer first.

## *About Dan Evertsz*

Dan Evertsz "The College Money Pro" delivers an engaging and informative packed lecture that empowers parents with the knowledge needed admit their children to college and access maximum financial aid and merit scholarships for working families. Dan is an expert speaker and down to earth energetic teacher. He helps parents focus on real life strategies that allow access to information not known to the general public. Parents will have a clear path to assist in funding college.

Dan Evertsz is the senior partner at Bay Area College Planners. BACP has helped hundreds of working class families Fund College. He offers practical methods that are easy to grasp and can be used immediately.

Dan's strategies and advise helps parents simplify a complex situation, crystallize the problem and offer a clear solution. As a parent of a recent college graduate, he understands the pitfalls, frustration and lack of information parents will encounter during this process.

Dan Evertsz
Dan@baycollegeplanners.com
Bay College Planning Specialist
www.thecollegemoneypro.com

# ~ Notes ~

# Debra Faris

*"What you do makes a difference, and you have to decide what kind of difference you want to make."*
*Jane Goodall*

## *Grow through your challenges*

Life isn't always easy, Debra grew threw a horrific childhood, her mother's suicide, divorce and loss of a child in her personal life.

As some would think of a home with a white picket fence in suburbia neighborhood or in her case they lived in an exclusive community with horses and a big beautiful home, it sounds like a blessed life. However abuse knows No financial differences, her father who was a very successful entrepreneur who traveled a lot flying here, there and everywhere in his private plane, while his 8 year old baby girl would be traumatized by her mother's violent rages from banging her head into windows to throwing her out in the middle of the night. Doctors would give her mother prescribed barbiturates, which only made her alcoholism craziness only crazier.

As years went by Debra would do her best to keep under the radar. She certainly knew that bringing any little friends to her home was never a good thing so, she figured out how to create friends on the outside and started honing in on her communications skills at an early age, she was like a little Dale Carnegie "How to win friends and influence people" becoming what people called the best little girl scout salesman!

Latter evolving from cookie sales to selling shoes. One day she had a customer that was a real estate salesman, she asked him about buying a house. The man replied "you can't afford a house but you would make one heck of a real estate salesperson". He had no idea that her father was very successful business man. All Debra knew was even though her father graduated from Stanford with double majors, he didn't believe girls went to college, he believed they married doctors. Debra thought Real Estate sounded like a great opportunity, studied the courses and passed the test, to only have her mother commit suicide a month later. Within days, the maid that her mother committed suicide over moved in. Debra decided to start her own education curriculum and enrolled into the Dale Carnegie course and within 6 months at 21 years old, she listed 21 properties in one month, she would continue to be one of the top producers for 24 consecutive months. She continued her personal development path by reading books like "Think and Grow Rich" and latter courses and seminars Tony Robins, Zig Ziglar, Brian Tracy, Wayne Dwyer, Mike Ferry etc.

She triumphed over market down-turns and career shifts in her business. Yet, the trials in her life were not over. Despite years of witnessing her mother's alcohol and drug addiction, her fate was to struggle with the addiction of two of her children, as well. Just as it seemed everyone was getting their lives back on track her son was beat up in a Christian program where he was taken to a hospital that gave him a prescription of oxy cotton, one thing led to another and he passed away days after he was beat up.

How does any parent move forward in the face of such devastating loss? Debra never lost her desire to help others and believes that it is her passion for helping others and that we all have a gift to serve which is connected to our purpose. Not that her road has been easy; quite the contrary. Her son who wanted to be an Anthropologist, she chose by getting out of her own pain, she focused a mentor program for college students to help them on their journey to success in their career path with LinkedIn, which has manifested into a book.

An interesting coincidence from her early years in real estate one of the top real estate coaches in the United States Mike Ferry contacted Debra through LinkedIn and hired her as his LinkedIn coach and took his connections from a few hundred to over 8,000, she also created and launched the "The Mike Ferry Realtor Connection" a group on LinkedIn. Debra coaches companies, entrepreneurs and professionals not just how to create an authentic empowering LinkedIn profile but how to build long term relationships, forging professional bonds, creating marketability/profitability of peoples vision for their business dreams.

*Debra Faris*

*Recipe for* SUCCESS!

1. When life seems crazy and the drunk monkeys are chattering in your head, slow down, take some silent me time, find a quiet place for a couple hours i.e. sit by the ocean, a creek, under a tree. Get back in nature with yourself and silence. When you get back home take another couple hours, put on some beautiful baroque/instrumental music, set a nice table with flowers, place matt's and everything for one, make a healthy scrumptious dinner for one, light the candles, sit down and tell yourself all the things you are grateful and enjoy your meal. Later get comfy with a good book for an hour. Followed by a bath with lavender sent and candles, enjoy the water and the silence. Finally before you crawl into bed be sure, the room is a little cool but comfortable, your favorite sheets and pillow, eliminate outside noises, enter your bed like a child and close your eyes and revisit some sweet childhood memories

2. Don't sweat the small stuff or I call it silly stuff, things that don't have special meaning, let them roll off your shoulder like water off a ducks back. Sometimes taking a step backwards maybe the one thing that puts you back in an opportunity to re-align yourself.

3. Questions are the Answer, the better the questions the better the answers.

4. Having resources is not always as important as being resourceful

5. If you want to feel abundant, start with the gift of giving by helping someone less fortunate

6. If you can't afford a mentor or coach ask someone successful who their favorite personal development person is and watch them on YouTube.

7. Write 50 actions ideas that will help you get where you want to be and get a accountability partner.

## *About Debra Faris*

My Goal is "It's all about you, to bring the very best out of you", to differentiate you from the pack; so your clients know they made the right choice! You don't need to be told what you already know. It's what you don't know that you need to know. I will show you how to Link yourself into unlimited possibilities!

I was the LinkedIn consultant for Mike Ferry world renowned Real Estate coach in North America, expanding his personal connections from a few hundred to over 8,000. This endeavor created and established the official LinkedIn group from zero to 800 in five months "The Mike Ferry Realtor Connections which was the progressive pathway to grow the Mike Ferry Organization presence on LinkedIn.

Do you just connect-connect? Let me, show YOU... how to Create YOUR own management system for your LinkedIn connections with a follow up Retention Program which Maximizes... Who you Know... to... Who Knows YOU! "Clients for Life Philosophy".

Debra Faris
debra.faris@yahoo.com
The Chief Networking Officer

# Barclay Fisher

*"Day by day in every way though the grace of God I am getting better and better"*
*W. Clement Stone*

## *Changes to  Changes to Positive Self Expectance*

The process began when Fred Laird hired him for Combined Insurance Company of America as sales person.  The founder, Mr. Stone, lived by the philosophy Of Positive Mental Attitude in everything that a person did. Barclay was a dry sponge that had been thrown into a vast lake of knowledge of how to live.  If was  during the next twelve years he spent with CICA that Barclay learned that he could teach and share the wisdom of the ages with others and they too could prosper from the knowledge that he had gained. He was honored as the top sales trainer with CICA and the top of his class as a manager trainee.

After leaving CICA he became a successful consultant teaching sales people proven techniques from the openings to closing of the sales process.

In 1986 he began to partner with Carl Frost in creating Publishers Discount Warehouse. The company sold magazines coast to coast via incoming 800 calls and he helped it grow from only 15 people to well over two hundred employees and from less than a million dollars to over twenty million in gross sales in less than five years.  This was accomplished by using the proven techniques and principles he learned through W. Clement Stone and Napoleon Hill teachings. These are the skills and mind sets he shares on his weekly show "Connecting to Your Greatness". Also available in his books and CD's.

Barclay Fisher
barclayf527@gmail.com
www.BarclayFisher.com

## *About Barclay Fisher*

I was raised by two wonderful people who taught me values that have stood the test of time. Because of hard work and treating others with respect I have always enjoyed being around people that share similar beliefs. After graduating from high school I joined the Army. While stationed with the 25th Infantry Division in Hawaii I played football and baseball earning All-Star awards in both sports.

After serving in the Army I walked on at Jacksonville State University in football and earned a full scholarship. I lettered three years in football and two in baseball. I coached at Jacksonville State in both sports before going into Motel/Hotel management. My life changed forever when I joined Combined Insurance. I spent 12 years learning not only how to sell and manage but how to teach others. I began to lead companies to great success. The coaching profession has allowed me to share my passion for building people and bushiness.

My personal life has been blessed by my wife Priscilla and her wonderful children, Melissa who is married to Blake, Lauren who is married to Brad and Brian her son. I have three great young men: Rodney who is married to Cristal, J.D. who is married to Chris, and Kelly who is married to Stacy. Together we have a total of eight grandchildren; Lula Mae, Shady, Scott, Luke, Theron, Samantha, Daniel and Tabatha.

# Kim Fuller

*"Be yourself; everyone else is already taken"*
*Oscar Wilde*

## *Slow Take Off, Smooth Landing*

Kim's business did not take off quickly. Her journey to living a fuller life and experiencing success in her business started during her internship as a marriage and family therapist.

She wrote down in her daily planner, "When I grow up I want to be a motivational consultant; a person who works with people who want to have fun in life." She shared this vision with colleagues; some laughed at her response since she was on track to obtain a psychotherapy license and was now, already looking to change her career.

Others encouraged her to follow her passion. Kim recognized that you need both sides in your life; one side whose intent is to discourage you from taking risks-while the other side encourages you.

Kim's approach to starting her business was to start slowly one client at a time, while holding on to her full time job. This plan was altered when Kim realized she was unhappy working full time in this field and having a long commute to work. She was taking out her unhappiness on her family. Turbulent changes in her personal life forced her to make the decision to jump into the coaching business with full force.

The number 1 problem of new business owners – how to get business. Just because she was now ready to Life coach full time, who knew she existed and how were the additional clients going to come to her? There wasn't a group of clients knocking down her door wanting her to be their Life Coach. A few strategies she used to increase her business and credibility included joining referral networking groups in her area, creating an online presence, seeking guidance from a small business development center, and shifting her career identity to Life Coach. This shift in identity meant, when someone asked her what she did for a living, she talked about being a Life coach and gave a brief description. She needed to be confident in her career and explain it clearly.

She faced personal and professional growth barriers along the way. The first barrier was credibility. There are many Life Coaches who have varied experiences that qualify them to offer their services. Kim wanted to improve her credibility and be different from others by obtaining additional education and credentials to pair with her current degrees and experience.

Another barrier Kim faced was being a self-promoter. Attending networking groups provided weekly opportunities to practice promoting her business and create relationships with other entrepreneurs which resulted in more possibilities for referrals.

Two things she wishes she would have done; nail down her target market early in her planning process and recognize the impact it has on all aspects of her business. She also wishes she had sought out and found a mentor earlier in the development of her business. Now, she is sitting comfortably and looking forward to a smooth landing.

*Kim Fuller*

*Recipe for* SUCCESS!

1. Choose something you enjoy

2. Seek out a mentor

3. Look at challenges and failures as an opportunity for self-growth

4. Learn about your target audience

5. Lead with confidence, learn with curiosity

6. Find your work/life balance and add fun!

7. don't make decisions based on fear

# *About Kim Fuller*

Kim is a certified professional life and business coach and has a bachelor's degree in psychology and a master's degree in Counseling. Kim is the owner of Fuller Life Concepts. Fuller Life Concepts provides life coaching services to professional women who want to live a Fuller Life: Healthy, Focused, and Fulfilling. She became a Life Coach and Motivational Consultant to work with people who are eager to change & willing to access their resource of courage to do so. She enjoys being a Life Coach and a catalyst for change. Kim shares her experiences and insights on her online talk radio show 'Change is Personal' that airs on Voice America Channel. Kim is a Certified trainer of the 'Enriching your relationship with Yourself and others' workshops which are based on the teachings and trainings of Virginia Satir. These trainings are held around the world and online through the Satir Global Network. Kim has been invited to share her expertise and insights at conferences and trainings. She has hosted workshops on topics that include; time management, procrastination, work/life balance, managing your relationships, dealing with trauma and de-stress techniques. Kim was featured in the August 2012 issue of Balanced Mom Magazine where she candidly shared her journey to business owner and the challenges she faced along the way. She experienced several life changing events in one year (marriage, mother hood, widow, business owner, solo parenting).

In addition to individual life coaching, Kim & business partner Terri Morgan started Mind Your Own Business in 2008. They co-authored a Fearless Management training series to train business executives & managers to become conscious of their own leadership style and learn effective management strategies to transform any business environment to improve productivity and passion.

Kim Fuller
kim@fullerlifeconcepts.com
Fuller Life Concepts
www.fullerlifeconcepts.com

## ~ Notes ~

# Claudette Gadsden-Hrobak

*"Never let someone else's opinion of you, become your opinion of yourself. –Unknown*

## *In Service; Helping Women and Children*

While growing up in Charleston, SC, Claudette was able to travel during summer and winter breaks from school to visit relatives. She realized as a teenager how much she loved to travel and five days after graduating from high school joined the US Navy to continue her travels. While traveling the world, she realized her purpose was to help people.

During her stay in Yokosuka, Japan her desire to help really kicked in. She met people who were feeling kind of lost having just left home for the first time and being so far away from family. She started to invite people over for dinner and conversation. Both of Claudette's parents were amazing cooks and she learned her way around the kitchen. She grew up believing that food made everything better, so she and her friends cooked and ate the lonely away. During these times friends always seemed to seek her out for conversation and advice. She helped people feel good about where they were and what they were doing, pointing out the purpose and benefits of being where they were.

Claudette formed a network to support wives left alone in a strange country, when ships were deployed. This network helped with kids, homework, and any other support or encouragement needed. During this time she even witnessed childbirth for the first time, while a new mother was away from her family and her husband was out at sea. The network cared for this young woman 24/7 for months, before and after the delivery, never leaving her alone to feel the fear kept at bay by these amazing women.

After moving back to the US, this knack for helping people just continued to expand. Claudette lived in San Diego, a big Navy town and people knew that they could call on her for assistance. She continued to help families adopt other families for support and encouragement, and most importantly to help with the children.

Just as Claudette has had many homes over the years, she has had many jobs. In all of these jobs, she supported, encouraged and motivated her co-workers. She ensured that everyone was celebrated for their accomplishments, both large and small.

In 2008 Claudette was laid off from Verizon and realized that it was the best thing that could have happened. This provided the opportunity to do what she loved most, help people. She became a licensed Neuro Linguistic Programming (NLP) Master Practitioner with certifications in Business Coaching, Life Coaching, Weight Loss and Social and Emotional Intelligence Coaching. Claudette's ideal client is women, particularly mothers and their daughters. She wants nothing more than for them to realize how absolutely amazing they already are.

During these years, I have learned to help people where they needed help rather than where I wanted to help them and to love people just as they are because diversity is what makes the world go around.

## Claudette Gadsden-Hrobak

### Recipe for SUCCESS!

1. Choose your niche. You cannot be all things to all people.

2. Be your authentic self, even if there are 10 personal/business coaches in the room, there is only one Coach Claudette

3. Build a Dream Team to help care for the things that you find challenging. Give them more than they expect. That something extra helps to make you memorable.

4. It's okay to refer a client to someone better suited for them.

5. Your word is your bond. If you say you will do it, do it and do it with a grateful heart.

6. Thank your clients for choosing you.

7. There are others in the same field and they could have chosen them.

## *About Claudette Gadsden-Hrobak*

Coach Claudette aka Claudette Gadsden-Hrobak is your Motivational Mentor, who has been a practicing life coach for countless years. She is licensed by the Society of Neuro Linguistic Programming (NLP) as an NLP Master Practitioner. She is a graduate of Global NLP Training with certifications as a Life Coach, Business Coach, Weight Loss Master Coach, and Social and Emotional Intelligence Coach.  For as long as she can remember, Coach Claudette has read books on and studied personal strength, personal growth and empowerment and takes pleasure in sharing what she has learned with others.  Iyanla Vanzant, who shares her own life stories and triumphs, is one of her favorite authors on the subject of personal strength and starting over.

After more than 25 years working in private, public and government entities, nationally and internationally, Coach Claudette understands how change and transition can impact someone's life.  During that time and through those years, she used her coaching skills to help people navigate through the maze of life to realize their dreams, visions and aspirations.  Coach Claudette decided to follow her passion of helping people realize their purpose, dreams and goals by becoming a Life and Business Coach.  Her direct, yet caring, approach makes it easy for her clients to learn new skills, identify barriers and take action. She takes pleasure in reminding people just how AWESOME they really are.

Remembering what life was like growing up in her village, Coach Claudette has opened a 'village' for young women.  The intention of the program is to help young women grow into their Greatness, one new thought at a time.   The program titled, I am a DOVe, Daughter Of the Village, teaches young women the importance of self-love, self-knowledge and self-respect in a group coaching environment.

Claudette Gadsden-Hrobak
Claudette@CoachClaudette.com
Personal/Business Coach
www.CoachClaudette.com

# ~ Notes ~

# Linda Giles

*" The key to realizing a dream is to focus not on success but significance - and then even the small steps and little victories along your path will take on greater meaning.*
*Oprah Winfrey*

## *It's Nice to Be Nice!*

As a young child growing up in a family of eight children, Linda really understood that she had a choice. She could become anything or anybody she wanted to be – because her parents told her that as long as she worked hard, cared about others, and focused on her goals, she would be successful. To this day, she still hears her Mother's voice saying, "It's Nice to Be Nice", and "Always strive to be the best – even if you are not the top BEST, you will be right up there with the Best".

Watching her parents work hard and make sacrifices and sometimes struggle to make ends meet, she promised that she would help them out as soon as she could work. In spite of the struggles, they had clean clothes, food, and she loved her childhood home. She started working in high school under a program for Future Business Leaders. So, at a very young age, she was preparing for her success. As the second born child, she knew that she needed to set a good example for her younger siblings.

Linda has always been passionate about being healthy. Her mother, Lena, a private duty nurse, was a vegetarian when most people did not understand what that lifestyle was about. At an early age, Linda learned the importance of natural herbs and healing remedies. As a result of her own discipline in health, she does not take medication, has great energy, and her doctor's reports are always great.

Recently, her optometrist told her that her eyes were doing what most people have surgery to do – self-correcting as she is growing older – 20/20 vision. Linda attributes this to her natural supplements, great diet, and clean healthy living. This is something that she wants everyone to experience. She really believes that the human body, which is God's greatest creation of all, has the ability to heal itself.

Linda's ability to be a great listener has helped her to be a better Wife, Mother, Sister Friend, and Confidante to so many. She speaks with her heart, and strives every day to make people feel good when they interact with her. She finds herself repeating to her children the words of her mother – "It's Nice to Be Nice!" This is how she leads her life – being kind to others, and giving back. She wants to have an impact on people as she lives out her purpose to help others be and live their BEST life.

Currently, she works a full time job in Corporate America, and balances her health and wellness business during her off work hours. She is passionate about people and loves to talk about health and wellness. Linda has had her struggles, but always has the courage to get back up and keep moving forward. Her ability to stay calm in the midst of chaos is clearly inherited from her mother, and serves her well. Her inner peace keeps her balanced and in love with

God and her life.

## Linda Giles

### Recipe for SUCCESS!

1. Always treat your clients and business partners the way that you want to be treated.

2. Be a product of your product. People can spot a phony salesperson for miles.

3. Regardless of the product or service that you sell, in order to be successful, you must always remember you are in the people business.

4. You are your best brand. People are buying into you - so always remember - It's Nice to Be Nice. It will go a longer way than being the opposite.

5. If what you are doing does not excite you, change the plan. You should be passionate enough to do it even if you did not get paid for it.

6. Always keep your life balanced when working your plan. It means nothing to have a lot of money and a great business, if you have neglected your family and loved ones along the way. Keep the main thing, the main thing.

7. Always remember that God has a purpose for each of us, and he will provide the means, the team, and the clients to help us live out that purpose. Always, always be in a spirit of gratitude!

## *About Linda Giles*

My biggest and most important job is Wife and Mom. My goal is to create a home environment that my family loves to be in – similar to my own childhood home.  In addition to the love and peace, I focus on nutrition.  My family leads a healthy life, and use products that I support in my business.

I inherited the entrepreneurial bug from my parents and I watched them balance family and business and do it well.  As the second child of eight, I learned to appreciate caring for others, sharing, and the art of negotiation.  As a business owner, these characteristics are very important – your customers have to know that you care, that you are willing to share, and, as necessary, negotiate.  In my business, I help people live a quality life, and I believe that the body is strong and has the ability to heal with proper nutrition and exercise.  Are you willing to commit to your health?  I look forward to partnering with you.

As I work with clients, my goal is to learn as much about their health goals, and any health issues.  We map out a plan of action, and I recommend products, and eating styles based on their needs.  My greatest reward comes when a client says, "You have changed my life!"  This is when I know for sure that I am working my purpose.

One of the things to do on my list is to write. I have a book in me, and I know that the words will help impact a life or two.  With two adult children as writers, I know that my editing staff is already in place.  I believe that I am here to heal, and I am a constant researcher of natural herbs and their power of healing.

Linda Giles
talkinghealthwithlinda@gmail.com
Talking Health with Linda
www.ardysslife.com/lsgiles

# Kingsley Grant

*"The more your understand, the less you judge"*
*~ Kingsley Grant*

## Life is what you choose it to be

It was May 13th, 2008. After months of praying and talking with family and friends, he finally made the decision to hand in his letter of resignation. Not only did he have difficulty falling asleep the night prior, but he remembered praying as he fought against his doubts and fears as they marched through the hallways of his head tugging at every door until they finally unlocked the one marked "second guessing yourself". Out stepped the giant called "Are you making the right decision?"

After one of the longest night ever and having prevailed over his giant, Kingsley walked into the office the next day, and handed in his letter of resignation. This was one of the most difficult decisions that he had ever made.

How do you walk away from a place that you invested 21 years of your life? How do you walk away from having a paycheck every two weeks along with benefits and other perks, to start a business without any benefits or steady income? How do you walk away from co-workers who had become like your own family?

This is not something you do very easily.

Why did he do that?

One of the reasons is having read a book written by Bob Buford entitled, "Halftime: Changing Your Game Plan from Success to Significance." Kingsley felt he was at the half-time point of his life. Having had success, he now wanted significance.

Another reason came as a result of listening to one of his favorite speakers, Dr. Myles Munroe. He heard him share with a group of college graduates as he gave the keynote speech, that while on his way to the college he passed by what he considered to be the wealthiest grounds in that city; the graveyard. Dr. Munroe explained that the graveyard was wealthy because there are people who were buried there with songs in them that were never sung, books that were never written, cures for certain diseases that were never developed, and on and on he went. He did not need to say more.

Author and poet Diane Ackerman made this statement, "I don't want to get to the end of my life and find I lived just the length of it. I want to have lived the width of it as well"
Kingsley decided that he did not want to add to the riches of the graveyard. He realized that he had some things in him that he wanted to get out. He wanted to have his own business; he has since done that. He wanted to write; he has since written two books. He wanted to become a better speaker so that he could inspire hope in others; he has done that.
He wants to die having emptied himself of all that is in him.

Has it been easy?

Certainly not!

He has had his shares of ups and downs along with a few setbacks. One of the major setbacks was undergoing quadruple by-pass surgery just six months after his resignation.

With much prayer, the support of family and friends, Kingsley was back on his feet a few months after and more determined to not let his dream die within him.

His mom did that.

She died on New Year's Day 2011. She was a schoolteacher all of her adult life.

She loved teaching.

He had the privilege of spending some time with her prior to her death. He used the time to ask many questions one of which was, "Mom, was there anything else that you wanted to do other than teaching?" Her answer surprised him greatly. She said, "I wanted to be a nurse". She never became one.

His mom died with that nurse within her. That nurse will never have the opportunity to make a difference in someone's life. The graveyard became richer, when she died.

His message to others is simply this, "Don't let your dream die within you" and "Your life is what you choose it to be."

## Kingsley Grant

### Recipe for SUCCESS!

1. If you can conceive it, you can achieve it

2. The more you understand, the less you judge

3. Learn to forgive all offenses

4. Believe in yourself; have faith in God

5. Be swift to hear, slow to speak

6. Walk in humility

7. Life and death is in the power of the tongue; use it wisely

## *About Kingsley Grant*

For over twenty years Kingsley worked with teenagers as a Youth Minister. During this time he has worked alongside parents serving as mediator, reconciler, and counselor.

He has written an Anger Management curriculum for teens, which has been used in both Middle and Senior High Schools in Miami Dade County as well as Life Impact Inc. He is the author of "Two Steps To ForGIFTness - Learning to forgive when your mind says yes but your heart says no", "This … Was Not Supposed To Happen - Finding the strength to persevere", and the "10-Day Devotional for teens and young adults while at a Retreat".

Over a period of five years he has received training from the Savannah Family Institute on teaching parenting classes to families with difficult teenagers. Since receiving this training, he has taught several parenting classes at various locations. He is a certified DiSC© personality profile administrator and a Certified Transitional Life Coach.

Kingsley is a licensed therapist in the state of Florida. He holds a Master's Degree from St. Thomas University in the field of Marriage & Family Therapy. He specializes in family counseling, which includes pre-marital, marital and individual. He has been married since 1985 and has two children.

He is a motivational speaker, who conducts workshops on Anger Management, Parenting, Interpersonal Communication and other relationship related issues. He also speaks at conferences, retreats, churches, and schools.

He is President and CEO of Helping Families Improve, an adjunct professor at Trinity International University and has served as the president of his Toastmasters club.

He can be contacted by email at kingsleyogrant@gmail.com or at http://www.helpingothershope.com.

Helping others hope is what he is all about. His motto is "Life is too short."

Kingsley Grant
kingsleyogrant@gmail.com
Helping Families Improve, Inc
http://www.helpingothershope.com

# El Ha Gahn

*"Be in peace but not in pieces"*
*El Ha Gahn 1979*

## Artist Healer Motivator Coach

EL Ha Gahn started his life as an artist. Painting, sculpting, and making things out of whatever materials he could find was his passion. Because of having a high creative mind it brought him into conflict in many instances when it came to complying with the rules and regulations of various schools he went to and jobs study had. He realized from an early age that he really didn't like to be told what to do. And having a tendency to be somewhat rebellious he decided that the job market was not for him. As a craftsman his ability to make items that people liked and enjoyed caused him to move into the venue of handcrafted candles which he did for several years. Being that most candle wax is a petroleum derivative, the first major oil crisis in the 70s made the price of wax cost prohibitive.

From that point El Ha Gahn moved into the field of jewelry making in which he is still active today. During his life as an artist he picked up many skills in areas like: wood carving, polymer casting, metal casting, welding, soap making, cabinet making, airbrushing, furniture making and quite a few more skills along that line.

Because of health challenges at an early age and being threatened that he would need surgery, prompted him to seek methods of repairing his own health conditions. He began to research herbs, remedies, and various modalities of healing support strategies. Not only did he rebuild his own health to a level of robust strength and efficiency that he enjoys unto this very day. He has been able to assist many on their quest for radiant health and well-being. Realizing that the road to health and the road to personal success in all areas of life are deeply intertwined El has been making a live case study out of every situation that has come into his field of observation. Formulating a precise system for self-evaluation and personal development. By being an artist he noticed that a person's life is orchestrated in a pattern. Some patterns make a complete and beautiful picture. And some patterns are incomplete and have gaps in them and elements that do not fit properly into the scheme of that person's life.

Comparing those observations over so many years and having gone through so many trials and tribulations of his own El Ha Gahn became good at detecting success cycle patterns

By analyzing the patterns going on in one's life compared to the rate of expansion or breakdown he can identify where to address gaps and fill in the missing patterns. He has thereby been able to formulate a unique system for self-evaluation and personal development which has helped hundreds of people move towards greater success in their daily lives.

At this phase of his 41 year journey of inner discovery he has become one of the most dynamic motivators and holistic life coaches of this time

El Ha Gahn

Recipe for SUCCESS!

1. Be thorough in all that you do

2. Make sure you build a reputation that you can stand on

3. If you mess up do it over

4. Openly admit your mistakes to yourself and all involved

5. Identify people who are having the kind of success that you would like and pattern yourself after them

6. Don't be afraid to go that extra mile

7. After you know you have done your best determine with might, to make your next project better

## *About El Ha Gahn*

El Ha Gahn is the Director of The Academy of the Cultural Arts & Life Sciences, a school that trains people in the art of natural living. He is a graduate of The Gibran Institute. He is also a Master instructor In the Institute of Certified Martial Artists.  He has been involved In the Essene healing arts for 34 years.  His Interest in this pursuit has taken him literally around the World on a journey of discovery about herbal systems, healing methods and wellness strategies.

Having a rich family background of African and Native American heritage, the contributions of wisdom from family members helped to inspire him in this direction. His travels and studies have taken him to such remote places as Jamaica, Nigeria, France and Israel and he has lived in several of the mountain ranges In the US.  For 12 years as part of El Hapiru Monastic Order he did organic farming In New Jersey and has had extensive training in forest and land conservation since a youth.

El Ha Gahn became Interested In wellness techniques as a result of a strong desire to get rid of chronic ailments he had as a teenager. The treatments he was receiving at the hospital were not helping, so he determined to conquer this difficulty. Additionally, seeing two of his family members suffer unto death and feeling helpless about it started the journey.  As a modern day Essene, El Ha Gahn has been a vegetarian for thirty six years. He is also an excellent culinary artist and can prepare some of the finest Raw and Vegan delicacies.

With a background In herbal essences and biochemistry, El Ha Gahn Is the originator and manufacturer of the ever popular Isle of Paradise Products. Versed In a vast array of the ancient esoteric arts like Yoga, Meditation, Naphtali Martial Art, Moroccan & Egyptian Massage Techniques, aura reading, etc., these all represent the focus of his dally life. As an Essene Healer he is dedicated to the re-education of people towards self-development and continued Natural wellness.  By combining his arts and sciences into a single creative Discipline, he is able to integrate his thoughts, ideas and experiences Into an Approach to life that reflects a harmony of confidence, peacefulness and Inner Strength.

El Ha Gahn
elhagahn@yahoo.com
PINGUIORIS AETERNA SOLUTIONS
http://bit.ly/Tlf6hn

# ~ Notes ~

# Cathy Hansell

*"Every great dream begins with a dreamer. You have within you the strength, the patience, and the passion to reach for the stars to change the world." Harriet Tubman*

## *Living Your Purpose*

Both of Cathy's parents worked when she was growing up, so her grandmother and great aunt watched her each day, until she was old enough to go to kindergarten. They instilled in Cathy a set of values, that some would say are "old fashioned". Not to her. They are the golden rules of being nice to others, working hard, never lying, not taking credit for the work of others; saying "please", "thank you" and "I'm sorry", appreciating nature and having great faith in God and Jesus Christ.

At a very young age, Cathy's father instilled in her self-confidence. He told her that she is very smart; she can do anything that she wants to do and not to be influenced by other's negative comments.

Cathy has carried these traditional values and advice from her father with her, all her life. It formed a drive within Cathy to serve others and to provide a greater good. She had various positions in business, all around health, worker safety, product safety and environmental protection. Cathy worked her way up to Vice President in four major corporations, and earned degrees in engineering, toxicology and law, and eight certifications.

Cathy's last career turned her attention to personal safety, where she found her purpose in life. She confirmed this to herself when she studied "A Purpose Driven Life". Cathy has passionately worked in the occupational safety field for over twenty years, where she has found great satisfaction in helping others to be safer and healthier.

Five years ago, Cathy found herself at another decision point and her first significant personal challenge. She chose to leave the corporate world and form her own consulting business in safety and health. Cathy founded "Breakthrough Results", a firm dedicated to helping people lead safer and healthier lives.

New work came slowly, and Cathy wondered how to reach more people. This was her next challenge: how does she market herself---my skills, products, services and availability. Cathy addressed this challenge in two ways. First, she accepted every speaking invitation with professional safety organizations. She created a website and jointed LinkedIn. She needed to be seen and heard. Second, she started a radio show: Safety Breakthrough Talk Radio. She heard Raven Blair Davis on a talk show, and Cathy immediately called Raven. Cathy knew that this was the way to reach many more people, through the radio podcasts.

"Safety Breakthrough Talk Radio" has been a wonderful venue to meet new people, to get safety messages out to many people and to increase business. Cathy has been privileged to interview national, global experts and government officials in many safety, health and sustainability topics.

Cathy doesn't believe in coincidences. She believes that she was meant to form her new safety firm, to find Raven and to launch "Safety Breakthrough Talk Radio". In the safety field, Cathy will never know how many people she positively influence and help to prevent an injury or illness. She doesn't need to. Cathy does this because she loves it.


Cathy Hansell
Breakthrough Results LLC
http://www.breakthroughresults.org
http://www.linkedin.com/in/cathyhansell

Cathy Hansell

*Recipe for* SUCCESS!

1.  Identify your passion! What do you love to do? That is your new business.

2.  Develop an initial business plan: know your immediate and ultimate goals and timeline; define which products and services you will offer for free and which you will charge; set a level of work to be obtained and if you work alone, hire employees or contract out work to other consultants.

3.  Develop and register your company and radio show domain name(s). Protect yourself by copyrighting your work products and materials.

4.  Get out and be seen! Attend and speak at meetings, even if you are not paid; aggressively network; set up professional accounts on LinkedIn and Twitter. Develop a website; it need not be perfect to start out, just get it operational.

5.  Organize your business: purchase a laptop computer and office equipment (fax, printer, scanner); contract for technical, accounting and legal support; set up 800 and conference numbers, Pay Pal account. For your radio show, you'll need radio recording and editing software.

6.  Maintain your integrity and stay true to your values, even if your clients would request or settle for less.

7.  Re-evaluate where you are, what's working and what is not. Change what is needed to keep on track.

## *About Cathy Hansell*

Breakthrough Results is dedicated to helping people lead safer and healthier lives. How? By providing a "one-stop shop" for expert safety and health information and guidance. Whether for yourself, your family or your business, Breakthrough Results (BTR) and its president, Cathy Hansell, will help you.

For over 30 years, Cathy has held senior VP and Director Positions in safety, health, environmental (SHE), product and manufacturing quality at several international corporations including AlliedSignal, Honeywell International, BASF, American Standard and Trane Company. She holds a BS in engineering from Cook College: a MS in environmental toxicology from NYU Institute of Environmental Medicine and a JD in law from Rutgers University Law School. Cathy is a certified Malcolm Baldrige examiner and holds eight certifications in safety, quality, six sigma and sustainability. Cathy was selected as the National Association of Professional Women 2010-2011 Woman of the Year in the Safety, Health and Wellness Field, and selected as "Top 100 Women in Safety" by the ASSE.

Cathy is a member of ORC Worldwide Consulting Group, and an affiliate with The Lawrence Bradford Group, and Breakthrough Marketing. She is a member of the American Bar Associations, ASSE and EHS Roundtable.

Cathy, through BTR, is working with manufacturing, chemical, energy, construction, pharmaceutical, aerospace industries, military, government and academic clients. Projects include developing and implementing a safety strategy and culture, educating leadership, integrating SHE into business processes, applying six sigma and lean tools to improve safety culture and performance. For each of these consulting service areas, training, self-assessments, programs, checklists, program and leading metrics are available.

To reach more people, Cathy launched a unique safety radio show, called Safety Breakthrough Talk Radio (SBTR). The show provides the latest information and best practices, along with expert advice from interviews with experts on many safety, health, wellness and sustainability topics.

Cathy Hansell
Breakthrough Results
chansell@breakthroughresults.org
http://www.breakthroughresults.org

# Carolyn Jones, M.A.

## *Freedom and Fulfillment through Entrepreneurship*

Carolyn has been helping small businesses master their finances since 1996 when she ended her career as a pharmaceutical chemist and got a part-time job in a pottery studio.

At the time, Carolyn just wanted to clear her head; little did she know it was the beginning of a lifelong love-affair with entrepreneurship.

One day the owner of the studio came in, tossed Carolyn an accounting program called QuickBooks and said, "learn it, live it, love it". Her analytical nature helped her become an expert in the program very quickly. But it didn't satisfy her desire to help people heal and become empowered in their lives, so she pursued my Master's degree in East-West Psychology.

Bookkeeping allowed Carolyn to keep a flexible schedule with decent pay while completing graduate school. She started to see how working with numbers can have a tremendous impact on people's lives. Here were these brilliant, creative business owners who felt helpless around their finances. What an amazing thing to witness them flourish when the weight of money management was no longer burdening them!

For the past 10 years, Carolyn has guided creative entrepreneurs and visionary small businesses through financial chaos to clarity and peace with their money.

All they needed was some hand-holding while they figured out where they stood financially and where they wanted to go...and then build a business that gets them there.

Planning now is what gives you the freedom later. That is what entrepreneurship is all about – having freedom – with how you spend your time, with how much money you make, and with how you will make your contribution to the world.

*Carolyn Jones*

*Recipe for* SUCCESS!

1. Love what your business offers to the world

2. Surround yourself with a community of inspired entrepreneurs

3. Find a mastermind group and a coach

4. Hire people that are smarter than you

5. Be selective with your clients

6. Put in place a heart-centered financial plan

7. Have fun and play often

## *About Carolyn Jones*

Carolyn is on a mission to help small business owners achieve their dreams through enlightened financial practices. She inspires creative entrepreneurs to reframe financial management as a task toward a much more significant pursuit: Living their dreams.

Serving hundreds of clients since 1996, Carolyn is a skilled financial manager, trusted advisor, and keeper of dreams. And she never loses sight of her client's creative and personal aspirations. With an uncanny ability to look at numbers and see a story, she can align that story with your day-to-day and longer-term

Carolyn Jones, M.A.
Financial Breakthrough Guide
Email: Carolyn@absolutenumbers.com
Website: http://www.absolutenumbers.com

# Faye Kitariev

*"Our deepest fear is not that we are inadequate. Our deepest fear is that we are powerful beyond measure. It is our light, not our darkness that most frightens us. We ask ourselves, Who am I to be brilliant, gorgeous, talented, fabulous? Actually, who are you not to be? You are a child of God. Your playing small does not serve the world. There is nothing enlightened about shrinking so that other people won't feel insecure around you. We are all meant to shine, as children do. We were born to make manifest the glory of God that is within us. It's not just in some of us; it's in everyone. And as we let our own light shine, we unconsciously give other people permission to do the same. As we are liberated from our own fear, our presence automatically liberates others."*
*(M. Williamson)*

## *Make the Impossible Possible*

Faye was born in the Soviet Latvia, to a family of Jewish heritage. Her mother Gita dreamed of her daughter, 'Faen'ka,' becoming a figure skating star. When 'Faen'ka' turned three, Gita took her for audition to the skating academy. However, short and stocky, dark complexioned Gita and her daughter didn't appear to be a good fit with pale, long-legged, blond Russian and Latvian girls. Faye was rejected on the premise of having "no potential." Gita was fierce, and refused to accept the verdict of the admissions committee for her daughter. She found the 'back door', and soon, Faye was learning the way of being on the cold slippery surface.

Ten years later, living through physical, mental and emotional abuse that was systematically applied and encouraged in the youth sports schools in the Soviet Union, Faye became a Junior Ladies Champion, proving that the label "no potential" didn't apply to her. She was still forced to retire from skating, as it was unacceptable to Soviet authorities to have a Jew representing USSR.

In 1988 Faye's family decided to take power in their own hands, and defected to the United States. They came to New York, and one early morning, Faye took her old pair of skates and went skating at the Rockefeller Center. Someone noticed her, and asked if she wanted a job at the rink. She accepted, and soon decided that coaching was her calling. Her family didn't approve, but Faye wouldn't take "No" for an answer, enrolled herself into the University of Delaware and got a degree in coaching figure skating. She became obsessed with not only bringing out the 'potential' in kids, that no one believed in, but doing it in the most empowering and inspiring way! She had a vision of teaching National, International, World and Olympic competitors.

As Faye started producing results, she had to face strong opposition from her competitors, and political system of the sport. It was a challenging time, where several times she had to start over again. Yet, her determination, will, focus, and perseverance paid off, and she became one of the top 1% of coaches in the US, working with such athletes as Sasha Cohen (2006 Olympic Silver Medalist) and Johnny Weir (2008 World Bronze Medalist), and training numerous athletes to medals at National/International competitions.

Over time she realized the benefits of mental training for success. At the same time, she observed the struggles athletes, their parents, and coaches were going through in hopes of grasping a moment of stardom, only to find themselves defeated and deflated as a result. Faye arrived at a place, where hard questions were being asked: 'Who am I', 'What is my purpose?' 'How can I contribute to the world?' These questions made her realize that professional sport is a metaphor for life and that a lot of people can benefit from her expertise and experience of coaching competitive athletes.

She created her company: Make The Impossible Possible, and is finishing her first inspirational self-help book, based on her experiences: 'Choreography of Awakening" available for purchase in March, 2013.

*Faye Kitariev*

*Recipe for* SUCCESS!

1. Create a daily ritual you can rely on, and stick to it. It will take you through the most difficult situations.

2. Eat wholesome, living foods and exercise. It will give you the energy to do what you want to do, and help you enjoy it as well.

3. Read inspiring literature daily! It will keep your goals and aspirations alive, and remind you why you do what you do.

4. Stay true to yourself. You know what you need, you know what you want, and you KNOW how to get there! Trust your most knowledgeable adviser-intuition.

5. Be original! You are one of a kind, a unique expression of the Divine. No one can be better at being you, than you. Don't look around. Stay focused and develop the best possible You, you can imagine!

6. Whatever you do, always seek for ways to inspire yourself and others. When you uplift someone, you lift yourself. Consciously look for something positive in those around you!

7. You can only live in the HERE and NOW. Past is filled with regrets-learn your lessons, forgive and let go. Future is filled with anxieties-be grateful for warnings and return into the NOW. NOW is the time to create.

## *About Faye Kitariev*

Faye Kitariev is a leader in coaching performance mastery, although, she likes to be called a 'life choreographer'. A former competitive figure skating coach, she coached numerous skaters to medals at national and international levels over the course of her 20 years+ career. The list of her students includes such athletes as 2006 US National Champion and Olympic Silver medalist Sasha Cohen and a 2008 World Bronze Medalist Johnny Weir. She was born and raised in Latvia (republic in the former Soviet Union), where she skated competitively since she was two years old, and was a Latvian Junior Ladies Champion. At age 18 she moved to the United States. She received a Bachelor's Degree in coaching figure skating from The University of Delaware, and Masters of Arts degree in Spiritual Psychology from the University of Santa Monica. In addition, she is certified in hypnotherapy, and Kundalini Yoga. She traveled extensively to study with spiritual teachers of different traditions and schools. Based on her experiences, years of study and inquiry, Faye have developed her own unique system of awakening the inner potential, finding the meaning and purpose in life, and manifesting the lasting change. Through her talks, workshops and seminars she inspires men, women and children to believe in themselves, and to take action towards realizing their heart-felt dreams. She lives in Irvine, California with her daughter Abbie and her husband Dmitri.

Faye Kitariev
coach_faye@me.com
Make The Impossible Possible
www.fayekitariev.com

# Dr. Dorine Kramer

*Our deepest fear is not that we are inadequate. Our deepest fear is that we are powerful beyond measure. It is our light, not our darkness that most frightens us. We ask ourselves, Who am I to be brilliant, gorgeous, talented, fabulous? Actually, who are you not to be? You are a child of God. Your playing small does not serve the world.  Marianne Williamson*

## *From Being Mom To Being Me*

Dr. Dorine chose to leave her medical career to be a stay-at-home mom raising her two amazing children, Stephanie and Benjamin.  When her almost 18-year old daughter left home to further her career out-of-state, Dr. Dorine's world collapsed.

Her 15 year old son had decided the previous year that it wasn't cool anymore to hang out with Mom, and so she became a de facto Empty Nester.

She knew it would be bad, but she didn't have a clue how bad.

Feeling isolated and alone.  Embarrassing tears over anything and everything.  Gaining weight because all she wanted to do was eat and watch TV.   Having bizarre or no conversations with her husband because he didn't or couldn't acknowledge the depths of her distress.  No interest in sex.  She was dragging herself out of bed, exhausted, every morning.  Dr. Dorine didn't know what to do with herself or how to make herself feel better.  She felt as if she didn't know who she even was when she wasn't doing "mom things".   And, thinking she had to sort it all out by herself.

When the kids left for college, Dr. Dorine's role as full-time mom finished and she found that she was confused and uncertain about her identity, the new role she had in life, and who and what she wanted to be in the future.  Her confidence plummeted and her health suffered, as did her marriage and her other relationships.  Having spent so many years putting her family's needs and wants above her own, she found it challenging to focus on herself.

After four challenging years of trying unsuccessfully to absorb the changes in her life, Dr. Dorine finally reached out for help.  That was the turning point.  She began to find ways to shift her view of herself and to find the motivation and the means to rediscover her true self redesign her life role and re-envision her future. Working with coaches and exploring a variety of disciplines, she reinvented herself and now enjoys her speaking and coaching business, her revitalized marriage and close relationships with her adult children.

In her BC (before children) life, Dr. Dorine demonstrated great achievements. Yet all those accomplishments paled in the face of her empty nest and loss of her main role in life at that time. Because of that experience, Dr. Dorine understands how our minds and emotions can play tricks and has us devalue our accomplishments, and has the tools to reverse that self-sabotage.

Dr. Dorine's passion is helping moms acknowledge their achievements and reinvent themselves easily and joyfully, without the struggle she experienced. Now, as a speaker, certified strategy and accountability coach, master NLP practitioner, hypnotherapist and author of the forthcoming book **From Being Mom to Being Me: 5 Steps to Purpose, Passion and Your Dream Life When Your Nest Is Empty**, Dr. Dorine has streamlined the same techniques she used for herself and uses them to help you in your own transformation.

## Dr. Dorine Kramer

### Recipe for SUCCESS!

1. Celebrate every accomplishment in some way, even if it's just a pat on the back.

2. You haven't failed unless you give up. Until then it's feedback and you can learn something useful, even if it's just that what you tried doesn't work.

3. Keep loving yourself, no matter what.

4. Talk about what you are working toward only with those people who support your vision.

5. Keep your focus on what you want, not on all the things that could go wrong.

6. Make yourself a priority over your work. That means, among other things, go pee when you need to!

7. Take regular breaks—get outside, pet your dog, or my personal favorite, watch the tops of trees blowing in the wind.

## *About Dr Dorine Kramer*

International Speaker and Author of the forthcoming book **"From Being Mom to Being Me";** Dr. Dorine Kramer is passionate about helping stay at home moms whose kids have left the nest to reinvent themselves so the next years are the best years of their lives.

Affectionately known as "Dr. Dorine" by her clients and colleagues, Dr. Dorine has created a unique process incorporating the life lessons from  her own experience of evolving from being a Stay at Home Mom to being an International Speaker, Author, Business Owner, Coach, and Leader in the community. Whether your children are about to leave, or they have already moved on to lives outside of the family home, Dr. Dorine is committed to helping you transform "from being mom to being me"  just as she did.  It is her great honor and privilege to help you find your own most rewarding life path.

Dr. Dorine enjoys her grown kids wanting to spend time with her, and helping other moms to value themselves so they can have the passion, health and future they want, including rewarding relationships with their adult children and other adults.

Dr. Dorine received her medical degree from UC Irvine.  She is Board-certified in Public Health and Preventive Medicine and has done work for the World Health Organization.  She also served as an epidemiologist at the world renowned Centers for Disease Control (CDC) during the early stages of the AIDS epidemic.

Dr. Dorine Kramer
drdorine@drdorinekramer.com
DGK Unlimited
www.drdorinekramer.com

# Gwen Lepard

*"Joy is what happens to us when we allow ourselves to recognize how good things really are."*
*- Marianne Williamson*

## *Joy is a Choice - Choose to Live a Joyful Life*

Gwen Lepard hails from the mountains of Western Montana. Growing up in this mystical place of natural surroundings and wonder, she gained many life lessons from simply enjoying her environment. She watched the river below her mountain home rise and fall each spring. The river became a metaphor showing change through dramatic flooding and then the default of joy in how the river found its bed again year after year.

She came into this world, as we all do, pure love, light, energy and joy! Her path has lead her through many experiences. Some joyful and empowering and others that some would allow to scar them for life or to put them into a mode of paralyzing victimization. However, Gwen has continually found her way back to joy! She calls it her default, the setting she came in with, that we all come in with.

In the 80's, she trained as a professional massage therapist and worked backstage and in the studio with well-known musicians. The 90's found her on the airwaves as an on-air radio personality, moving music, timely information and occasional inspiration.

In the early 2000's, she co-founded a small record label and was personally responsible for getting an album placed on the Grammy ballot.

Her deepest passion was inspired after healing from what she'd discovered was verbal abuse during her marriage. When she was cringing from yet another verbal whipping, Gwen never imagined that her husband would actually physically whip her and yet he did. That day she left her mountain home and began a journey back to joyful empowerment.

She shares with her audiences, "If you feel like you're being abused. You are being abused!" She was told that she needed to "toughen up and this is how it is in the real world". Not in my world, she thought! AND she was right when she made the choice to recreate her life from her default of joy.

Through excellent mentors and inner healing work, she realized that she'd created this situation to show her how she had verbally abused herself. That realization had her looking around at the world and at her client's patterns of anxiety, fear and shame, and... she "got it"!

With this insight came the passion and purpose to create a movement. A movement of joy that brings to public awareness that verbal abuse to another or to you is damaging... AND there is something that can be done about it. Every individual has the ability to choose. They can choose to change this pattern!

Gwen says, "There is healing to be done! So much more joy can be brought into this world and it starts with the words you say to yourself and to others. It also matters how you say those words and how your body responds to them... Choose to see joy, speak joy, hear and feel JOY!"

### Gwen Lepard

### Recipe for SUCCESS!

1. Show Up

2. Trust that You are Always in the Right Place at the Right Time

3. Gratitude... Practice, Journal, Walk do Daily

4. Believe in Yourself

5. Prepare & Practice

6. Do the Work on Yourself First

7. Allow Your Default to be Reset to JOY! (Everything in Life Flows Easier When You Come From a Place of Joy...)

## *About Gwen Lepard*

Gwen Lepard is Host of Joyful Living Radio, a Master Healer, a Speaker, an Authority on Joy, Master NLP Practitioner and Trainer, Master Hypnotherapist and Bestselling Co-Author of "The Gratitude Book Project, Celebrating 365 Days of Gratitude". With close to 30 years of healing experience, she's impacted thousands of people through touch, voice, words and music.

In her 9 years as an on-air radio personality she was featured in over 1500 shows and spoke in front of groups of hundreds and even thousands during a fundraiser featuring Heart's acoustic group, the Love Mongers. She's directly worked one-on-one with a number of well-known musicians backstage and in the studio.

Gwen also co-founded a small record label that included an album she personally placed in over 400 stores and through her efforts that album made it to the Grammy ballot in four categories.

As a Master Healer and an Authority on Joy, she brings joy and healing through awareness of verbal abuse, works with private clients, speaking to groups, running workshops and through hosting Joyful Living Radio. She is shining light on a new way to have more energy, better health, happier relationships and how become more attractive to the abundance you desire.

Creator of the "Be the Sun, 3 Keys to Joy" and the Quantum Joy Experience, Gwen Lepard helps divorced women who have been victims of verbal abuse and suffer from anxiety, fear, shame and loss of self-esteem heal, recover and rediscover their joy.

Gwen Lepard
gwen@joyfullivingradio.com
Joy Centered Life
www.joyfullivingradio.com

~ Notes ~

# Debbie Luxton

*"You are never too old to set another goal or to dream a new dream."*
— C.S. Lewis

## You Can't See the Inside From the Outside

Debbie is the mother of four, step-mother of one and grandmother of 8.  She is retired from a 30 year Fortune 500 corporate career, an entrepreneur and small business owner. Debbie is a ministry co-leader, Board of Director's volunteer and author.

Although "retired", she believes strongly in giving back and she has lived the challenges many women face of balancing family, career and life.

Debbie spent much of her life working a high-profile and high-stress corporate job.  And, just like so many women today, she wore too many hats in constantly juggling it all.  By all appearances she was very successful and handled her overloaded life well.  Debbie wore her masks well.  Unfortunately, you can't see the inside from the outside.

Debbie learned many life lessons the hard way as she began making poor life choices to deal with her stressful life.  She was constantly overwhelmed at trying to control everything and everyone around her.  Debbie believed she couldn't let anyone know that she needed help.  She felt she couldn't say "no", after all she had always been the person that everyone could come to and counted on.  As a corporate and family leader she could show no weakness; she had to "have it all together".  This meant, she had to maintain her perceived level of perfection.  The fallacy was in thinking she was helping herself, when all she was doing was adding fuel to the fire of her overloaded life.

By God's grace, Debbie was saved from herself and all of her masks were removed. She found the true joy and peace that living an authentic life has to offer.

Debbie excelled in her corporate position.  She was the "go-to" person for building successful teams.  One key to her success was the care she took in helping each person on her team to be the best they could be.  To this day, Debbie's heart is in giving freely and partnering with others to live authentically and free of self-defeating burdens.

Debbie was sought out to serve on the Board of Directors for the Missouri Recovery Network, voted to serve on the Executive Committee and she co-chairs the Organizational Development Committee.

Beginning a new or second phase of her life, Debbie has become a successful solo-preneur, dedicated volunteer and writer.

Debbie believes that Jesus is the Truth and He alone provides the pathway to a life that is traveled in freedom. She has personally experienced the freedom that only He can provide. Her desire is that you too will know His grace, love and mercy. And, that you would know the truth that He created you for nothing less than greatness.

### Debbie Luxton

### Recipe for SUCCESS!

1. Take care of yourself - you can't help others if you are not well in heart, mind and soul.

2. Always be honest - especially when it hurts.

3. Be authentic - transparency speaks volumes.

4. Pray continually - lift up every part of your business.

5. Stay humble - never forget that it's not about you.

6. Give freely - do not expect something in return

7. Keep your priorities straight - your family always comes first.

## *About Debbie Luxton*

Debbie Luxton is a Christian Life & Leadership Coach, Retreat Leader, Speaker, Workshop Leader and Author. She is a small business owner of Debbie Luxton Coaching (formerly, Truth for Life's Journey), a Blessings Unlimited Independent Team Leader and a Founding Partner and Independent Coach, Teacher and Speaker with the John Maxwell Team.

Debbie's passion is in working with executive and professional women. She very much understands the pressures and complexities of being a wife, mother and professional woman.

Debbie co-leads, with her husband, a Celebrate Recovery Ministry, serves on the Board of Director's for the Missouri Recovery Network (Executive Committee and Co-Chairs the Organizational Development Committee), is writing her first solo-authored book, is a contributing author in the 2011 published book, "Inspired Women Succeed" and the 2012 published book, "How to Create a Rich, Successful and Fulfilling Life: Dynamic Tools for Overcoming Obstacles and Creating Rapid Transformation".

Debbie is a retired director from a 30 year corporate career where she built and led many teams to success. Debbie partners with her clients to relieve constant stress and anxiety, reverse self-sabotaging thoughts and behaviors, achieve deeper relationships and discover their unique purpose. She knows firsthand that you CAN renew your heart, mind and soul to live a successful life based on your true authentic priorities.

Debbie has written and conducts two annual life enriching women's retreats: "The Serenity Retreat" and "The Authentic Influence Retreat". She offers individual and group coaching on 5 John Maxwell leadership programs and multiple life coaching programs.

Debbie Luxton
dluxton@sbcglobal.net
Debbie Luxton Coaching
http://www.debbieluxton.com

## ~ Notes ~

# JoAnn Martin

*" ...Be ye transformed by the renewing of your minds, that ye may prove what is that good and acceptable, and perfect will of God."*
*Romans 12:2 Holy Bible*

## Choose Well---Choices Are The Key

Growing up in Texas in the 40's and 50's gave JoAnn many opportunities to be transformed by the renewing of her mind. That verse and a second one about all things working together for good were very useful in moving her through life to positive ends.

She was back and forth between her Dad and a single frustrated Mother. After high school graduation she started college and met the man who she married. After a year in Germany with her military husband the first of three sons was born. Soon after his birth they returned to the US and settled in California hoping for a better life than Texas might have provided.

It soon became clear that she needed to supplement her husband's inadequate salary. California proved to be less progressive than expected for black men. Without a college degree her salary was also inadequate so against great odds, now with three babies, she embarked upon the task of earning a college degree. After spending several years teaching she was recognized among peers as someone who was knowledgeable about personal relationships, wellness issues and finance and was often approached for coaching. This led to weekly meetings in her home and ultimately, to workshops and seminars.

This "aura" continued when she relocated to Texas after retirement and she is often called upon to speak, write or teach/interface to address a challenge. It is with great joy that she accepts these opportunities. Currently she hosts a Talk Radio show and is working on writing for publication and adding to her poetry collection. Her wish is to expand the Institute of Wisdom, Wellness and Wealth into a well-known Retreat Center and help more people make better choices. She has a passion for expanding the concept of Oneness thereby creating peace.

*JoAnn Martin*

*Recipe for* SUCCESS!

1. Be One with Source/Higher Self

2. Believe in yourself and dream Big

3. Know the power of words. Speak success

4. Be surrounded by successful people (support group)

5. Focus on desired goal and decide to attain it

6. Ask for what you desire and act as if...

7. Give gratitude and praise!!!

## About JoAnn Martin

JoAnn Martin BS, MA. Transformation Coach, Certified Healer assists others in being transformed by changing their minds, and leads them to the healer within. She was dubbed as a "born teacher with kind eyes and healing hands" early in her life and started her work life teaching and healing. Her greatest joy is sharing information to inspire and motivate others to new levels of expression. After 30 years of teaching school in California she returned to Texas, her home state and settled for her retirement years. She is often called upon to speak, teach and write, and happily shares the awareness of wisdom, wellness and wealth that she has gathered along her journey through life. She keeps busy writing, speaking, hosting a Talk Radio Show and planning Retreats.

JoAnn Martin
wisdomwellnessandwealth@gmail.com
Applied Awareness Systems Institute
www.wisdomwellnessandwealth.com

# Louisa Mastromarino

## *Energy Coaching Business Success*

Louisa Mastromarino, certified educator and certified counselor, intuitive consultant and medium, is a business owner with over 10 years of solid experience building a holistic practice worldwide.  Her business Mastro Holistic Consulting and Specialties Programs has now expanded to include a distant energy medicine division, Distant Holistic Arts at www.distantholistic.com and a career coaching division, Resume and Career International at www.resumeandcareer.com designed to service the needs of populations seeking to create positive lifestyle changes with mind, body, spirit modalities directly online.  With her attention on customer service, Louisa has seen changes that include stronger customer communication, innovative program development, and worldwide access to services that accommodate changing market places and customer requests.

As an entrepreneur, Louisa's business has now outreached into products where in the beginning of her startup, she never would have foreseen.  With a winning attitude and stout planning, she was able to use her writing talents to create meditation scripts for guided meditation programs and her intuitive abilities to design custom artwork.  These items are now for sale on her web sites.  She has also been able to create positive and productive metaphysical classes that foster client education and empowerment in the areas of complementary medicine and energy anatomy.  Small business works and it does not matter what individuals feel they can offer, even during financial and economic changes.  Everyone has the ability to translate what he or she loves into successful living.

Louisa learned to succeed with love and a positive approach that includes self-determination and self-motivation along with division expansion and customer friendliness.  Listening to client needs always is a key resource when developing products and services.  Customer service is the most important attribute of successful entrepreneurship. For example, in order to reach more customers and worldwide access, Louisa created Distant Holistic Arts and Consulting so clients faced with difficult conditions or life stress can order right online and receive the benefits of holistic medicine in the comfort of their own homes.

As a certified counselor educator, Louisa was inspired by areas of her life that offered education as a service to customers.  Her teleconference courses and private coaching sessions teach skills to all ages and populations seeking to learn mind, body, spirit awareness applications for stress management. Mind, body, spirit awareness is becoming more mainstream and can be accessed by everyone seeking new opportunities for personal growth.

*Louise Mastromarino*

*Recipe for* SUCCESS!

1. Start fresh. Don't copy anyone. Be yourself and be friendly.

2. Renew your loves. Enjoy your new found interests. Interests change over time and all of our interests can make valued business ventures.

3. Read. Enjoy being well read and see the truth behind the words.

4. Business can be play. Do what you love and play 24-hours a day.

5. Be kind to yourself. Self-kindness fosters self-motivation and self-motivation allows small business ventures to rise and flourish.

6. Be true to your words. Allow people to know you are honest and willing to work with them on all levels.

7. Accentuate the positive. Positive thinking and resurrection is key in fulfilling lasting dreams, no matter what age.

## *About Louise Mastromarino*

Louisa Mastromarino holds a Bachelor of Arts degree in Communications and a Master's degree in Counselor Education. Louisa owns Mastro Holistic Consulting, a leading holistic practice in Staten Island, New York. After receiving her Reiki Master certification in 2001, Louisa continued to foster her spiritual training in other energy medicine systems and intuitive development programs. She holds additional certifications as a medium, intuitive consultant and esoteric healing practitioner. She also holds specialist certifications in biofeedback, stress management, pain management and bioenergetics from the Natural Therapies Certification Board, a leading certification board recognizing advanced modalities. Currently, her company Mastro Holistic Consulting, www.mastroholistic.com, and its two divisions: Distant Holistic Arts, www.distantholistic.com and Career and Resume International, www.resumeandcareer.com offer quality distant services in spiritual coaching, energy medicine modalities, intuitive consulting, mediumship training, career and resume development worldwide.

Louisa provides teleconferences and training programs that enhance client learning for spiritual concepts and holistic awareness. She is a proponent of the power of positive thinking, expands gratitude every day for entrepreneurial achievements, and enjoys creating programs for her new found radio show "Distant Holistic Talk Radio" airing on Raven Blair Davis' network. She has also contributed inspirational quotes in Making Marriage a Success by Jaleh Donaldson and has had her clients featured on television shows airing on the Biography channel. She finds learning from her clients is the best learning that a business owner can do in terms of business development and enhancement. Client service is the highest recognition that offers a quality return as a holistic specialist and energy coach.

Louise Mastromarino
distantholistic@gmail.com
Mastro Holistic Consulting
www.distantholistic.com

~ Notes ~

# Consuelo Meux, Ph.D.

*"I woke up early this morning and paused before entering the day.
I had so much to accomplish that I had to take time to pray"*
**Author Unknown**

Consuelo started her first business in the eighth grade as a musician for the neighborhood church. By college she was an entrepreneur, paying her way to a degree in marketing. For decades, Consuelo worked successfully teaching and consulting in organizational and business development and women's leadership helping others to learn business and build their operations. She is a former Peace Corps volunteer who lived and worked in West Africa building food cooperatives, has been a faculty member at various universities and active as a speaker and teacher in women's ministries.

At the height of her career, things took an abrupt turn. In 2004, she moved to a new location expecting to join the community and continue her career. Instead, she became the full-time care provider for her ailing mother for the next 2 ½ years. During this time, she was isolated with few resources or support. The alone times only magnified some of the ugly situations she had silently survived over the years without ever seeking help. The effects of those days along with the isolation caused her to develop a fear-based mentality that threatened to keep her stuck. She also developed several health issues as the consistent high-level stress in her life started to wear her down.

Fortunately, Consuelo had always had a strong interest in natural health and wellness issues since experiencing digestive problems as a child. She had taken courses on how to use food for better health, learning to prepare healing dishes to care for others. Yet, while she was going through her major life transitions, she experienced serious health symptoms that gave her a wake-up call to get really serious about changing her life and health behaviors.
Despite all of the problems, her strong faith in God let her know that there was a purpose for what she was growing through and she began to put one foot in front of the other to face two major challenges:

1.  Not being able to continue in a career she had spent decades to build was devastating. But she had to face the current reality and learn to find a way to make a total change in her life and get moving again.

2. She also absolutely refused to get "old" too soon through illnesses and needed to work on reversing the bad effects that were already taking hold of her body.

Consuelo knew many other boomer women were experiencing similar life transitions and many others were also facing health issues. She decided to focus on developing areas she felt were parts of her true life calling by using her background in health and wellness. She learned to create websites, wrote and self-published information products and books, and started teaching courses online. She became a Certified Holistic Health Coach, Creativity Coach, Life Breakthrough Coach. Consuelo shares that all of the success in the world will be for nothing if you don't have a daily practice of prayer along with good health and wellness.

Consuelo started her first business in the eighth grade as a musician for the neighborhood church. By college she was an entrepreneur, paying her way to a degree in marketing. For decades, Consuelo worked successfully teaching and consulting in organizational and business development and women's leadership helping others to learn business and build their operations. She is a former Peace Corps volunteer who lived and worked in West Africa building food cooperatives, has been a faculty member at various universities and active as a speaker and teacher in women's ministries.

At the height of her career, things took an abrupt turn. In 2004, she moved to a new location expecting to join the community and continue her career. Instead, she became the full-time care provider for her ailing mother for the next 2 ½ years. During this time, she was isolated with few resources or support. The alone times only magnified some of the ugly situations she had silently survived over the years without ever seeking help. The effects of those days along with the isolation caused her to develop a fear-based mentality that threatened to keep her stuck. She also developed several health issues as the consistent high-level stress in her life started to wear her down.

Fortunately, Consuelo had always had a strong interest in natural health and wellness issues since experiencing digestive problems as a child. She had taken courses on how to use food for better health, learning to prepare healing dishes to care for others. Yet, while she was going through her major life transitions, she experienced serious health symptoms that gave her a wake-up call to get really serious about changing her life and health behaviors.

Despite all of the problems, her strong faith in God let her know that there was a purpose for what she was growing through and she began to put one foot in front of the other to face two major challenges:

1. Not being able to continue in a career she had spent decades to build was devastating. But she had to face the current reality and learn to find a way to make a total change in her life and get moving again.

2. She also absolutely refused to get "old" too soon through illnesses and needed to work on reversing the bad effects that were already taking hold of her body.

Consuelo knew many other boomer women were experiencing similar life transitions and many others were also facing health issues. She decided to focus on developing areas she felt were parts of her true life calling by using her background in health and wellness. She learned to create websites, wrote and self-published information products and books, and started teaching courses online. She became a Certified Holistic Health Coach, Creativity Coach, Life Breakthrough Coach. Consuelo shares that all of the success in the world will be for nothing if you don't have a daily practice of prayer along with good health and wellness.

Consuelo Meux

Recipe for SUCCESS!

1. You don't have to feel like it or want to... Just Do It!

2. Take care of yourself – this is the only body you get

3. Good health and wellness will make you a successful professional

4. Never stop learning – keep up with the times so you are ready for any challenge

5. You have to live through many experiences before knowing your true life calling

6. Embrace life transitions – these times open doors to new adventures that are greater than what you've already known

7. Don't worry, pray and remember – God's Got It!

## *About Consuelo Meux*

Consuelo Meux, Ph.D. provides expert holistic health coaching for seasoned (Baby Boomer) women who struggle with the lifestyle changes necessary to make health and wellness a practical, easy-to-do practice in their daily life. She is the founder of Seasoned Women™ Productions that includes Seasoned Women™ Wellness programs. As the host of Seasoned Women™ Health Radio (SWHR) she shares her diverse experiences and expertise and interviews experts from around the world on health and wellness issues relevant to seasoned (Boomer) women.

Consuelo has a doctoral degree in Human and Organizational Systems, is a Certified Holistic Health Counselor (CHHC) and member of the American Association of Drugless Practitioner (AADP). She studied with the Institute for Integrative Nutrition (IIN) and the School for Natural Health Sciences (SNHS) and is becoming a Raw/Vegan and Personal Fitness Chef. Consuelo is a health columnist at Examiner.com and produces the Seasoned Women™ Wellness Expo and Retreat.

Consuelo Meux
info@seasonedwomenwellness.com
Seasoned Women Wellness
www.seasonedwomenwellness.com

# Michelle M. Miller

*"When you change the way you look at things, the things you look at begins to change."*
*Dr. Wayne Dyer*

## *Seizing The Audacity to Shift Gears*

From as early as eight years old, Michelle was a curious-minded child. She believed there was something extraordinary about dreams and about life. Having successfully navigated the life-altering experience of caring for her ailing mother and younger siblings, from the young age of 19yrs, she recommitted herself to exploring all of life possibilities.

She learned that life is not a static but a dynamic experience. We each have a unique purpose to fulfill and specific path to travel. Every struggle serves to build our strength. If we desire to realize our dreams, we must be willing to shift and expand our perception.

Over the years, she enjoyed many incredible job opportunities, leading to Assistant Vice President in an offshore bank. Despite much external success, she yearned for a genuine sense of fulfillment and had to reassess what matters most. Embracing self-discovery, she redefined how she desired to show up in the world; shifting towards helping, others realize their life dreams. It was a pool of inspiration springing from her early role as a young caregiver for her mother and siblings.

She studied extensively, becoming a Certified Life-Coach, Leadership Trainer, Author and Radio Personality. Trusting her faith, she left her corporate life and opened *Take The Lead Coaching Business.* She learned about the complexities of human behavior and the power of our emotions. Ultimately, she sees life as a crash course in choices and consequences. Her task is to inspire individuals to broaden their perception in order to make quality choices.

Working with young girls, parents and professionals, her coaching strategies address how information fundamentally influences our choices and behavior. She challenges her clients to take the lead for their dreams by taking charge of their choices. To define who they are and how they show up in the world. This means taking personal responsibility, shifting towards better life outcomes.

In every moment, we can choose whether we live fearfully or fearlessly. In a rapidly changing world, many live the matrix of misconceptions, which hinders their shifting capacity. She reminds individuals that their life moves according to their directives. Fearless living requires seizing the audacity to alter one's thinking. When we feel more secure about our ability to overcome our life challenges, we aptly engage our power to shift life gears. Authenticity is one of her core values. Having learned to take the lead at a young age, she knows that at anyone can learn how to shift and improve his or her life.

Michelle's ideal clients are young girls, parents or professionals, who are ready to shift, redefine how they show up in the world and take the lead for their choices. She challenges them to take control of their whole self by intrinsically moving towards meaning and authenticity. She knows for sure that everything we need to realize our dreams already exists within. Our task is to learn to shift life gears in order to expand who we are and the way we see the world.

*Michelle Miller*

*Recipe for* SUCCESS!

1. Be honest in examining who you are and what you believe is possible for your life

2. Clarify what you want, why you want it and how you intend to achieve your dreams

3. Identify the skills you possess, the skills you need and know when to ask for help

4. Take control of your choices; you are either in control or you are out of control

5. Set goals and create a strategy; goals require an action-focused strategy

6. Carpe diem is not just a Latin phrase it is a life principle. Your time is your greatest resource; seize every moment participating in quality activities

7. Be willing to shift gears; nothing changes in your life until you change.

## *About Michelle Miller*

Born and raised in The Bahamas, she is Founder of the Girls Leadership Coaching Club (GLC) and Author of **Take the Lead** – *For Girls with Dreams.*  Standing on the strength of her experience, she offers individual and group effective coaching strategies.  She also facilitates **Take the Lead** **– for Your Dream** workshops and boot camps.

The core focus of her strategy session is to engage clients in the process of awareness and acceptance to enable them clearly determine their forward track.  Individuals who benefit most from her strategic approach are Teens and young adults who are on the brink of entering the working world, as well as parents and professionals between the ages of 27 to 67yrs seeking more meaning.  These individuals are ready to take responsibility for themselves, ownership of their lives and unleash their full potential.

Michelle M. Miller
**Take The Lead Coaching Strategies**
coaching242@yahoo.com
http://taketheleadbook.com

# ~ Notes ~

# Mari Mitchell Porter

*"Go confidently in the direction of your dreams. Live the life you have imagined."*
*~ Henry David Thoreau*

## *Don't Give Up*

Mari just realized one of her dreams; publishing her first book, "Diary of a Hopeless Romantic." Although written as a novel, her purpose was to give people the tools to form healthy and fulfilling relationships. She has several testimonials from men and women who have used the suggestions in the book with great results.

For most of Mari's adult life she worked as an administrator. She excelled in this field which she had entered even before graduating from college, but never felt fulfilled.

After she married and the birth of her first child, she took a hiatus from working. She became a full time mother and continued at home when her two daughters were born. The entrepreneur in her though, always had a side business going.

As her marriage began crumbling after 17 years, she and her husband separated. Mari moved to South Florida with her two young daughters and encountered the struggles of being a single mom. Administrative work paid low wages and meeting the bills was a challenge.
Mari finally worked her way up to a high paying position managing a doctor's office. Although her finances were now secure, she longed to work in a field she was passionate about. In the meantime she was working on herself to learn where I had gone wrong in my relationships and how to find the love I yearned for. With the help of a therapist, she coached myself through the pain of divorce and the challenges of dating.

Mari met a wonderful man and a year later was engaged. Now that she had peace, joy and wonderful relationships, she wanted to impart what she had learned to others, so she trained to become a certified professional coach. Mari launched her coaching business while still working at the doctor's office, but yearned to do her coaching and writing full time. In September 2010 she left behind the security of a good paying job in order to give her full attention to coaching and writing.

Mari did have moments when she regretted leaving her job and doubted her ability to be a successful coach. Then her mother became gravely ill early in 2011 and she had to neglect her business in order to help take care of her. She died that April and with a heavy heart Mari put her focus back into the coaching. Then in July her husband broke his hip and again she had to put her coaching aside. Once he recovered she went back to fully focusing on her business.

Slowly her client base grew. Men and women came to her hurting and unhappy, but by the end of their sessions they were smiling, hopeful and willing to take the steps necessary to get what they want in their lives. The greatest fulfillment Mari receives from coaching is experiencing people's lives transforming right before her.

Believe in yourself and don't give up, is what I've learned through the struggles and what I teach my clients.

*Mari Mitchell Porter*

*Recipe for* SUCCESS!

1.  Believe in yourself. This is <u>key</u>. If you don't believe in yourself and the service and or products you have to offer, others cannot believe in you. Also, many people will try to tell you why you can't do what you dream of doing, so a strong belief in yourself is necessary

2.  Quiet your mind. I call it quiet time. Sit quietly for a time preferably at the start of your day to give your mind a rest from thinking and be open to receive inspiration and direction. The more you do this, the more confidence you will have in the decisions you make and the directions your take.

3.  Be Authentic. Authenticity is not much talked about, but it's so important to be you. Most of us grew up having everyone telling us who and what we should be. The only one we can be happy being is us. Be yourself and you will draw to you the people you can help because you have been gifted with what they need.

4.  Follow your heart. There are many programs, methods, ideas and plans out there. You must follow your heart when deciding what's right for you and your business. Others may have very good ideas, but they may not necessarily be for you.

5.  Be teachable. There are many ways of doing things and we can always be open to learning new things. If you're teachable, you won't miss out on learning new things every day that can increase your business or be helpful in some way.

6.  Share your knowledge. Don't be afraid to share what you've learned with others. If you keep everything to yourself you can't expand and grow.

7.  Keep your word. If you promise to do something, keep your promise. If you say you're going to do something, do it. This is how you build your reputation. Beautiful websites, cards or brochures cannot speak about your reputation. It's how you serve your clients that matters.

213

## *About Mari Mitchell Porter*

Mari is a relationship coach, life coach, author and speaker based out of South Florida. She became a certified professional coach after coaching herself through divorce, the struggles of being a single mom and beginning to date again.

Mari's passion is working with people one-on-one and giving them the support, encouragement and tools necessary for bringing love and fulfillment into their lives. Her workshops and seminars are both informative and practical, giving people simple steps to follow in order to improve their lives.

Her first book, **"Diary of a Hopeless Romantic",** a self-help novel about how to form healthy relationships, was just published in early October 2012.  She also just launched her line of "Quotes for Living Photos", inspiring quotes on beautiful photographs.

Mari Mitchell Porter, CPC
http://www.lifecoachmari.com
mari@lifecoachmari.com

# Carol Neu

*"Whatever the mind can conceive and believe, it can achieve."*
**Napoleon Hill**

## *From Canvas to Computer*

Having Spinal Meningitis at age 3 and a need to refine motor skills and attention span, Carol's father built an easel, bought primary colored paint by the gallon and purchased end rolls of newsprint from a local newspaper for the canvas. She received encouragement from her Mother also talented in several artistic industries.

Carol has been painting and designing ever since. She painted limited edition duck decoys for a company that was contracted by Ducks Unlimited. Her first computer experience was designing stencils and creating the vector images to create the dies to manufacture the stencils. Carol styled hair for several years and finally opened an arts and craft store and started teaching classes in acrylics and oils. The classes she taught in the store were beginner to intermediate. When ask if she would ever teach advanced, her reply was "No, I still have more to learn".

She became a published artist of several painting books and magazine projects and at a late age in life turned to computer graphics as her husband owned and operated a computer repair store and needed some advertisements done. She had been involved with a video email company for about 6 years and realized the need for graphic artists at an affordable price. As a small business owner herself, she knew how hard it was to succeed when you are up against corporate America.

Carol started her latest company NeuWorldDesigns. To further her education she attended LV-PITA in Las Vegas, NV and became an Adobe Certified Associate at the ripe age of 61. Like she says, "You can teach an old dog, new tricks"! Carol has always been a very giving person and her mission now is to help all small to medium businesses succeed.

*Carol Neu*

*Recipe for* SUCCESS!

1. Do what you love and love what you do.

2. Believe in yourself and you will attract those that are confident.

3. Always be honest

4. Always be fair.

5. Be grateful and thankful (to your spouse, family, co-workers, customers).

6. Accept the 3 "C's" ( change, criticism and compliments

7. Always have an open mind to learn.

## About Carol Neu

Carol is an Adobe Certified Associate, owner of NeuWorldDesigns, Mother of 3, Nana of 4 and married to the most wonderful supportive man in the world!

Carol Neu
carol@neuworlddesigns.com
NeuWorldDesigns
http://www.neuworlddesigns.com

# Danise Peña

*As we let our own light shine, we unconsciously give other people permission to do the same.*
*— Marianne Williamson*

## *Beyond Fear is Fun*

Danise never considered that she would start her own business!

It was during a class on Emotional Freedom Techniques (EFT, also called meridian tapping, or just tapping) that Danise's life changed.

Up until then, she was content with her life, her stable corporate job, and her small, close-knit circle of friends.  While others in the class wanted to work on "serious" things, all Danise wanted to use EFT for was to finally be comfortable with the sexy dance moves that all the other women seemed to do so easily in the salsa clubs.  She had struggled with being shy and uncomfortable with the moves for almost 10 years.

Through the class she discovered she believed it wasn't safe to be sexy – that if she were sexy on the dance floor, and something "bad" happened, it would be her fault.  She was aware that other women had this belief, but was shocked to discover that she had it buried deep down inside her, too!  Using EFT to uncover, then release this belief helped her realize that the negative, limiting beliefs she had about her body and her ability to dance (or lack of ability) all served the same purpose:  to keep her safe.  And that all the negative, critical voices that told her she couldn't or shouldn't do what she longed to do actually came from a loving and protective place, and that they could be transformed into positive, supportive voices!

She used EFT to clear those beliefs.  And then life became more exciting in all kinds of pleasantly unexpected ways – she enjoyed getting dressed up to go out; she accepted invitations to parties and happy hours and looked forward to meeting new people, rather than dreading social events as she had in the past; her steady, dependable job came to feel more suffocating than safe; and the itch to help others grew stronger.  She earned her EFT certification and started her own business.

When she made that decision, the challenges started all over again.  All of the work involved in the creation of a new business often seemed overwhelming and insurmountable.  And at her first networking event, she vacillated between bright-eyed excitement and "please let me hide in my hotel room" fear, intimidated by all the "real" businesswomen out there!  And that's when she realized her struggles with salsa dancing and starting a business were largely the same. She had been afraid to draw attention to herself on the dance floor, and was afraid to put herself out there professionally. The difference was that this time around, she was inspired by a mission to help others, she had a powerful tool in EFT, and she knew how to use it!

Today, Danise is thrilled to work with people from all over the world, in person, by phone, or Skype, to release the fears and beliefs keeping them playing small when they know they are meant for a bigger stage – creatively and professionally.

## Danise Pena

### Recipe for SUCCESS!

1. There's Truth with a capital "T". Everything else is a belief, and beliefs can be changed. Choose empowering ones.

2. When things get tough – be inspired by your vision.

3. Always give other people the opportunity to say yes to you.

4. Stay in the game! It's not lack of experience that takes a person out of the game, it's the self-judgment about it that does.

5. Make the shift from "I can't" to "I wonder how I could..."

6. Be gentle with yourself.

7. Done is better than perfect!

## *About Danise Peña*

Danise is a speaker, teacher and certified EFT Practitioner.  Her work is EFT, her passion is salsa dancing, and her gift in working with her clients is her ability to dismantle the story that's telling them it's not safe to go after what they want.

The core element to her work and what she teaches and talks about is overcoming the fear of putting yourself out there – whether in a professional sense by taking on a highly visible project or job, speaking up in meetings, or taking "the big leap" in business; in a personal sense by asking the guy or girl out or stating what you really want in a relationship; or, of course, on the dance floor!  Danise takes people deep into how this fear plays out in their lives and their work, and helps them break through their limiting beliefs and really free themselves to step into their lives and take the chances they need to live the way they long to do.

Danise can help you live your hero story!

Danise Peña
danise@danisepena.com
www.DanisePena.com

~ Notes ~

# Ruby Renshaw

*" You are the mighty ocean in the drop"*
*~ Rumi*

## *Give Your Soul The Last Say*

Uncovering an aptitude for accounting, Ruby started a small-accounting practice in the Midwest in the mid-80's that grew to a successful business offering bookkeeping, payroll and tax services.

Ruby discovered that while her business was successful, she was working long hours with stressful, ongoing deadlines --many self-imposed. She also noticed that this was the case for many of her clients.

Armed with a deep desire for a balance in her life that included a healthy lifestyle, family, friends and spiritual devotion, Ruby made some radical decisions about her business.  Letting go of her staff, raising rates, and moving into a home-office paid-off.  She found she enjoyed her practice much more and was able to assist her remaining key clients to another level within their business by offering consultancy beyond accounting.

Having the opportunity to go to graduate school, Ruby set off to obtain her Master's Degree in Business. She found the experience beyond her expectations and was surprised by the level of self-analysis required.  She found she had skills and interests not typical of an "accountant" and she began to explore new areas of business. By the time she had graduated, she was passionate about an up and coming topic "Business and Spirituality".

A move to Houston with her husband and young daughter, forced the decision to sell her accounting practice and delve into the world of management consulting. Combining her accounting background and new found passion, Ruby was fortunate to work with the organizational development teams of many Fortune 500 companies to develop metrics of success that went beyond profit and encompassed such indicators as fulfillment, happiness, and joy.

221

After five years in the corporate world, the messy demise of an "once-in-a-lifetime" project and the end of a 20-year marriage, Ruby was stopped her tracks. Discovering that her spiritual model only supported her in the good times, she set out to broaden and deepen her understanding of what it means to be spiritual.

Today, Ruby is once again working with small business owners. She has developed programs incorporating "listening to the soul or highest-self" as an integral tool for business success. She believes that the challenges of entrepreneurship uniquely provide the groundwork for growing passions, the fulfillment of highest destiny, and the potential to transform the world.

### Ruby Renshaw

### Recipe for SUCCESS!

1. Know that everything you need to be a powerful force is contained within you

2. Trust in what you believe and what you want

3. Create a plan for your business, even if it is 2 pages long and all in picture

4. Know your values and align your business objectives with them

5. Sit everyday with your soul (i.e. meditate, pray, be in nature, dance)

6. Listen to what your soul says

7. Always give your soul the last say

## *About Ruby Renshaw*

Ruby Renshaw, founder of Strategy Stream, is an experienced and inspiring business growth facilitator. She has been speaking, writing about, and developing business success models that integrate business and spirituality for over fifteen years.

Ruby is committed to empowering home-office-based-business-owners to prosper by transforming mindsets about success, balance, and power.  At the same time, she gives her clients the tangible tools and connections they need to build a successful enterprise and sustain desired goals.

Ruby, the author of the eBook "Becoming a Source of Good: seven success practices to transform your business and the world", is also a certified yoga instructor, living in Santa Fe, NM.


Ruby Renshaw
ruby@strategystream.com
Strategy Stream
https://www.strategystream.com

# ~ Notes ~

# Sandhan

*Watch your thoughts: They become your words*
*Watch your words: They become your actions*
*Watch your actions: They become your habits*
*Watch your habits: They become your character*
*Watch your character: It becomes your destiny*
*(Unknown)*

## *"There's Never Been a Better Time To Be Alive!"*

Ever since she can remember, Sandhan has had a burning desire and thirst for wisdom and self-enquiry, searching anywhere and everywhere for nuggets that might better herself as well as empower others to greater happiness and success ~ success that most certainly includes, but is not limited to, creating financial abundance.

The burning question that directed the majority of her life began as, "Isn't there more to life than this?" stemming from deep dissatisfaction and disillusion which she calls Divine Discontent. Weaned on fairy tales, she even used to believe she was a foundling!

Paradoxically this extreme dissatisfaction has not only become her most significant driving force, but has led her to help others become the best they can be too. It certainly kept her moving out of her comfort zone time and time again when the going got really tough, which it frequently has ~ emotionally, financially, physically and even spiritually sometimes.

It is obvious that with such passion, a career as a seeker, healer, teacher and coach would eventually be born; yet it took many years and several attempts at hiding her light under a bushel by denying her greatest gifts before Sandhan realized that she really DID have something valuable to share with the world, and that doling out free advice around the kitchen table was a skill she must capitalize upon. It seems that our greatest skill is usually to be found in the place we feel the most wounded and insecure!

For Sandhan spent years hating the sound of her speaking voice and believing she had nothing of value to share, but still has become a gifted presenter and public speaker. She certainly knows what it's like to feel misunderstood and undervalued yet one of her gifts is to find the radiance in others when they cannot see it for themselves and reflect it back to them.

Leaving home at a relatively tender age, to 'find' herself, it was a huge struggle to follow her heart and not got sucked into pleasing others or follow the crowd simply because it was the easiest route. Tears were shed and she was even disinherited by her family who feared she had joined a cult when she spent time in India in the ashram of the enlightened Master, Osho. Yet she not only survived but thrived!

She has owned several (relatively!) mainstream businesses, some more profitable than others and has had her fair share of ups and downs but through it all has gained a philosophy that while pain is an irrefutable part of life's rich tapestry, suffering is definitely optional!

The circumstances of unique lives may well vary, but we all share common hopes, fears and patterns. By working through her own dark places, Sandhan has become a 'pattern recognition specialist' and is able to gently steer others to higher ground.

So many people these days are on a deep spiritual inner search to discover what will give their life REAL purpose. Yet if you look around it's easy to get brainwashed by the scaremongering in the media.  Life is about the meaning you give to it, so you can either focus on the better feeling thoughts or choose to see what's happening right now as an opportunity for massive expansion for the human race.

It's no longer a case of "What's happening on Planet Earth?" but rather, "What can we expect next? How can we best prepare ourselves? And how much more exciting can it possibly get?"

## Sandhan

### Recipe for SUCCESS!

1. Spend more time BE-ing and less time doing so learn to relax and breathe more

2. Happy people are more successful, so get happy!

3. Take (calculated) risks and stretch your boundaries

4. Think better feeling thoughts as much as possible

5. Asking quality questions will provide superior results

6. Practice daily random acts of kindness and be grateful for EVERYTHING

7. Fill your own cup first by nurturing yourself

## *About Sandhan*

Born in the UK, Sandhan is a seasoned traveler.

A "citizen of the world", she has lived in Germany, India and France and is now resident in Australia.

Passionate about personal development, transformation and responsibility, she has dedicated her life to her own Spiritual path as well as helping others to walk theirs.

In India she lived in the Osho Commune International for over 10 years, working as a healer, facilitator and therapist as well as cook, cleaner and "ashram shopper", which she says was her favorite job! Concurrently she ran a meditation and healing center in the South of France.

Since arriving in Australia she is a graduate of Tony Robbins' Mastery University and Leadership programs as well as NLP, professional speaking and numerous entrepreneurial courses, saying that it all adds another more practical and pragmatic dimension to walking her talk and her search for Truth. She is also a certified Law of Attraction coach.

Over the last 35 years she's been immersed in the teachings of some of the world's masters of personal development and spirituality and been lucky enough to be coached by some of the foremost teachers in their fields. She's absorbed an unbelievable amount of information but above all the knowledge has hopefully become wisdom and intelligence.

Additionally, she's a trained massage therapist, Reiki Master, energy healer and part of the Oneness University and happy to share her wisdom with anyone who wants to know more.

She's spent years learning how to make the most of new internet based technologies and LOVES how we are able to connect with like-minded souls all over the planet and spread the love.

Moreover she has written several books available online.

Sandhan
sandhaninc@gmail.com
www.thrillbootcamp.com

# Alycia Schlesinger

*"This is the true joy in life: the being used for a purpose recognized by yourself as a mighty one; the being thoroughly worn out before you are thrown out on the scrap heap; the being a force of nature instead of a feverish, selfish little clod of ailments and grievances complaining that the world will not devote itself to making you happy." George Bernard Shaw*

## Divine Surrender:   Sometimes the only step forward is inward!

On June 7, 2007, there was only one thing Alycia wanted to do with her life and that was end it!

Just a short 14 months prior to that moment in 2007, Alycia had been at the peak of her game in seemingly every area of her life and going after it all with a zest she had never before experienced.  She had launched a successful entrepreneurial project rebranding her father's company, was in the process of getting her Master's degree in Spiritual Psychology, and was head over heels in love.

Yet, after a series of unforeseeable circumstances created what Alycia calls the perfect storm, it all came crashing down in what seemed to be a matter of months. After finding herself suddenly heavily in debt, experiencing a series of close personal betrayals both in her romantic and family life, having slept an average of 3 hours a night for the previous 8 months with her body burning from Post-Traumatic Stress and seeing no realistic solution in sight, Alycia felt the most compassionate thing to do for both herself and her family was to consider suicide.

After a series of spiritual experiences and a "Conversation with God" helped her to re-consider her options, Alycia summoned all her strength and her courage and made both a decision and a commitment to move forward at all costs.  Having been told that she was a healer when she was 29 years old, she began to view this crisis as an opportunity to put her money where her mouth was by using all of her life experience up and all of her training in personal development to become the hero she had been waiting for.   Once coming to understand that the suicidal impulses and depression she was experiencing was a combination of both the pain of the recent betrayals and the pain of repressed traumatic memories from her childhood firing off simultaneously in her nervous system, she became convicted in finding a homeopathic solution.

Fiercely intent on recovering without the use of medication, Alycia spent the next 4 1/2 years using all of her training and every healing modality available to her including NLP, hypnotherapy, spiritual psychology, prayer, meditation, breath-work, inner-child work, yoga, nutrition, bodywork and cleansing to naturally clear her own consciousness and to fall deeply in love with herself.

She credits her full recovery to the development of her empathic and intuitive abilities, her deep thirst for self-knowledge, her intimate relationship/experience with the Divine, (the Universal Love she calls God), along with her unwavering commitment to lead by example by realizing her own healing, freedom, and heartfelt dreams first followed by the burning desire to help others to do the same.

Once again fully empowered in her own life, Alycia now works insatiably to light the way for fellow entrepreneurs who find themselves at any transition point in their lives. Using her unique intuitive style, she works one on one and in group settings to assist others in becoming aware of and in clearing any blocks residing in their unconscious and in supporting them in creating the most authentic and highest vision for them. She walks with them as they call their visions forward and reminds them, as they take action towards it, to remember that no matter what the challenge they face, all things are truly possible.

# Alycia Schlesinger

## Recipe for SUCCESS!

1. To thy own self be true. You and God are the only two you have to answer to at the end of your life. When you can remember that, it tends to put all things in perspective and priority.

2. Decision and Commitment are power; if you have truly decided on what you want and are 100% committed to the outcome, it's as good as done.

3. The power is in the why! The greatest thing you can do for yourself in reaching any goal is to link every part
of your life into why you must achieve it; there is nothing you can't do when you do that!

4. Trust your inner knowing; it's the wisest source of information at your disposal, and it has vision with scope far beyond what your conscious mind can entertain.

5. You have a very specific purpose and specific talents and gifts that align with that purpose. Make it your mission to find out what that is and use your gifts towards it. The by-product of that is more joy and fulfillment that you could ever imagine

6. Create a support network including coaches, peers, and like-minded individuals who can hold you up and keep you accountable to and lovingly supported in the pursuit of your vision.

7. No matter what the challenge, obstacles, or odds against you, never, never, ever, ever, ever give up!! There's a miracle waiting for you just around the corner.

Alycia Schlesinger

## *About Alycia Schlesinger*

Alycia Schlesinger is an inspirational storyteller and empathic healer/transformational coach who uses both speaking and writing to convey her message of transformation and who has spent the last 14 years of her life dedicated to mastery in the fields of personal development, consciousness, health, and spiritual evolution. Fearless about transparently sharing her own pain and life challenges, she uses her advanced intuitive abilities and her personal story both in one on one and group work as her primary tools to assist people into their own personal revelations.

While she holds a Masters in Spiritual Psychology with an emphasis in Consciousness, Health and Healing from the University of Santa Monica and is trained as a Master Practitioner of Neuro-linguistic Programming and Transformational Coaching, she believes her experience with applying these healing modalities to her own life is her greatest asset in helping others to realize their own unlimited potential. As she cleared the pain in her own consciousness and began to find peace in her inner world, she found that her outer world began to shift accordingly which served as confirmation of one of her most firmly held beliefs: outer experience is a reflection of inner reality. When we surrender to the truth of who we really are, our worlds transform accordingly.

Alycia has been passionately sharing her story since 2008 and has used her heightened intuitive abilities in working with hundreds of people since 2004 both in one on one sessions and in group settings. Her energy is presently focused working on her first book and on expanding the scope of her audience to maximize her ability to serve as an instrument of hope and transformation. She currently resides in Los Angeles, CA.

Alycia Schlesinger
amsbreeze@yahoo.com
www.nextgreatetspeaker.com  SEARCH #32

# Linda M. Schulman

*"Does this path have heart?"*
*from The Teachings of Don Juan by Carlos Castaneda*

## Making It Worthwhile

When Linda M. Schulman was in the process of creating a home-based business for her retirement, she thought it was possible to become a national success; or at least if that didn't happen, then at least a regional success.

In her dreams, Linda saw herself out of the red and into the black with a growing business that would supplement her Social Security income by the time she retired.

So of course it was a surprise and disappointment when she realized in spite of everyone saying they loved her product and buying it, there was no great grassroots uprising of thousands of people spreading the word like a gospel tidal wave flooding across the country.

Linda knew how difficult it would be to do this business, but it was one thing to make an educated guess about the business process and another to work through it.

There has been so much frustration, disappointment, and aggravation that without friends who were artists and writers to commiserate with, she would have thought her problems unique.

Without any experience or connections in her field, she came to realize that creating and implementing a bigger plan might be impossible and beyond her reach and revising her dream was the only way to stick with her commitment and get some of the benefits she envisioned when she decided to move forward.

And there were plenty of successes such as finding the right printer, book signing events, and being featured in newspaper stories; and of course the complete satisfaction of making all the artistic and business decisions.

The biggest successes that Linda M. Schulman enjoyed were tied to her two biggest challenges:

writing and illustrating children's book.

To date, she has written and published two books.  In order to finish them, she sacrificed long-standing routines and interests to make time and space, she drank too much coffee with sugar to give her energy, and had to learn how to focus her creativity within a certain time slot of her life.

When she was done and in those brief moments of completing each illustration and section of the book, there was the satisfaction of an accomplishment unlike any other because of how hard it was to do.

What was it that made it worthwhile for Linda M. Schulman to write two books and self-publish them?  What was the over-riding reason that made her commit to this business knowing how difficult it would be?

There were two choices she faced.  In one scenario, she'd just grow older.  In the other, she was doing everything to be at her very best and have purpose.  The choice was easy and so chose being an illustrator, writer, and publisher.

## Recipe for SUCCESS!

1.  Make a Commitment: Researching everything about your project, creating a comprehensive pros and cons list, realizing the sacrifices that have to be made, and solutions about handling the down side of the business. Do the pros outweigh the cons and in spite of how difficult this will be, are you willing to commit wholeheartedly and not give up?

2.  Adjustments to the Plan: The plan cannot take into consideration everything that can and does happen during in the execution of your plan. Being flexible, creative, and committed, it's possible to negotiate the bad times. For example, switching your focus to a different part of the plan because you are stumped trying to execute a part of the plan that is not working out right.

3.  Take Advantage of Opportunities: These are the little gifts that come along which enable you to take your business a step further unexpectedly, possibly opening up new avenues to sell your product.

4.  Take a Break: If there is too much aggravation, frustration, and difficulty, take a break. Pull back on projects. Pull back on spending money. Connect more with family and friends or whatever brings you back to your normal level of balance. After your vacation, you'll come back refreshed, energized, and creative.

5.  Deal with the Unexpected: Things go wrong whether they are simple or complex. Up until the moment when that part of the plan is complete, anything can happen and frequently does. Expect the unexpected and hone your skills in damage control. Being calm, persistent, and professional works real well. Dealing with the problem immediately and with the most diplomatic and frank assessment will lead to the best solution and best outcome.

## *About Linda M Schulman*

Linda M. Schulman was born in the Bronx, New York. When she was in grade school in the 1950's, the choices for girls were this: wife and mother, teacher, nurse, or secretary.

She started off wanting to be a teacher, but then changed her mind. She ended up as a Secretary, which then led to being an Employment Counselor, and then to being an Insurance Agent which she has been for the last 30 years.

But that's what she did for a living, not who she was.

At the age of 8, Linda decided to become a writer. She wrote stories and poetry in high school and during her college years continued with more poetry. In the 1980s Linda's articles, reviews, columns, and press releases were published in various newspapers in Northern California. In the 1990's she composed music and wrote song lyrics.

When Linda was 14, her Mother convinced her to apply to the High School of Art & Design in Manhattan. She did and was accepted. This was where she received her art training.

Linda M. Schulman is married to Sam Schulman and they live in Northern California. Sam is the love of her life and was the key to opening the door to her business as an illustrator, writer, and publisher.

In 2010, Linda's first book Tales of Woofie was published by her own company, Weingart Book Publishing, and in 2011, her second book in the Woofie series, The Rabbit Chase was published.

Currently, Linda is working on 2 major projects, a storytelling video, and the third book in the Tales of Woofie series.

Linda M. Schulman
weingartbookpublishing@hotmail.com
Weingart Book Publishing
http://www.talesofwoofie.com

# Veronica Schultz

*"Our deepest fear is not that we are inadequate. Our deepest fear is that we are powerful beyond imagination. It is our light more than our darkness which scares us. We ask ourselves – who are we to be brilliant, beautiful, talented, and fabulous. But honestly, who are you to not be so?"*
*Marianne Williamson*

## *Passing Through Midnight*

As a child, Veronica remembers searching for a profound sense of purpose in her life. Although she would love to say that she had an amazing childhood, the reality was that her environment and life situation created personal struggles that would encroach upon her adult life. She couldn't connect with her reflection in the mirror, as though her own skin were a stranger to her, the ugly truth of how she felt about herself always stared back at her.

Out of desperation, Veronica learned to become a chameleon, surreptitiously finding a way to survive in the many different areas of her life and career. With no direction, she continued this lifestyle until a major life shift emerged that brought up all the anger and bitterness that had been accumulating for years. Breaking down, she sought God through her anger and tears, asking Him to reveal her path and bring healing to her soul and heart. "I felt so empty, hurt and angry. All I wanted was to find happiness and some purpose that made sense. This desire fueled me to pursue answers and change. I never gave up! I always knew there was an answer out there for me and that God would help me find it. And find it, I did."

Nine years later another major life shift happened and tragedy struck her family. Their homes fell into foreclose, she and her husband separated, their son had a car accident shattering both legs, everybody in the home lost their jobs, Veronica's husband almost died from respiratory failure, their daughter fell ill and their grandson was born with a hole in his heart. With dedication and diligence, Veronica's family made it through and within the next year they began to get back on their feet. Life felt different! Purpose began to be realized in Veronica's heart. "It was very difficult to go through the tragedies of that year and honestly, without God, I don't know how we would have made it. I developed a grateful heart and every day I pursue to know myself better. With this new purpose I began to explore a new path." By the age of 45, Veronica had been coaching for 10 years through different ministries. She decided to go back to school and get her BLC Certification in Life Coaching. It was then, the name "the Soul Whisperer" stuck.

Most people consciously acknowledge that they are responsible for where they are in life, even if they may not realize how they got there. Most also understand that the first step of getting out of messy situations is fixing our mindset and then taking the proper actions. Just acknowledging something isn't enough. Veronica creates an environment that will help you see yourself in ways that you haven't been able or haven't wanted to see. Her goal is to empower you and help you script the life you want for yourself.

*Veronica Schultz*

*Recipe for* SUCCESS!

1. Be healthy! Think, live and eat healthy. We are what we eat!!

2. Become familiar with your inner voice and follow it. Be brave about trusting yourself.

3. Get clarity. Take control and script how you want your life.

4. Make it your goal to think only on positive things. Develop your affirmation list and make it a habit to make them a part of your everyday life.

5. Take action. Just recognizing your need is not enough. For the rest of your life, make it your mission to improve yourself.

6. Develop a heart of gratitude. Never ever take for granted anyone and anything you have now. They could be gone tomorrow. Appreciate yourself as well.

7. If you're scared... Do it anyways. You only become stronger by stretching your boundaries.

# *About Veronica Schultz*

Veronica Schultz, LBC aka the Soul Whisperer, Herbalist - is a Holistic Master Life Coach & Health and Wellness Mentor. Her vision is that YOU reclaim YOUR personal power by designing your life. Holistic meaning "holism" or being "whole" means that we explore and make the necessary changes that include body-soul-mind-spirit. You can think of it as improving your whole being from a multi-directional approach. Veronica Schultz is the CEO/Founder of Joshua CC Inc (The Joshua Project) & Optimum LIFE-Design where she serves to assist others in helping them to design the life of their dreams. She creates an environment that helps people see themselves in ways they were previously unable to, catapulting them into finding their personal power. Veronica moved out from the East Coast as a teen and now resides with her family in Northern California.

Veronica Schultz, LBC, the Soul Whisperer Certified Life, Health, Wellness Mentor, Certified Life, Health and Wellness Coach
ExceptionalLifeNow@gmail.com
www.veronicaschultz.com

# ~ Notes ~

# Cathy Sexton

*"Insanity: doing the same thing over and over again and expecting different results.*
*~ Albert Einstein*

## *Working Harder or Working Smarter*

Have you ever had a workload that felt insurmountable? Have you started out your day with so much to accomplish that it seemed impossible to get it all done? It is common and most people have.

In 2000, Cathy Sexton found herself in this endless cycle with a constantly increasing workload. At first, she started going to work a little earlier to try and catch up. This tactic seemed to work for a while, until Cathy began starting earlier and earlier. Then, she would add extra hours to the end of the day. Cathy was starting earlier and ending later than anyone else that worked with her. Instead of working smarter, Cathy was working harder and putting in longer hours. In return, she became frustrated, stressed, and still unable to catch up with all of her work.

After all was said and done, Cathy was diagnosed with a life threating medical condition that was triggered by her stress. She ultimately realized that if she did not make changes, her daughter would grow up without a mother and her husband would lose his wife. Cathy had to take a stand.

One day, Cathy decided to reassess her work life and make serious changes as to how she was spending her time. Cathy realized that her work was the immediate factor to her health issues. The next step was to take responsibility. Cathy was in control of her situation and habits, and only she could change them.

Habits are difficult to change, but they CAN be changed. The goal in changing a habit is to replace an unproductive routine with a productive one. Cathy learned to organize her workload, increase her focus on the project at hand, and delegate some of the overwhelming workload she had in order decrease the stress in her life. By understanding and working in her "Natural Productivity Style" everything began to come together in a new productive way. After Cathy was able to break the bad habits that she held in her workplace, she realized that,

241

through her own accomplishment, she could help others with the same issues. She is passionate about helping others live a healthy and stress free lives.

Challenge: Working harder and harder will only cause stress, frustration and overwhelm while getting less done. Learning to work smarter will allow you to accomplish more with less effort.

Challenge: Knowing you need to make a change and actually taking on the challenge to live and work differently is the key to living the life of your dreams

*Cathy Sexton*

*Recipe for* SUCCESS!

1. It's not what you should do it's what you will do that matters

2. Value your time... outsource and save time and money

3. Working in your "Natural Productivity Style" you accomplish more with less effort

4. t's NOT about changing habits it's about improving actions

5. Only things we can control is our Time, Money, Energy & Behaviors / Attitude

6. If you can't find it...when you need it...it's lost its value

7. 15 minutes of planning at the end of the day will save you 60 minutes the next morning

# *About Cathy Sexton*

In 2003, Cathy launched her productivity consulting business that offered organizational and productive skill training to business owners, professionals, department managers, and individuals. The Productivity Experts help individuals to ignite their performance in their work environment as well as with family and friends. Helping those who are stressed frustrated and feel their days spinning out of control while working too many hours. Working with Cathy they find clarity, focus, improve productivity and work less hours while they make more money. During her productivity and organizing career, Cathy has helped change the lives of many people looking for an escape out of their stressful, unorganized lives. By using her 6 step I.G.N.I.T.E process to help individuals find their natural productivity style, The Productivity Experts have been able to help hundreds of small businesses and individuals achieve a better, happier, more productive, and less stressful lifestyle.

Cathy is a co-author of "Focus, Organization and Productivity," "Exploring Productivity." and "7 Point of Impact" with 2 other books currently in process.

Cathy's past and current professional affiliations include Member of National Speakers Association (NSA), Certified Life Style Design Coach. The Network for Productivity Excellence (NPEX), Experts for Entrepreneurs (e4e), National Association of Professional Organizers (NAPO) St. Louis Chapter, the American Society of Training and Development (ASTD), Mastermind Network of St. Louis and the Fenton Chamber of Commerce Board Member. She has been featured in NBC.com, KSDK TV, Entrepreneur Magazine, Return on Performance Magazine, St. Louis Post Dispatch, St. Louis Small Business Journal, St. Louis Business Journal, Lawyers Weekly, It's Your Biz, and the St. Louis Women's Journal.

Cathy Sexton
cathy@theproductivityexperts.com
The Productivity Experts
http://www.TheProductivityExperts.com

~ Notes ~

# Carrie Sharpshair

*" Eternity is in love with the creations of time"*
*William Blake*

## *The Sharp Cookie*

Carrie was always curious —constantly trying to figure out how to get the answers and get things done. That's probably why, from an early age, her Nana called her "The Sharp Cookie."

Her career has been incredibly eclectic, and she's enjoyed both corporate and entrepreneurial experiences. After helping her husband complete his degrees and licensing requirements for his profession, she decided it was time to go back and finish her education. At the time she was working full time at a Fortune 500 biotech company supporting a vice president, a director, and 40 engineers. Oh yeah, and she had a one year-old as well!

When she finished her degree (adding another baby along the way), she moved into project management where she excelled at putting all the pieces together to deliver complex, successful projects.

In 2003 Carrie started a personal chef service and discovered after a couple of years that she liked the "business of the business" more than she was enjoying the actual services she was providing. She recognized that her vision of success meant that she had to build her business on her terms, integrating per personal and professional lives in a way that served her and her family the best. So she sold the business in 2006 in order to begin focusing on helping others achieve success on their terms.

Carrie has enjoyed working with service professionals to get their businesses launched and streamlined. She even helped launch a grass-roots non-profit organization and had the great fortune to travel to Africa to see the results of her efforts.

While her experience and knowledge were in high demand, 2009 brought a sharp decline in clients willing to pay for her services, and she began to struggle. Self-doubt and insecurities crept in (very un-sharp-cookie-like), and she lost sight of her big picture.

Never being one to get down for too long, though, she rebounded and learned quite a bit about herself in the end. She learned to reach – reach up, out, down, and out - and discovered what she was really passionate about. She's connected with hundreds of like-minded individuals who are looking to change the world in a big way.

Her passion is to be an elegant and determined spark of inspiration for those ready and willing to see their entrepreneurial dreams become a reality. She believes the impact of this passion is to fuel the flow of innovative commerce and to provide personal fulfillment and sustainable prosperity the world over.

Carrie lives in Southern California with her husband, Ron, and their two sons, Evan and Brad.

*Carrie Sharpshair*

*Recipe for* SUCCESS!

1. Decide to be a professional

2. Be clear on your visio

3. Understand what success means to you

4. Realize your strengths and weaknesses

5. Know when to ask for help

6. Hang out with other successful people

7. Don't take yourself too seriously

## *About Carrie Sharpshair*

Balancing right-brain creativity and left-brain logic, Carrie Sharpshair has the ability to quickly tap into her clients' business vision and to guide their creation of strategies and actions, inspiring and teaching them how to get grounded, create momentum, and enjoy success on their terms. She's known by those around her as "The Sharp Cookie," and she's comfortable being equal parts brainy and zany!

Carrie's passion is for showing new entrepreneurs how rewarding being a business owner can be. She frequently speaks with local high school students to expose them to entrepreneurship and the realities of launching and running a business in today's economy.

Before going into business for herself Carrie spent over 20 years in the corporate world with a variety of organizations including both Fortune 500 organizations as well as boutique consulting firms. Her experiences include developing and delivering in-depth training programs, managing multi-million dollar projects, and growing start-up organizations.

While working alongside hundreds of small business owners, Carrie has honed her philosophy on envisioning and achieving success. This led her to start SimplyStrategicSucces.com where she works with business owners to achieve success on their terms.

A key foundation to her mentoring involves learning how to integrate a business and personal life while staying sane!

Her eclectic personality and background enable her to strike up a conversation with just about everyone, and her clients love the combination of her no-nonsense approach coupled with a sense of fun and adventure.


Carrie Sharpshair
carrie@brecsmail.com
BRECS Corp.
http://yescarrie.com

~ Notes ~

# Kimberly Sherry

*"Some gifts can never be taught. Heightened awareness distinguished exceptionally perceptive practitioners from the norm."*
**Kimberly Sherry**

## *Healer Heal Thyself*

Kimberly believes just about anything can be healed. She speaks from personal experience having gone from near suicide to now living a life of joyful ease, peaceful empowerment, grounded clarity, radiant health, with a thriving business and an abundance of love.

You'd never know it by looking at her or even knowing her, but Kimberly has had an intense life. She was given plenty of material to prepare her for her gift as a highly intuitive energetic healer.

Born of the baby boomer generation in San Rafael, California, she was one of five children and the youngest of three girls. Her challenges started early when she was sexually abused by her alcoholic father for years as a toddler. This became the direct cause of a lifelong bladder and kidney issue that would eventually require surgery.

Her mother sought refuge in a religious cult that became her source of emotional support. While having good intentions, she had no idea of the future impact of being raised in the shadows of fear, guilt and shame on her children.

Kimberly had a very lonely and isolated childhood devoid of friends outside of the cult even though she was expected to be in and among the world. She was also not allowed to celebrate any holidays or birthdays, which became an annual reminder that she was not worth remembering. She was forbidden to participate in competitive sports or go to college. All of this led to a very shy, low self-esteem.

She married into the cult to a man who cheated on her for 23 of the 25 years they were married. Adultery was the only way out of the marriage then but you had to be able to prove it. His highly controlling, jealous, emotionally abusive, and threatening ways left Kimberly feeling very trapped, helpless and suicidal. Her lowest point was when she walked into a sporting goods store to buy a gun to end her life. The realization hit her that she could not do that to her two children.

Little by little doors opened and she began to trust in a power much bigger than herself. The long journey of self-healing led her to books such as "Feel the Fear and Do It Anyway" by Susan Jeffers and "Heal Yourself" by Louise Hayes. She left the cult and started a support group for ex-cult members for 9 years. It was a great catharsis and she got tremendous satisfaction from saving lives and helping others.

Knowing she would become a single mother without any financial support, she prepared for the inevitable. She got her certification for massage in 1999. After just her third month in business, ready or not, it was time to fly on her own. She filed a restraining order and for divorce.

Kimberly attended the previously forbidden psychic school at Aesclepion Intuitive Training in San Rafael, CA. This became a good replacement for the weekly meetings she was used to attending her whole life. She trained at Aesclepion every week for 12 years to learn to trust what she knew, saw, and felt. Her training became her healing as each person who sat before her became a mirror of the places she was healing in herself.

Kimberly's biggest challenges to overcome were deprogramming her upbringing in the cult and learning how to make friends and meaningful connections. Her second biggest challenge was healing her heart. All of this has been the door to deeply knowing how to help others heal.

Today she believes each of us is perfect, luminous and brilliant beyond belief. She believes healing is necessary, not because we are broken, damaged, and defective, but because some of our essence is buried among the lies and misconceptions we believe about ourselves. We entered this world with radiant innocence and no judgments. The judgments we now carry do not belong to us, and can be easily released. This opens a space within our heart that allows all healing to take place. Hearts Expanding Allows Love is the acronym for H.E.A.L...as love is the ultimate healer.

*Kimberly Sherry*

*Recipe for* SUCCESS!

1. You are a walking testimony so practice what you preach.

2. Feel the fear and do it anyway.

3. Do things imperfectly and don't compare yourself...there is always someone doing it better.

4. Trust your intuition...you have your answers.

5. Surround yourself with those that support your vision of success.

6. Hire a business coach.

7. Practice daily self-care and nurturing.

## *About Kimberly Sherry*

Affectionately known as the healer's healer, Kimberly has spent the last 15 years full-time helping 1000's of people overcome their fears and sabotaging thoughts to lead more productive lives in their joyful passion.

Kimberly loves to travel and has had the opportunity to heal the indigenous Mayan people of Guatemala, participating in their ancient 4-day ritual of bringing in the New Year. Her travels have taken her from the ancient temples in China and Tibet to the mosques of Istanbul. She has visited the wondrous historical site of Machu Picchu twice in Peru, stone circles and ancient Druidic sites in Ireland, and the home of the famous Oracle of Delphi in Greece. She has explored seven of the islands in French Polynesia, three of the Hawaiian Islands and Florence, Italy. In all of these places she received healing and collected ancestral healing information. She has also participated extensively with Native American ceremonies for the past 15+ years. Her most recent trip took her deep into the Amazon jungle of Peru to work with the Shipobo Shamins and their plant medicines for two weeks.

For years Kimberly hid her healing gifts behind her amazing massages. With the help of her business coach, Kimberly now brings her gifts to the world as an internationally recognized energetic healer, seer, and spiritual advisor doing remote, long-distance healing via the phone and Skype throughout the globe. Local clients get the added benefit of having hands-on work and experiencing her most powerful sessions through transformational breathing.

The Dream Architect Workshop is Kimberly's signature system for creating the most powerful vision boards ever. This is complimented by her 48 page workbook that outlines her system for transforming lives.

Kimberly received her massage certification and weekly psychic training through 12 years at Aesclepion Intuitive Training in San Rafael, CA. She has also received training in orthobionmy, Touch for Health, and Effiji Breath as a group practitioner.

Her ideal client is the awakening and conscious woman who already has a spiritual practice but knows that sometimes an expert set of intuitive eyes is necessary to see those blocked places that lurk in the shadows. These blocked places reflect in their life as lack of motivation and clarity, paralyzing self-judgment, overwhelm and burnout. They come to her for energy clearing so they can live calm, grounded, empowered lives. They are ready to unburden themselves of old painful energies and programming that keep them from moving forward. The process is unusually simple for her and the results profound.

"When I first met Kimberly, I was a real skeptic. But after our first session, I had so much clarity that I knew exactly what to do. I decided to take my at-home business helping newly divorced women handle their finances and go full bore outside of the home. This was against the advice of all of my friends and family. I have now doubled my income and could not be happier." L.P.


Kimberly Sherry
kim@kimberlysherry.com
Intuitive Healing
http://www.hearts-expanding-allow-love.com
FaceBook: https://www.facebook.com/KimberlyCampbellSherry

# Ng "Khai" Siung

*"If you can dream it, then you can achieve it. You will get all you want in life if you help enough other people get what they want"*
*Zig Ziglar*

## *From Zero to Internet Content Publishing Hero*

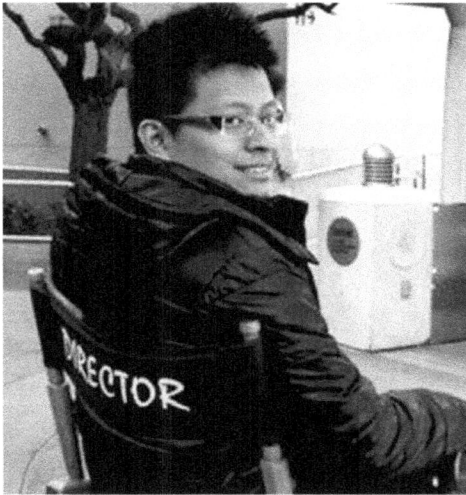

Khai Ng is one of the biggest publishers in the personal development niche having created and sold thousands of e-books, audio tools, video recordings and training materials in the personal development market.

But things weren't always this good for him. He is a college dropout and an underachiever during the early years of his life.

After trying many different business opportunities, programs and attending countless seminars, he has found his niche in online content publishing and coaching others.

It really isn't about skill, talent or having a business degree. Khai Ng has proven that with hard work and determination, he can succeed well faster than many others who had more talents compared to him.

*Ng Khai Siung*

*Recipe for* SUCCESS!

1. Business integrity

2. Authentic communication

3. Determination

4. Innovation and creativity

5. No excuses

6. Giving value

7. Over Delivering

## About Ng Khai Siung

Khai Ng is one of the biggest publishers in the personal development niche having created and sold thousands of e-books, audio tools, video recordings and training materials in the personal development market. His publishing empire - http://inspirationdna.com has the largest following of personal development enthusiasts who are eager to publish content on personal development - having helped thousands to do so.

NG KHAI SIUNG
khai@aboutkhai.com
http://www.inspirationdna.com

# Lesley Sive

*"Education is the most powerful weapon which you can use to change the world."*
**Nelson Mandela**

## *Tax Knowledge Can Be a Life-Saver*

Life for Lesley has always been a constant way of discovering things about the world, other people and herself.

Lesley was born in Johannesburg, South Africa, a place that profoundly influenced her views of life and the world. Not wanting to grow up in the shadow of apartheid, at the age of 21 she emigrated on her own to the U.S. to continue her college studies. She graduated from Michigan State University with a Master's degree in Exercise Physiology and moved to California to work with nutritionist, Nathan Pritikin.

Two years later, she decided she wanted more challenge in her life and was accepted to law school. She attended night school at Loyola Law School, Los Angeles, and worked during the day as a law clerk. After graduating in 1985, she practiced law in Los Angeles working in both the private and public sectors.

Her daughter was born in 1997 and Lesley decided she needed a break from the grind of lawyering so that she could spend more time with her. She tried several jobs in the sales and marketing area in order to have more flexibility in her work hours. By chance, she landed a sales job with a company that helped people and businesses resolve their tax problems. When the company lost an attorney in their legal department, Lesley moved into the vacant attorney position.

Unexpectedly, she found she really enjoyed the work and, particularly, the opportunity to help people on a more immediate basis than in her previous legal positions. She learned quickly about how tax problems can severely affect people's lives and can lead to serious financial, emotional and sometimes physical issues. In some cases, she has worked with clients whose tax problems weighed so heavily on them that they became suicidal. She often has to calm and reassure people and act as a "therapist" with them.

Since finding her niche, for the past decade Lesley has focused her practice on tax law. The big change in her career came in January, 2011, when she was laid off the company she had worked with for six and a half years.

A few months later, the company filed for bankruptcy. After working for other people for all her working life, and finding it difficult to find another position she really wanted, she decided the time was right to start her own tax law practice. As an entrepreneur, she has had to constantly learn about marketing her own business and staying afloat in a weak economy. She has continued to expand her areas of expertise while building her practice. She not only helps both individuals and businesses resolve their tax problems, she also helps her clients stay out of trouble by educating them on tax issues.

In handling thousands of cases, she has found that women, in particular, often do not have the basic tax knowledge needed to help them make informed decisions in order to stay out of tax trouble. Many of her women clients have found they owed taxes because the people they trusted most to make tax decisions for them, did not necessarily have their best interests at heart. Through public speaking, seminars and writing, Lesley's goal is to help as many women as possible understand taxes in a basic, interesting and practical way. Tax knowledge can indeed be a life-saver for many people.

*Lesley Sive*

*Recipe for* SUCCESS!

1. Have confidence in your ability to learn new things

2. Never give up on your dreams

3. Open your eyes, ears and mind to the people and world around you

4. Know that you have so much inside you that is just waiting to show what you can do

5. Broaden your focus by using all available resources to learn

6. Find a mentor or someone you can look up to and learn from

7. Keep pushing forward and around the obstacles that sometimes block your path

## *About Lesley Sive*

Lesley Ann Sive is a graduate of Loyola Law School, Los Angeles, and member of the State Bar of California. She has practiced as an attorney since 1985 and focuses on tax compliance and tax controversy law. Her firm, Lesley A. Sive, Tax Consulting, represents individuals and businesses before the IRS and state taxing agencies, encompassing all 50 states of the U.S. Lesley not only focuses on helping her clients resolve their tax issues, but also educates them on how to comply with tax regulations to prevent future problems.

Lesley is admitted to practice before the United States Tax Court, as well as the United States District Court, Central and Southern Districts of California.

Lesley is also a public speaker and seminar leader on tax issues for employers, community organizations and individuals. She enjoys writing and is working on publishing her first book.

Lesley's law practice is located in Los Angeles, California where she lives with her daughter, a dog and two cats.


Lesley Sive
info@lesleysivetaxconsulting.com
www.lesleysivetaxconsulting.com

# ~ Notes ~

# Vanora Spreen & Diane Koz

*"Coming together is a beginning. Keeping together is progress.*
*Working together is success."*
**Henry Ford**

## The Art of Teamwork

The Art of Teamwork was first conceived by Diane Koz. Diane had been working in the corporate community, building organizations and forming teams for most of her career. One day, she came to the realization that she could help more companies and service organizations if she set up shop and shared her knowledge in team building, planning and organization.

After carefully considering her experiences, both personal and professional, Diane realized there was a common thread in a dysfunctional team. And that thread is bullying! Having experienced all sides of bullying – having been bullied, observing someone else being bullied, and also being accused of being a bully, Diane set her sights on eliminating the bully from the workplace. The unfortunate reality is that most of us have experienced bullying. In fact, if we have participated in office gossip, we can also be accused of bullying in the workplace!

Diane's knowledge of and interest in eliminating bullying is being compiled in a book designed to help business leaders recognize the workplace bully (even if they are the one being the bully) and stop the bully in his or her tracks.

At the same time, Vanora was in a state of transition herself. Vanora decided to serve entrepreneurs and independent contractors through her business called Success Empowerment. This meant leaving a successful career in real estate sales management for a well-respected brokerage.

During her time in real estate, Vanora had many challenges to overcome. These challenges included a teenage child who did more than experiment with drugs and alcohol, marital discord, and a demanding profession. A good friend challenged Vanora, suggesting that one can only control one person and that person is yourself!  This prompted Vanora to delve into personal development and that is where she found her passion and purpose and the recipe to save her family!  Wanting to share her knowledge, Vanora authored the best-selling book, Living The Big Picture, One Promise At A Time.

In January 2012, Diane and Vanora met at a business networking event.  Immediately there was a connection between them and they began discussions to work together – as a Team!

Originally, they thought they would do occasional seminars together, but it wasn't long before they recognized that together they could both achieve more!  By April, they decided to formally join forces and together become The Art of Teamwork, serving small to midsize companies, evolving groups of employees into highly functioning energetic teams!

Working from their kitchen tables, and drawing from their respective strengths, they developed a winning series of modules for small to midsize businesses, modules that when combined create a synergistic effect on a team.  The result is their program, The Nine C's of Successful Teams.  The first step an organization can take is doing a Team Assessment.  Check out TheArtofTeamwork.com – there is a Team Assessment that you can do online, no charge or obligation!  Find out if your team is functioning at its peak or if there is room for improvement.

*Vanora Spreen*

*Recipe for* SUCCESS!

1. Take the time to assess your team.

2. Communicate with clarity.

3. Seek first to understand, and then be understood.

4. Ensure that you as the leader are acting as part of the team.

5. Leave your ego at home.

6. Develop a team culture, through caring, recognition and celebration.

7. Recognize the bully's and stop them in their tracks.

## *About Diane Kos and Vanora Spreen*

Diane Koz and Vanora Spreen are on a mission. Their mission, at The Art of Teamwork is to provide the tools and guidance necessary to businesses and organizations so they can create powerful, productive, innovative, free-thinking teams to establish a competitive advantage. The Art of Teamwork brings two distinct career paths together to offer a unique package for business owners and team leaders.

Diane's professional experience encompasses corporate, public and private sectors, with experience and success in strategic planning, marketing, community and stakeholder engagement, business and project management, training and adult education. As an experienced facilitator, Diane is adept at managing change initiatives through the use of her skill set in change management, quality and process improvement, project management, collaboration and team building. Diane is an enthusiastic, results-oriented individual with exceptional interpersonal, presentation and communication skills.

Vanora's professional experience is in real estate sales and management, recruiting, and professional coaching for independent contractors. Being responsible for a sales team of varying numbers, Vanora's nurturing and encouraging communication style has helped her influence the careers of many sales professionals. An accomplished author, Vanora's best seller, "Living The Big Picture, One Promise At A Time" guides the reader through a series of promises to living their life with meaning.

Diane's keen sense of organization and structure complimented with her ability to bring people together are balanced with Vanora's focus on developing the individual's sense of purpose and service. The result for the business owner is an evolution from a group of individuals, working at the same organization, to a highly functioning and motivated team of employees working with collaboration rather than competition. Our vision is to build businesses from the inside out, creating a sustainable competitive advantage.

Vanora Spreen
Vanora@TheArtofTeamwork.com
The Art Of Teamwork
http://www.TheArtofTeamwork.com

# ~ Notes ~

# Dona Storey

*"When the student is ready the teacher will appear."*
*-Buddhist Proverb*

## *Selling to the World's Biggest Customer*

Doña learned about true success from her father.

Some of her earliest memories involve sitting at the kitchen table, listening to her father's lessons of success, failure and the importance of seizing a vision and making it into a reality.

Doña's father emigrated to the U.S. from the Philippines as a teenager at the end of World War II. He was recruited by the Navy and joined as a Steward. Doña's father had heard of the "American Dream," and he was determined to make it his own.

An avid news reader, he heard of a revolutionary new concept being tried out on the West Coast -- coin operated laundries. He took that idea and ran with it. Doña's father became one of the first people to bring the concept to the East Coast, and was a successful business owner by age 30.

Doña's father died at a young age, but he left her all of the tools she needed to honor his legacy with her own success.

Out of all those kitchen table lessons that Doña learned, one stands out—there is no fear in failure. If something doesn't work the way you thought it would, you pick yourself up, make some changes and then go even bigger than before.

Doña was working as a management consultant when a client first suggested she do business in the federal marketplace. After doing some research she decided to make her entrance as a consultant, after all, that was what she knew. However, she quickly realized that consultants in the federal sector didn't quite fit her description. They were admirals, generals and other high ranking former government officials.

Instead of letting this discourage her, Doña changed course. She didn't wait for failure. If she couldn't sell her consulting services, she'd just sell something else. Doña researched opportunities, and found her niche. With the help of her sister, Doreen, Doña started a facilities project management company.

As Doña's business prospered she was invited to speak and show other company's how to succeed as she had. At one point, she participated in a mentor-protégé program designed by the Department of Defense.

Doña is now the president and CEO of GOVtips, LLC, what she calls her retirement project. She gets to take all of her years of experience and all of her father's secrets for success and mentor companies that want to grow as she did. GOVtips helps companies identify opportunities and sell to the Federal Government, the world's biggest customer. The government buys everything but many small companies don't know how to market their products or services to the federal sector. Doña helps simplify the process. She breaks down the steps and sheds light on the myths that keep many people from attempting to sell to the federal government. Doña also helps her clients set their sights on big successes. She teaches them how to go after millions even as a small business to go after millions even as a small business.

*Doña Storey*

*Recipe for* SUCCESS!

1. America is truly the land of opportunity for those who choose to acknowledge it, seize upon it and use it as their path for growth and opportunity in their own way.

2. Integrity is the strongest intangible that brands you.

3. Have a clear vision for success.

4. Success is not measured by dollars alone, but by prosperity at all levels

5. Think big, win big

6. Calculated risk can be a successful path for some entrepreneurs.

7. Entrepreneurs aren't any smarter and don't work any harder than many people in the marketplace. The difference is how we manage our fear when taking risk.

## About Doña Storey

Doña Storey, owner of GOVtips, has been a successful business owner for 32 years.

As an expert on federal and corporate procurement and creator of www.GOVtips.biz and the World's Biggest Customer book series, she is a frequent contributor, writer and resource for media nationwide including the Washington Post, Wall Street Journal, Forbes, Inc., Enterprising Women, and blogs on small business issues.

Doña is the American Express OPEN Advisor on Procurement and through her experiences as an active woman-owned small business contractor, she lends her expertise to help small businesses navigate the procurement maze and find success.

Doña Storey
dona.storey@govtips.biz
GOVtips.biz
www.govtips.biz

# ~ Notes ~

# Marilyn Taylor

*"Go confidently in the direction of your dreams and live the life you've imagined."*
*Henry David Thoreau*

## *Priorities and Passions*

Marilyn describes herself as a holistic professional who is a visionary, independent thinker, self-starter and highly motivated to empower others to live a life of passion and authenticity. She herself has been on an incredible life journey to combine her career goals with her personal goals, especially her commitment to her family. Her desire to spend time with her children as they were growing up and now her grandchildren led her to create businesses that allowed flexibility for a working mother.

She received her BS in Psychology and Secondary Education and immediately went into a career as Certified Childbirth and Early Parenting Educator. She taught privately for many years and became part of a community of health educators at a women's prison. As part of her services she was also a doula and attended the deliveries of many beautiful babies coming into the world.

Continuing to pursue her interest in mind/body healing, she became a Licensed Massage Therapist and continues to have a private practice in her home office. Drawing from all of her previous careers, she was certified as a Life and Wellness Coach in 2002 and founded her current business CONFIDENT DIRECTIONS Life Coaching.

Communities have been a strong theme in Marilyn's careers and it seems so especially now. She leads several ongoing Mastermind groups for entrepreneurs, founded and facilitates The Wellness Roundtable Holistic Practitioners Networking Group, and created SPIRITED WOMEN, a monthly inspirational forum. She loves to create workshops, retreats and is a sought after speaker. All of this from Home Sweet Home.

*Marilyn Taylor*

*Recipe for* SUCCESS!

1. Create time every day for some type of self-care practice. Self-care creates an atmosphere for low stress and clear thinking.

2. Be aware of energy and time drains that pull you off course (ie: checking emails, talking on the phone, multitasking).

3. Take your career seriously! Map out a strategy to keep you on track with your goals and stick to it or change it when it no longer seems to be working.

4. Participate in a Mastermind Group or work with a Coach, who can inspire, support and hold you accountable to action.

5. Surround yourself with positive people who believe in your dreams and have been successful in living theirs.

6. End each day with a review of what you accomplished and plan out the next day to begin it with a focused agenda.

7. Include a gratitude practice somewhere in your day. Better yet, be grateful throughout the whole day.

# *About Marilyn Taylor*

Marilyn Taylor is the owner of CONFIDENT DIRECTIONS Life Coaching offering workshops, individual sessions, retreats and presentations in both the private and business sector.  She also has an active private practice as a Massage Therapist in Southborough, MA and frequently combines life coaching with bodywork sessions and stress management skills. She emerged into these professions with a background in Psychology and Education and spent many years teaching privately as a Certified Childbirth and Early Parenting Educator for physicians and in women's health and wellness programs in correctional settings.  Her volunteer work with Jewish Family and Children's Services Visiting Moms Program was recently filmed as a mini-documentary by the Hallmark channel. She created "SPIRITED WOMEN" a monthly community of women seeking to explore their connection to living a more mindful life.  The workbook will soon be available; She is founder and facilitator of The Wellness Roundtable, Holistic Practitioners Network, providing educational and monthly networking opportunities for holistic practitioners and providers.  In 2008, she authored CONFIDENT DIRECTIONS LIFE COACHING CARDS, a 48 card deck inspiring and empowering people to be CALM, CLEAR, CONFIDENT AND COURAGEOUS.

She is an active member of the International Coaching Federation, and the American Massage Therapy Association.

Marilyn Taylor
http://www.confident-directions.com
Marilyn@confident-directions.com

## ~ Notes ~

# Elise Thompson

*"If we are to better the future, we must disturb the present."*
**Catherine Booth**

## *Starting From Here... Starting NOW!*

Elise was raised in a small town in North Carolina, but always dreamed of a "big" life outside of it. Although she received scholarship offers from Ivy League colleges, she did not seem to be able to press her way past the boundaries of her hometown. Then, she saw an open door called the Navy! Elise enlisted and was stationed from one side of the country to the other. Soon, after discharge, she found herself returning to the unhappy life she had finally escaped to take care of family members. Since Elise could remember, she had a passion for helping others and thought it was necessary but only temporary. (Even at the tender age of two, she began to teach other children how to read and write – which also kept her inquisitive little mind busy.) However, rejection haunted her and low self-esteem became the guiding compass of her life, even leading her into violent relationships.

 Yet, Elise had a propensity to have a positive outlook...no matter what! Almost everyone Elise knew came to her for administrative help and spiritual guidance. She was zealous about helping others fulfill their dreams. She had a passion for strong family, ministerial, and corporate structures. Elise could create policies and procedures, by-laws, and business plans with ease for others. She found the courage to start a staffing agency, but soon discovered that the local economy would not support it. So, her inability to see her own worth prevented her from breaking through invisible barriers of disappointment, shame, and financial woes.

However, there came a time when the children were adults and the parent so loved was gone. It almost seemed as if a single, monumental moment suddenly occurred, and she realized she was simply existing...never having actualized her own dreams and visions. She called it an "Oh, No!" moment, but Oprah Winfrey has coined it as an "Aha!"moment. Then, Elise met some great mentors who heard the cries for help from within and told her that it was time to go to work. This time it was not to help others fashion their gifts into marketing or business plans, but rather to stir up her own gifts to create her ideal life. It was time to disturb her present.
So, Elise began a journey from where she was at that very moment. Now, she sees herself as G-d had always intended. Elise is a carrier of His Light in this world. She brings hope as a licensed minister and ordained Apostle, facilitator with two women's organizations, a public speaker against domestic violence, and talk radio host. Elise has learned that she can actually

thrive by gifting herself as a positive force in the world. Every aspect of her ministry and business revolves around creating a better society/world…a better future. With each venture, Elise is taking her dreams to visions and fulfilling realities. She gives all Glory to G-d for His Grace and Mercy as she traveled along the road and building her "starting from here".

*Elise Thompson*

*Recipe for* SUCCESS!

1. Believe in and value yourself - even if you have to first believe the positive reports of others.

2. Be true to yourself and others- even when it hurts.

3. Create something that is going to be a blessing to others.

4. Write your vision, make it plain, and keep it where you can see it daily.

5. Find one to three true mentors. Take the actions required by the mentors you receive. (Yes,   they are a gift.)

6.  Allow yourself to be creative.

7. Work diligently.

## *About Elise Thompson*

Elise Thompson is a powerful Teacher of the Scriptures, Author, and Conference Speaker. Elise is a licensed minister and ordained Apostle. She is the CEO/Founder of The Women On the Move In Ministry & Business; the Spiritual Leader of "Tikkun Olam Global Ministries" and "The Jewels of Jasper"; and co-facilitator of "For Her Worth Far Above Rubies". She is also the Executive Producer/Host of "Women On The Move In Ministry & Business Talk Radio".

She has spent decades tutoring children (privately and in afterschool programs); dedicated her time to working with the Department of Social Services assisting in programs geared to reuniting children with parents who have lost their custodial rights; spent hours in the courtroom as Guardian Ad Litem in child abuse cases; and most of her adult life counseling youth and young adults in matters of social, sexual, and spiritual matters.

Elise Thompson loves her fellow women and men, and is a advocate for the downtrodden. She loves strategizing community development efforts involving government entities, faith-based communities, and the citizens being affected. She believes in the power of network marketing and that it is a means of achieving financial success no matter what your social status. Elise focuses on creating positive solutions to destroy the negative impacts that have already been made in the world and deter any that could be created.

Elise Thompson
info@wommb.org
Women On the Move in Ministry & Business
www.wommb.org

## ~ Notes ~

# Dr. Huesan Tran

*"Focus on the core, leverage the branches."*
*Dr. Huesan B. Tran*

## *From Vision To Reality*

One of the greatest joys in life is doing what you are meant to do in life – to be who you are.  After 15 years of preparing and integrating different puzzle pieces, Dr. Huesan Tran breaks free to create a purposeful and mission driven business that is unique, profound and transformational.

Her divine message "The Meridian Of God" is shifting human consciousness from the old paradigm to a new paradigm of human evolution around the globe through the Messenger Network.  Her spiritual wisdom and unique perspective on "Financial Enlightenment" is published alongside Deepak Chopra, Jim Stovall and many leading experts.   And, she is launching her seminar platform to teach spirituality and healing in business, finance, economics and all aspects of life.

All these are divinely orchestrated to happen in the last quarter of 2012 as part of the greatest transformation in human history.

Turning vision into reality takes patience, persistence, and perseverance.  It starts from clarity and direction and making no concession for anything that deviates from the divine vision, purpose and mission.  Regardless of how many comments about how things couldn't be or should be done a certain way, good luck, etc., Dr. Tran is doing it her unique way and having fun in the process.  Turning negativity into positive growth can be done.

The world is full of experts teaching niches with information coming at random and out of sequence.  That is why most people are living in overload and overwhelm.  Dr. Tran saw the problem with this approach that the experts with years of experience overlooked.  She realized the differences between going narrow and deep versus going wide and broad so she integrated both to create her unique hybrid approach.  Like any architectural building or software system, the overall design, master planning and integration is the essential foundation.  That is her role.

275

She is a visionary, master planner and integrator collaborating with leaders and experts of different industries to turn the divine vision into reality.

Great vision starts from seeing the forest before its existence. Then, the process is planting seeds to grow one tree at a time to create the forest, not to focus on the tree and miss the forest. That is how the divine vision of the New Paradise starts and becomes the reality. Two major challenges for Dr. Tran were: (1) deciding the priority of focus so she won't go off tangent and misalign with the divine vision, and (2) navigating through the overwhelm of overloaded, random, and fragmented information to identify the right sequence of implementation. Clarity of direction is when her priority is focused on the core – the most unique thing only she can do. And, her sequence of implementation is natural when she reversed the process to start with the end in mind and back steps to the present. Her overwhelm stopped when she let go and went with the flow to let the divine plan unfold. Most importantly, she is fulfilling her divine purpose and mission in life.

*Huesan Tran*

*Recipe for* **SUCCESS!**

8. Clarity of Vision/Mission/Purpose of what you are here to do in life.

9. Know your uniqueness, value and contribution.

10. Identify the biggest problems you are solving for the world. Focus on the biggest transformation, outcome and impact you can bring.

11. Prioritize the solutions/products/services you offer starting with the most urgently needed, easiest to implement, and the most profitable

12. Identify the Ideal Clients you Love to work with who are willing, ready, and able to pay.

13. Develop a Master Plan to implement in the right sequence and be flexible to adjust.

14. Do the best you can. Let go and have fun!

# *About Huesan Tran*

Dr. Huesan Tran (HuesanTran.com), transformational author/speaker, spiritual teacher and visionary leader of the New Paradise, incorporates energy healing philosophy into business, finance, and economics to transform the old paradigm to a New Financial Paradise™. Her signature work in energy healing is the discovery and teaching of The Meridian Of God™ that unites both spiritual and physical realms as one to solve problems, overcome deadlocks, and transform to a new phase of human evolution. She has invented and teaches the revolutionary New Wealth Model™ that integrates spirituality to create wealth with divine purpose and mission. Her New Financial Paradigm™ platform and Financial Healing Series™ educational program provide both conceptual understanding and practical solutions for healing, rebuilding and creating a New Financial Paradise™. She is the founding premier member of Women Speakers Association. She speaks to organizations and appears on media to bring new awareness and solutions globally.

Huesan Tran
Info@HuesanTran.com
New Paradise Publishing
www.HuesanTran.com

~ Notes ~

# Bonny Valentine

*"Everything Circles in Season and Bears Fruit in its Time"*
**Anonymous**

## *Purpose Fulfilled!*

Growing up and dreaming and knowing that she was called to do a specific work. As Bonny grew into her adult life, she had no tools, resources or anyone available to tell, or teach her about there being purpose in life, so there soon was a void that was not getting fulfilled in her life.

Before she went on to college she experienced that in life when you have no goals, direction or purpose anything is bound to happen, and it did. Bonny was devastated when she found out she was pregnant briefly following her Father and Grandfather's passing within a two week period and then losing the baby a month later.

Well, Bonny graduated from Barber Scotia College receiving her BS in Biology and furthering at Christian Life School of Theology, where she received her BS in Theology.

Bonny discovered, through prayer and searching from within, her purpose in life, and was able to find that out, through understanding and knowing who she was as an individual. Tools, resources became inevitable as Bonny became to step out on faith and trust God in knowing that her purpose was that of helping, pushing and challenging others to get to the next level, through finding out their purpose in life.

Bonny, now a certified Life Coach and President of her own Coaching Business and Radio Show, Aspiring You Today Internet Show, has not allowed distractions to overtake the plans that she has in helping others to succeed and find Purpose. Bonny understands that things will happen along the way unexpectantly and expectantly, but you have to maintain focus for success, growth and maturity in life and Business. Bonny has a passion for Ladies her age and younger wanting and searching in life for fulfillment.

Through her life experiences Bonny has come to understand that we who are strong ought to bear the infirmities of the weak. She is a vibrant, illuminating, and a divine

Speaker/Coach.  Activating and charging the atmosphere with her wisdom, knowledge, and years of experience, Bonny holds nothing back and is known as a deliverer to those who hear receive her wisdom.

*Bonny Valentine*

*Recipe for* SUCCESS!

1. Have a plan with objectives simply stating how you are going to make it happen

2. Be Realistic

3. Be Patient

4. Prepare

5. Be diligent and consistent with aiming forth

6. Share your story

7. Always put forth effort daily

## *About Bonny Valentine*

Bonny is a certified Life Coach of IWin, and Radio Producer of Aspiring You Today (It's Real Time Talk). Bonny is very passionate about helping others get to the next level in life, by finding Purpose. She teaches you to get going, and will move you into the right direction, very strong encourager and motivator impacting lives and making things happen.

Bonny Valentine
bonnye@everwinning.org
IWin, Inc.
www.everwinning.org

# Amethyst Wyldfyre

*"If you can dream it you can do It"*
*Source Unknown*

## Succeeding Inside Out

Amethyst's story is really quite an unusual one – maybe as unusual as her name (where she got that is a story all by itself – for another book and another time!). Up until 2002 she was a Real Estate Developer and Common Interest Community Consultant and at that time was also the National Chairperson for her trade association representing 1 in 8 homeowners in the country and with a membership of over 30,000. She was at the end of developing and selling an award winning multiuse commercial and residential development project of 51 single family homes, 56 apartments and an office building when she experienced a spiritual awakening.

Lying on the ground outside during a yoga class the veils between the worlds parted and she was shown a golden white staircase with angelic beings traveling up and down the stairs – the experience was so profoundly moving and intense that it lasted for several hours and every person around her including people driving in cars she perceived as golden white orbs of light. Following this experience (and several others of equal power and vision) she knew deep within her that she could no longer continue in her business partnership or doing the work she had been doing.

What followed was a journey of exploration and discovery that lasted several years. Amethyst became a healer and discovered that she was also an artist and a messenger here to help other people and especially women to learn how to honor and value their unique gifts and to bring those gifts and blessings to the world through entrepreneurial ventures. After opening and closing an art gallery and healing arts center and then producing a street festival for two years in a row she found the internet and began to create a business that would allow her to serve people all over the world and would also allow her to be totally mobile and free to create her own schedule and lifestyle.

The online business that Amethyst created (in her PJ's!), combines her 30 plus years of award winning entrepreneurial expertise and a decade of deep inner spiritual work. She generated multiple six figures in under 2.5 years almost entirely from speaking virtually (meaning on line on radio shows or telesummits or calls to people's private lists as a guest expert) and bringing potential clients into a very powerful one on one phone conversation where they decide to invest at high levels for group or private work with her.

Amethyst's business is a "boutique" style business catering to visionary women entrepreneurs offering them highly customized and personalized breakthrough experiences. In her small group programs she enjoys helping women to Find Their Voice and Crystallize Their Message and become confident, capable, empowered and excited to serve by learning and practicing The Inner Game of Sizzling Sales (tm pending). Private clients have included a wide range of women leaders from NY Times Best Selling Authors to Hay House Radio Show Hosts to international clients from around the world.

## Amethyst Wyldfyre

### Recipe for SUCCESS!

1. Find your personal ESSENCE - meaning connect with your heart, your source of inspiration

2. Crystallize your MESSAGE - meaning don't just figure out what you want to talk about - figure out how to translate what you want to talk about into a message that your intended audience can hear!

3. Find your PEOPLE - who exactly are you here to serve - your solution should fit their problem like a hand in a glove

4. ORGANIZE yourself - set yourself up to succeed by knowing what it takes to have a viable business - this means making money too - know how to sell yourself and your work and feel powerful doing so - if you aren't selling you aren't serving!

5. Weave a WEB of connection - no man or woman is an island - do not for one minute think you are going to get your great work out there all by yourself. Ask for help - often!

6. EXPOSE yourself - meaning get out there and speak, write, connect, network, collaborate - be willing to show your stuff and risk failure or embarrassment

7. Reap the REWARDS!! Celebrate when you have a success - don't be focused all on the work and none on the play and celebration or you will burn yourself out completely and lose your passion for your work

## *About Amethyst Wyldfyre*

The Empowered Messenger Master Mentor is an internationally known Speaker, Spiritual Leader and Transformation Artist. She is passionate about serving visionary leaders and conscious entrepreneurs who want to LEAP fearlessly into their highest level of service to the planet and who want to profit handsomely from following their Spiritual path.

With programs, products and services designed to serve the empowerment of women as global messengers of change and enlightenment, Ms. Wyldfyre believes that when people everywhere (and especially women!) feel safe speaking their truth, powerful asking for money and prepared internally to be seen and heard then the world will naturally change for the better.

A successful and award winning entrepreneur since her mid-20's, prior to her journey into the realm of personal and professional empowerment Ms. Wyldfyre was active in Real Estate Development and Community Management Consulting and worked as a consultant with the US Agency for International Development, the World Bank, the Department of Housing and Urban Development and several Fortune 500 builder/developers. Active in her community – Ms. Wyldfyre has served in many volunteer leadership positions and been an avid supporter of the arts for years.

Amethyst Wyldfyre
amethyst@theempoweredmesssenger.com
Amethyst Wyldfyre Enterprises, LLC
http://www.theempoweredmessenger.com

# ~ Notes ~

# THE ACHIEVEMENT OF YOUR GOALS IS ASSURED
# THE MOMENT YOU COMMIT YOURSELF...

*"Until one is committed, there is hesitancy, the chance to draw back, always ineffectiveness. Concerning all acts of initiative (and creation), there is one elementary truth the ignorance of which kills countless ideas and splendid plans."*

*"The moment one definitely commits oneself, then providence moves too.*

*All sorts of things occur to help one that would never otherwise have occurred.*

*A whole stream of events issues from the decision, raising in one's favor all manner of unforeseen incidents and meetings and material assistance, which no man could have dreamed would have come his way.*

*Whatever you can do, or dream you can, begin it. Boldness has genius, power and magic in it."*

*Begin it now.*

*Johann Wolfgang Von Goethe*

# Commitment Agreement

**Are you ready to make the necessary commitments for the growth of your business – starting today?**

List your top 5 commitments below and make this agreement with yourself!

I commit to _____ by _____ (date)

I commit to _____ by _____(date)

I commit to _____ by _____ (date)

I commit to _____ by _____ (date)

I commit to _____ by _____ (date)

*NOW IS THE TIME TO SAY YES TO SUCCESS!*

OK – are you REALLY committed?  Sign here: _____

# Quick and Easy Recipes
# for the Busy Entrepreneur

Even when we have the opportunity to work from home, the time flies by and before we know it, it's time to fix a meal.

On the following pages, you'll find an eclectic selection of recipes from those contributing to the book.

Most are quick and easy making it possible for all of us, to sit back and enjoy a good meal.

Let's Get Cookin!
*Bon Appetite!*

*Most of the following take 20 minutes or less to prepare!*

**Carolyn Jones, M.A**

**Penne with Sausage, Basil, & Arugula**

16oz. dry penne pasta
2 tbsp. olive oil
1 clove Garlic – pressed
4 Italian sausages (pre-cooked like Aidell's
1 pint cherry tomatoes
2 tbsp balsamic or red wine vinegar
½ tsp. salt
¼ tsp. ground black pepper
½ cup loosely chopped basil leaves
1 cup arugula
¼ cup grated Parmesan cheese

Cook pasta according to instructions on package. While pasta is cooking, heat the oil in a pan over medium-high heat. Add the garlic until is browns slightly. Add the sausage and cook for about 8 minutes. Meanwhile you will drain the pasta and set aside. Add the tomatoes and cover the pan until skins start to pop, about 10 minutes. Add vinegar, salt and pepper and stir. Add in the pasta, basil, arugula, and stir gently until arugula wilts slightly. Top with Parmesan and enjoy!

---

**Beverly Basila**
**Beverly's Sautéed Brussels Sprouts**

Wash Brussels Sprouts.
Lightly steam until tender and cut in halves.
Sautee in ghee and sea salt over a medium fire.
Add finely chopped pecans or walnuts and serve warm.
Absolutely Delicious!  :)

---

**Michelle DeBerge**
**Stuffed Chicken Breast**

This is a very easy dish to make that has a lot of flavor.  I have made this for company often and I never seem to have leftovers.  The fat from the skin of the chicken cooks with the wine and creates a gravy full of flavor.  The provolone cheese adds another layer of flavor.  The skin gets nice and crispy on the outside while the breast is juicy and delicious.
1 chicken breast with skin on
¼ cup fresh spinach 1 thin slice of provolone cheese
½ small yellow onion sliced 3 cloves of garlic sliced

6 crimini mushrooms sliced
½ cup of white wine
salt and pepper
1 tablespoon
½ teaspoon olive oil
Prep Time: 10 minutes
Cook Time: 45 minutes Serves: 1

Wash and pat dry the chicken breast.
Butterfly open skin side on the left.
Lightly salt and pepper the inside of the chicken.
Place ½ of the cheese slice on the right side of the chicken breast.
Put the spinach on top of the cheese and cover with the other half slice of cheese.
Fold the left side of the chicken over so that the skin side is up.
Place the onion, garlic and mushrooms in small baking dish and toss with 1 tablespoon olive oil and a pinch of salt and pepper.
Pour white wine over the mixture and top with the chicken breast.
Rub ½ teaspoon of olive oil over the chicken breast and sprinkle with a small pinch of salt and pepper.

Bake 350° for 45 minutes.

Serving Suggestions:   Serve the chicken breast with the onion mushroom mixture on the side. Pour the sauce over the chicken. This dish can be prepared ahead, covered and refrigerated for one day. When you take it out to cook, let it stand for 15 minutes at room temperature before putting in the oven.  This recipe is from "Family Favorites for One" a cookbook with 140 recipes for the solo diner by Michelle DeBerge

---

**Linda Doyle**
**Lentil & veggie soup**

1 cup lentils
1 cup chopped carrots
1 cup celery
4 cups broth- chicken, beef or veg stock your choice
Optional :   1 cup chopped smoked turkey sausage
Cook on low .... This is a high protein crock pot meal...

---

**Kim Fuller**
**Salmon Cakes**

(Adapted from e-diets.com)

2-4 servings | Active Time: 15 minutes | Total Time: 30 minutes

3 teaspoons extra-virgin olive oil
 2 tablespoons breadcrumbs
1 small onion, finely chopped
1 tablespoon chopped fresh parsley
3 ounces canned salmon, drained
1 ½ teaspoon egg replacement
1 ½  teaspoons Dijon mustard
¼ teaspoon garlic powder
¼  teaspoon oregano
¼ teaspoon crushed red pepper
1 lemon, cut into wedges Preparation

1. Heat 1 1/2 teaspoons oil in a large nonstick skillet over medium-high heat.   Add onion and cook, stirring, until softened, about 3 minutes. Stir in parsley; remove from the heat.

2. Place salmon in a medium bowl. Flake apart with a fork. Add egg and mustard; mix well. Add the onion mixture, breadcrumbs and pepper, garlic and crushed red pepper; mix well. Shape the mixture into 2 big or 4 small patties.

3. Heat remaining 1 1/2 teaspoons oil in the pan over medium heat. Add 4 patties and cook until the undersides are golden, 2 to 3 minutes.

4. Serve with lemon wedges.

---

**Claudette Gadsden-Hrobak**
**Chicken Alfredo**

1lb chicken breast
1lb pasta of your choice
1tb olive oil
1 jar of Alfred sauce (Bertucci is great)
Boil pasta following directions on the box
Cut chicken into cubes and brown in Olive Oil
Add Alfredo Sauce to chicken
Combine chicken with drained pasta

Plate, sprinkle with Parmesan and enjoy! Prep time 15 minutes Serves 6

---

**El Ha Gahn**
**El's Breakfast Power Smoothie**

1 Large red D'Anjou pear
¼ pineapple
Large green D'Anjou pear
3 tablespoons goji berries
¼ ounce fresh ginger root
1 tsp. licorice root power
2 Stalks of Yu Choy Greens
½ tsp. juniper berry power

Slice up the ginger into quarter inch pieces and place them in a blender.
Next add the goji berries.
Now chop up both pears and add them.
Cut off a piece of pineapple about one fourth and then cut that down into half inch chunks. Put them in. Chop up the Yu Choy greens and them.
Now fill the blender half full of water.
Turn it on high for 3 minutes.
Stop it and let it settle for a minute.
Add the licorice root and juniper berry powders.
Then start it up again on high and let it blend until smooth.
You may add more water to thin it down if desired.

---

**Gwen Lepard**
**Joyful Nourishing Chocolate Shake**

1 Banana (ripe)
1/2 Cup Blueberries (frozen)
2 T Almond Butter
2 T Flax Meal
1 Scoop Rice Protein
2 T Raw Chocolate (powder)
1 Stalk Celery (cut in 1 inch pieces)
1 Handful Parsley (rinsed)
1 Avocado (ripe) adds creaminess and great oils for your skin and brain
Stevia Drops to Taste Water to desired consistency (Joyful Water)

Start with some water in the blender and add all ingredients.
You can blend in stages for the best consistency and make sure you use plenty of water. (Joyful Water – see website www.joyfullivingradio.com/water for how to put joy in your water)

The more water the thinner it will be.  I love to make mine thick and sometimes even eat with a spoon.  Some blenders need more time and it's good to do in stages with lots of water

---

**Debbie Luxton**
**Crock Pot Chicken Cacciatore**

3 pounds chicken breasts, boneless, skinless
Celtic sea salt and pepper to taste
2 onions, chopped
1 pound fresh mushrooms, thickly sliced
2 cloves garlic, minced
1/4 cup almond flour
1 cup chicken broth
2 tablespoons tomato paste
1 14 1/2-ounce can diced tomatoes, drained
Fresh basil to garnish

Directions
Add chicken to crock pot, and then top chicken with remaining ingredients.
Cover and cook on Low 7 to 9 hours.
Garnish with fresh torn basil.
 This recipe makes enough for 6-8 people, so I served it for dinner, had some for lunch the next day, and the other half went into the freezer for reheating next week.  Isabel De Los Rios Certified Nutritionist Certified Exercise Specialist

---

**Carol Neu**
**Basic Crepe Recipe**

1 c flour
2 eggs
½ c milk
½ c water
¼ tsp salt
2 tbl melted but6ter

Mix – let set – then pour into heated omelet or crepe pan.  Swirl till brown.  Set Aside

Use for any kind of crepe – breakfast, lunch, dinner or dessert!

**Ruby Renshaw**
**Golden Milk**

An ancient yogic recipe:

Particularly good for women and helps you to sleep!

1/8 tsp Turmeric
1/4 cup Water
8 oz Milk
2 Tbsp Almond Oil Honey or Maple Syrup to taste

Instructions:   Place water and turmeric in a small sauce pan and bring to a boil, stirring to a paste for 8 minutes.
Place milk and almond oil in a separate sauce pan and heat until the milk just comes to a boil, then remove from heat.
 Add the turmeric paste to the milk and stir until the milk becomes completely yellow.
Add honey or maple syrup to taste. Drink Warm.

---

**Tuck Self**
**Better Than Sex? Yes!**
Courtesy, Paula Deen

1 18-ounce package chocolate cake mix
1 8-ounce tub of Cool Whip
1 14-ounce can sweetened condensed milk  4 Skor candy bars, crushed
1 6-ounce jar caramel or hot fudge topping

Prepare cake according to package and bake in 9x13 inch pan.  Pierce warm cake all over with toothpick.  Pour condensed milk over cake.  Pour caramel over cake.  Chill.

Before serving, top with whipped topping and sprinkle with crushed candy bars.

---

**Carrie Sharpshair**
**Grandma's Peach Cobbler**

1 stick salted butter
1 cup flour
1 cup sugar

1 tsp. baking powder
½ tsp. salt
1 egg
½ tsp. vanilla extract (or almond is yummy, too)
Milk (enough to make a pancake-like batter)
1 jar sliced peaches

Preheat oven to 350 degrees.
While oven is heating up, place stick of butter large baking dish (9x12) and put in the oven to melt.
Mix flour, sugar, baking powder, and salt together.
Add egg and enough milk to make create a consistency like pancake batter.
Stir in extract.
Remove baking dish from oven with butter is melted and pour in batter (do not mix with the melted butter).
Drain peaches and place throughout batter.
 Bake until golden on top (about 30 minutes – ovens will vary).
 PS – it's great with vanilla ice cream!

---

**Vanora Spreen**
**Quick & Easy Salmon Spread**

This is my stand-by dip when friends drop by unexpectedly!
The best part is that the recipe includes ingredients that are staples on most people's shopping list.

1 can salmon, drained
1 cup cream cheese
1 dash lemon juice
1 green onion, finely chopped

Combine all ingredients.
If you have time, you can refrigerate and mold.  If not, serve this in a small bowl with a variety of crackers or vegies!  Enjoy!

---

**Elise Thompson**
**Quick Energy Smoothie**

Two scoops of protein powder
 1 Tbsp of Maca
1Tbsp of Spirulina Pacifica
1 Frozen/Peeled Banana
1/2 Cup Mixed Berries
1/2 Cup of Carrot Juice

Just enough water/ice to blend to consistency.

Drink and feel refreshed!!!

---

**Veronica Schultz**
**Sushi Roll**

1 cup uncooked sushi rice
1 cup water
1/4 cup rice vinegar
1 tablespoon Organic Agave Nectar
A pinch of sea salt
4 Organic carrots shredded or thinly sliced lengthwise
8 sheets nori (dry seaweed)
2 1/2 tablespoons sesame seeds
1 Organic cucumber, cut into thin spears
2 Organic avocados - pitted, peeled, and sliced the long way

1. Wash the rice and drain well. Place in a rice cooker with 1 1/4 cup water and select white rice to cook.
2. Mix the rice vinegar, sea salt and Agave nectar in a small bowl and mix well. Add to the cooked rice and stir to blend well.

3. To roll the sushi, cover a bamboo rolling mat with plastic wrap. Lay a sheet of nori, shiny side down, on the plastic wrap. With wet fingers, firmly pat a thin, even layer of prepared rice over the nori, leaving 1/4 inch uncovered at the bottom edge of the sheet. Sprinkle the rice with about 1/2 teaspoon of sesame seeds, and gently press them into the rice. Carefully flip the nori sheet over so the seaweed side is up.

4. Place 2 or 3 long carrots, cucumber spears, 2 or 3 slices of avocado in a line across the nori sheet, about 1/4 from the uncovered edge. Pick up the edge of the bamboo rolling sheet, fold the bottom edge of the sheet up, enclosing the filling, and tightly roll the sushi into a cylinder about 1 1/2 inch in diameter. Once the sushi is rolled, wrap it in the mat and gently squeeze to compact it tightly.

5. Cut each roll into 1 inch pieces with a very sharp knife dipped in water.

6. Use sweet soy sauce and sambal for dipping sauce (optional)

---

**Linda Giles**
**Blackened Grilled Grouper Sandwich and Grilled Sweet Potatoes**

Courtesy – Publix Apron Meals

**Ingredients**
1 medium tomato (rinsed)
1 1/2 lbs grouper (or mahi) fillets (thawed, if needed)
cooking spray
2 tablespoons blackening seasoning
4 Bakery Kaiser rolls
4 tablespoons tartar sauce
8 lettuce leaves (rinsed)

1. Preheat 2-sided tabletop grill. Cut tomato into 1/4-inch-thick slices. Cut fish into 4 portions. Coat both sides of fish with cooking spray then sprinkle with blackening seasoning.
2. Place fish on grill (wash hands); close lid and cook 5 minutes or until fish is opaque and separates easily with a fork. (If using regular grill, double cooking time, turning once.) Cook time may vary depending on thickness of fish.
3. Cut rolls in half, if needed. Spread tarter sauce on bottom half of each roll. Top with lettuce and then tomato slice.
4. Add fish; top with remaining lettuce and top half of roll. (Assembling with lettuce next to the roll helps to prevent soggy bread.) Serve.

Ingredients
2 medium sweet potatoes (rinsed)
cooking spray
1/2 teaspoon blackening seasoning
1/8 teaspoon pepper

1. Preheat 2-sided tabletop grill. Cut sweet potatoes in half lengthwise. Coat cut side of potatoes with cooking spray, then sprinkle with blackening seasoning and pepper.
2. Place potatoes on grill; close lid and grill 5 minutes or until grill marks are visible. (If using regular grill; double cooking time, turning once.)
3. Arrange potatoes in microwave-safe dish. Microwave on HIGH 10 minutes or until tender when pierced with a fork. Serve.

**Consuelo Meux**
**Daily Green Smoothie!**

The idea of a "green smoothie" may not sound appealing at first. But you will soon love this power-packed drink to start your morning.

Here's the basic recipe:

1 Banana (peeled)

1 Apple (chopped for easy blending)

1 large handful of spinach ( washed and put in blender)

2 cups fresh, filtered water

Ice – optional

Put the fruit and spinach into the blender. Add the water.  Blend and drink. How easy is that?

You can also add strawberries, blueberries, or another favorite fruit.

Be sure to use the freshest fruits and vegetables and use organic if possible

---

**Karen Tompkins**

**Egg and Sausage Breakfast Dish**

From *River Road Recipes II, the Junior League of Baton Rouge, Louisiana.*

1 pound cooked, drained sausage

6 eggs, slightly beaten

2 cups mil

1 teaspoon mil

1 teaspoon dry mustard

2 slices crushed, day old bread

1 cup grated Cheddar cheese

3 tablespoons chopped onion

Mix ingredients and let sit overnight in a 11x 7x1 ½-inch pyrex dishBake at 350 degrees for 45 minutes.

This is a great Sunday brunch.  Serves 6

---

**Cathy Sexton**

**Taco Soup**

2 # ground beef

1 package Taco Seasoning mix

1 can Pinto Beans

2 can Red Kidney Beans

2 cans Corn with juice

1 can diced tomatoes

1 can Rotel tomatoes & Chilies

1 can tomato sauce

Brown and cook ground beef add all other ingredients bring to boil, simmer for 20 min. Serve with taco chips and grated cheese

---

**Carmen Cook**
**Unforgettable Chocolate Orgasms**
**A Favorite of Carmen Cook since 1995**

(Recipe adopted from Rosie's All-Butter Fresh Cream Sugar-No-Holds-Barred Baking Book)

**Brownies:**
3 1/2 ounces unsweetened chocolate
12 tablespoons (1 1/2 sticks) of unsalted butter at room temperature
1 1/2 cups sugar
3/4 teaspoon vanilla extract
3 large eggs at room temperature
3/4 cup + 2 tablespoons all-purpose flour
1/2 cup + 2 tablespoons chopped walnuts

**Frosting:**
1 1/2 ounces unsweetened chocolate
1/4 cup evaporated milk
1/2 cup sugar

**Brownies:**
Preheat oven to 350 degrees and grease an 8-inch square pan lightly.  Melt chocolate and butter in a double boiler; cool 5 minutes.
Mix chocolate and sugar with electric mixer at medium speed till blended (about 30 seconds).
At low speed, add vanilla, then eggs one at a time, blending briefly after each.
Add flour and mix briefly.
Finish mixing by hand and stir in 1/2 cup of nuts (if desired).
Spread batter in pan and sprinkle remaining nuts over top.
Bake 25 to 30 minutes (inside should be moist).
Cool 1 hour.

**Frosting:**
Melt chocolate in double boiler. Mix evaporated milk, sugar and chocolate in electric blender on medium -low until thickened (50 seconds).
Frost brownies and let sit for 1 hour before cutting.

---

**Karen Tompkins**
**Chicken in Wine Sauce**
from The Lady and Sons Savannah Country Cookbook Paula Deen

4 large skinless boneless chicken breasts
6 ounces Swiss cheese slices
One 10 ¾ ounce can condensed cream of chicken soup
¼ cup white wine (more if desired)
Salt and pepper to taste
1 cup herb-flavored Pepperidge Farm stuffing mix, crushed
4 tablespoons (1/2 stick) butter, melted

Preheat oven to 350 degrees.
Place chicken in shallow buttered casserole.
Layer cheese on top.
Mix soup, wine, salt, and pepper, pour over cheese.
Sprinkle stuffing mix on top and drizzle with melted butter.
Bake for 45 – 60 minutes.

---

**Saskia Jennings- de Quaasteniet**
**Lunch favorite: Shrimp & Goat Cheese Quesadillas**
Courtesy Clean Eating Magazine

Serves: 4 can easily be doubled; can be assembled up to 12 hours in advance.

Ingredients:
6 oz. frozen cooked shrimp (peeled,
deveined, tail off), thawed, drained and
coarsely chopped (about 1 cup)
4 oz. goat cheese, crumbled ( ½ cup)
½ cup jarred sliced roasted red peppers,
drained
¼ cup jarred sliced green olives, drained
1 tbsp. chopped fresh basil
4 small whole-grain tortilla's (each 6-inches in diameter)
2 tsp. olive oil
¼ tsp. ground black pepper

Instructions:
1. preheat oven to 425F

2. In a medium bowl mix shrimp, cheese, roasted peppers, olives and basil.
Lay tortillas out in a single layer on a flat surface. Scoop quarter of shrimp mixture into center

of each tortilla. Fold tortilla into a half-moon shape, pressing gently to flatten filling evenly inside tortilla.

3. Place tortillas on a parchment-lined baking tray. Brush tops of tortilla with ½ tsp. olive oil and sprinkle with black pepper.  Bake for 6 minutes, until quesadillas are golden brown.  Remove from oven and let rest for 2 minutes.  Cut each quesadilla in half and serve immediately.

Serve with your favorite healthy green salad. Enjoy!

---

**Sherry Prindle**
**Low-fat Jalapeno Poppers**

12 jalapeno peppers (large whole)
1 block low-fat cheddar cheese
1 block Neufatchel cheese
1 package turkey bacon
1 can bread crumbs

Important: use gloves when handling jalapenos

Halve the jalapenos, remove the seeds and soak in cold water (the longer you soak them the less spicy, so just rinse if you like the burn).

Drain and spread on paper towels to dry.

Stuff each pepper with a sliver of cheddar cheese covered with Neufatchel (the cream cheese keeps the cheddar from leaking out during baking) and dipped in bread crumbs.

Top each pepper with a half slice of turkey bacon
Bake at 350 degrees for 20 minutes

---

**Nancy Lee Bentley**
**Nancy Lee's Signature Sunsé Seed Mix**
Quick, nutritious, basic seed mix goes from 0-60, sweet to savory, snack to salad, crunchy casserole to dessert topper with complete variations in Nancy's cookbook, *Truly Cultured*, www.TrulyCultured.com

2-½ cups raw, hulled sunflower seeds,

½ cup hulled sesame seeds

½ cup pumpkin seeds or green pepitas

½ cup flax, chia or *edible* hemp seeds

1. Combine seeds.

2. Store in covered container in refrigerator or freezer for up to two months.  Yield: 4 cups

Variations:  Nancy's favorite Savory Golden Sunsé:

Delicious as snack or salad, baked potato or casserole topper

In heavy, dry skillet, lightly toast Basic Sunsé over medium heat, stirring constantly until sesame seeds start to pop. Remove from heat.  Add ½ cup dry mixed vegetables or vegetable soup mix blended to a powder, 2 Tbsp poultry seasoning, 1 Tbsp thyme leaves, 2 Tbsp nutritional yeast, 1-1/2 tsp Spike or Celtic sea salt. Stir to mix.  Cool.  Store in covered container in refrigerator or freezer.  Good for 6-8 weeks.

Notes: For optimum health, all seeds should ideally be raw and organic, soaked, sprouted and dehydrated

**Find this delicious, versatile, easy-to-make seed mix along with over 175 more healthy recipes you and your family will actually WANT to eat in Nancy Lee's evergreen cookbook and nourishment guide, *Truly Cultured* at www.TrulyCultured.com.**

# ~ Notes ~

# In The Kitchen With....

**Wow – you have to be hungry now!** While you wait for your dish to finish – why not lay back, relax, grab yourself a hot cup of coffee and enjoy the articles that follow!

**Brought to you by:**

# In The Kitchen with Kelly Poelker

## The Right Way to Outsource Social Media Management

Nothing can get a good debate going more than a discussion on social media and outsourcing. In fact, the topic of outsourcing social media management is questionable from the very start. By this I mean that:

1. Outsourcing is no doubt a hot topic, especially as it relates to social media. As you can see below, many believe it negatively impacts those here in the U.S.

2. There are many people in the social media world who question the authenticity of "managing" social media, especially when automation is employed. They question whether you lose the personal touch when it's not done correctly.

So who's right? Never the type to shy away from the hot topics, we, at Another 8 Hours, believe that outsourcing and social media management can be done with the upmost quality and we are proud to offer this service to our clients. After all, it's a service we provide on a daily basis and our clients are very pleased with the results we get them.

By taking a step back and looking at the often heated debate about outsourcing and the management of social media, we will expose our core beliefs and basic techniques concerning them.

**First: Outsourcing.**

If you have listened to a minute of domestic news in the last few years, you know that outsourcing is debated and argued at almost every turn. The crux of the argument has usually centered on the practice of sending work (and therefore jobs) overseas rather than providing it through American workers.  Politicians, business leaders, unions and others have joined in the debate and fed the argument.

This is the center of the outsourcing storm.

The idea of productivity stemming from farming out your work to cheap, overseas "assistants" has been met with its share of criticism, particularly from U.S.-based Virtual Assistants (VA). It seems the promise of working less, making more, and paying as little as possible for your business operations is overshadowed by the desire for quality. In reality, many who have ventured into the land of outsourcing overseas have returned to the more qualified, more capable domestic VAs after experiencing the challenges of cultural differences, language barriers, time zone issues and more—some things ended up costing more money!  The grass is not always greener on the other side.

**Second: Social Media Management**

Social media is hot and it is not going away anytime soon. Each of the top social media platforms like Facebook, Twitter, YouTube, Google+ and Yelp is experiencing tremendous growth. Here are some fascinating user statistics to consider:

*As of September 2012*

- Facebook: 955 million users
- YouTube: 4 billion views per day
- Twitter: 140 million users
- Google+: 250 million users
- Yelp: 30 million reviews

What started as a weird way to carry on a conversation, has transformed into a multi-billion dollar industry. And it isn't slowing down anytime soon.

With stats like that, it would be a disservice to our clients if we didn't provide that service. That's why at Another 8 Hours, we do help businesses with their social media. We work alongside individuals and companies who have made the decision to purchase this service instead of providing it internally. They have decided to outsource.

They do this in an atmosphere of contention from some in the "social media world" as to the ability for someone to "do" social media for someone else. The use of automation through such tools as Hootsuite, Tweetdeck, Buffer and SocialOomph is deemed as inauthentic and impersonal.

In light of the debate, why do we do what we do? Because….

1. People ask for it. Pure and simple, individuals and companies see the need for our services and ask us to help them develop a strategy to meet the needs of their growing businesses.  They are often too busy to do it otherwise and therefore, without our help, it just wouldn't get done.

2. We believe that each argument in the debate can be overcome with our core beliefs and values related to the outsourcing of social media management.

**Here are those core beliefs/values:**

**It's about partnership**

From the moment we are contacted about our services, we begin talking with the client about partnership. We stress that they will need to work side-by-side with us in order to develop and implement a social media strategy that has the greatest impact for them or for their business. They cannot dump their stuff in our laps and run for the hills.  They need to be a part of the equation and even though they are not doing the work, they must be committed to offering input.

**It's about providing value**

We have learned over time that the best way to see success with social media is to set yourself up as the trusted provider of valuable information that people are looking for within your given niche. People need help. It's our job as a partnership to provide them with value that meets and transforms their need.

**It's about quality**

Many folks are discovering again that cheaper is not always better. The price tag of a business service should not be the only factor these days. We believe that quality work is the key to success and longevity in the social media management world. When you outsource to a company, you should do so because of the partnership they form, the value they provide and the quality of their work.

**It's about building relationships**

Lastly, we believe that a key ingredient to impactful social media management is the need to build relationships with those that you reach with your social strategy. It's called "social" media for a reason. It requires more than just simply advertising products and services. We stress to our clients the fact that people buy from people they trust through a successfully built relationship. It is their job to interact and build those relationships as we help them with their strategy. It's a combination of all of the above that makes it successful.

Social media management and the outsourcing aspect of it is a powerful way to see success as you build your business and seek to meet the needs of potential clients or customers. We believe it can be done quite successfully with the right skills, the right team, and the right partnership with the clients.

## About the Author

After 17 years in the corporate arena, Kelly Poelker, left her cubicle behind to start her own empire as a virtual assistant.

Kelly was in the forefront of the VA industry when she started her company, Another 8 Hours. Since 2000, she has been partnering with clients to keep them out of overwhelm. Her client list includes Fortune 100 and 500 companies; TV and radio show hosts, internationally recognized speakers and coaches as well as award-winning authors.

Kelly is co-author of Amazon bestseller and VA industry bible, *Virtual Assistant - The Series: Become a Highly Successful, Sought After VA*--the longest standing book in the industry that has helped thousands of virtual assistants get started in business. Her VA-The Series book and workbook are the most widely used training material in college VA programs across the country.

Kelly Poelker

Another 8 Hours, Inc.

106A East Fourth Street

O'Fallon, IL 62269

Tel: 618.624.3080

# In The Kitchen with Lynn Hidy

## Goal Setting - The Flip Side; Why We Don't Achieve Them

What's Stopping You? (from reaching your goals)

Over the years coaching salespeople, I've come across quite a number of reasons for missing goal. Small ones, big ones, financial objectives, personal aspirations; you name a goal - I'll show you someone who has achieved it AND someone who hasn't.

We all have our own deep dark secrets about why we aren't doing the things we know we need to. People have shared with me over the years lots of different reasons; here is my Top 10 Countdown.

10. A skill set, piece of knowledge, or expertise were missing and gaining "it" was missing from the plan.

9. Inside they didn't believe they deserved it.

8. Achieving the goal would set a higher expectation of their future achievement (*and that is scary*).

7. Milestones were missed and they gave up instead of regrouping.

6. Old habits are easy to fall back into.

5. They didn't visualize what it would be like once they'd achieved their goal and couldn't get excited about the work to be done.

4. They figured out in the middle of the process, that their objective had changed - so abandoned the original goal AND set a new one.

3. The bite size pieces they had cut to achieve the goal were too big and they gave up.

2. It wasn't their goal in the first place, but one they felt they "should" care about.

And the #1 reason salespeople do NOT achieve the goals they've set for themselves is (*imaginary drum roll please*)...

**the reward for reaching their goal DOES NOT outweigh the pain of change**

Your objective for the week is to determine what your reasons might be, what is holding you back from achieving the big audacious goals you've set for yourself.... or the micro-goals that would propel you forward.

I would then make a gentle suggestion to reevaluate: your goal, the plan, and yourself to figure out what it will take to overcome the obstacles you've built. Plus set a few rewards for your own good behavior - most of us are willing to beat ourselves up for NOT achieving something, yet have difficulty celebrating success!

What could that look like?

- Sleeping in an extra hour
- A special meal
- Buying yourself a gift - commiserate with the size of your accomplishment
- Celebrating with friends & family

Enjoy the journey and achieve your goals.

# In The Kitchen with Saskia Jennings

*Careers from the Kitchen table…famous for the "cooking without the cooking"*

Let me help you right now with this great new recipe you have in your mind: your own home business!  Want some guidance from the 'Chef', the Expert? Well, let's get cooking!

Imagine this: you got a great idea and you want to make it a success….how do you do that?

Well, it's like cooking. I can hear you asking: what do you mean Saskia?

You're invited to join me in the kitchen and bring that great recipe that you have in mind for your Home Business.

What do you do first?

Really know WHY you want to cook this specific recipe, that's #1 ingredient for success!
Write down all the specifics, all the details that you see for your business, look at it from all sides, envision it and ask yourself: WHY do I want to create this?

This is the SECRET ingredient: your **WHY**. How about:  your passion, your inspiration, your drive, your success and your fulfillment. Your –financial- freedom and independence. What are your unique gifts and talents? What difference will you make in the world? In order for you to succeed with your Home Business, it's essential that you understand your WHY.

What other ingredients would you need for your own recipe?

How about a list of what you need for your business. And think of: product or service, suppliers, your support team, work space, information you need, money, professionalism.

There's no need in the beginning to communicate your recipe on luxurious paper and glossy cards…. A website and business cards are mostly not the #1 focus.

Create from your Heart, Be Passionate. And when you start cooking, make sure your 'kitchen' is clean and keep it that way. Have a great workspace, which can be a simple desk and keep it neat. Too many piles of unorganized paper make your brain fuzzy.

Built your recipe step by step and take the time for all the prep work before you start cooking. Sometimes you may use the 'wrong' ingredient and your recipe fails. Don't panic, just do it again, and again.

Brain Tracey states: fail often and fail fast. Why? You will move forward faster as you take note of where you failed and make a change. I assure you, those are wise words and experience.

Do you meet someone who doesn't like your recipe? Don't take it personal!
If someone offers you a platter of appetizers, do you always take one? Your favorite one might not be on the platter, or you're on a diet…you decline. So do people who you offer your product or service. There's a whole world out there that will certainly say yes!

When you cook at home, make sure that your family knows what you're doing and what your needs are.

You want them to enjoy the outcome of your recipe as much as you do, don't you?

Listen, you don't need to have all the education and skills to create an awesome recipe, your business. You have unique gifts and talents, use them! Make sure that your business is unique in a way, that you love what you do!

The saying, "Do what you love, love what you do" should not be taken lightly. Your business is going to be your livelihood - you should have a good time doing it. If not, it will be difficult to get motivated at times.

If you are excited about your business, your customers will notice and it will be easier to get them excited, too. Plus, completing the steps to starting your small business will be fun and much more enjoyable.

As you start the cooking, you'll be mostly on your own. Make sure you don't put 100 hours of work in your business per week while neglecting your own personal needs.

Take one step at a time and-very important: focus on only 1 thing. Do that well and then add something new.

If you keep <u>insisting</u> on doing it all at once, then recognize that as a defense mechanism that will actually stop you from succeeding and moving forward. Yes, you can read that again!

Members of your family, at least those still at home or any family members, who may need to make sacrifices or lifestyle changes in order to accommodate your business, need to know what you're up to and how it might affect them. If you have a spouse or significant other or children living with you, your home business will be a big part of their lives too.

I love to share with you some of my great Recipes for Success

- Believe in yourself and be authentic
- Have a coach or mentor to support you (call me ☺, yes I'm serious!)
- Let go of fear and self-doubt and take positive action

- Stay focused on serving your clients the best you can
- Prioritize your tasks
- Care for yourself: exercise regularly, eat healthy

Saskia Jennings is Cert. Holistic Life Coach, Intuitive Healer and Radio Talk Show Host.

She is an expert and passionate about helping women entrepreneurs in midlife to transform their Midlife Crisis into Midlife BLISS!

www.creatingbeingwell.com | saskia@creatingbeingwell.com

*"Be free from overwhelm and meet your own needs, double your free time and make more money NOW!"*

# In The Kitchen with Raven Blair Davis

## Podcasting for Your Online or Offline Business

Unleash The Power of Your Voice with The Power of Podcasts and Elevate your Business Faster Rather Than Slower

Podcasts were thought to be the hobbies of computer freaks and people who spend hours in front of the screen trying to do everything possible with the available range of options. Nowadays this medium has garnered sufficient attention in the corporate world with business concerns taking note of this unique device of communication and using it to the fullest to create advertising effects like never before.

Podcasts serve the basic cause of promoting your enterprise. But this promotion can proceed via several avenues without making it look like too brazen an attempt to advertise your firm. What is possible is intensive information sharing via podcasts that help your firm pass on all the relevant information to the customers without running the risk of over advertising.

Thus, podcasts can serve the dual role of advertisement for the company and service for the customer. Examples would include medical firms offering health related advice and educational institutions providing weekly advice to students on podcast.

The further use of a podcast in a commercial enterprise is that it can be used to train employers and all they will need is an mp3 player or a laptop to access the training information and thus go through it right there without going through elaborate training schedules. This saves your money and your employee gets some time.

Like any other device, podcast comes with costs and expenses to be borne. The nature of these expenses is particular to the product and in case of podcast you will need people with technical knowhow and along with people who will be the content on the podcast. This cost could be managed by attaching costs to the podcast the customer views on your website.

Or you could start a service for which the customer receives podcast updates from you for a fee. These measures really depend on the success of the podcasts or else the customer might just bypass it if he or he has to pay a price for it.

Podcasts are amazing innovations that you can put to good use to help your enterprise. They could be used for advertising, passing on information, training employees or even for bonus customer service that you want to offer.

Given this wide range of things that a podcast could do for you, it can only be an asset to your firm and nothing less. But key to a better functioning of such apparatus is that you maintain high

When you are offering a product or service to prospective clients, the client should be acquainted with what you are offering as well as its traits or characteristics. If minute details are given, the client's decision can be faster. This is why advertising is indispensable for generating sales and subsequent gains from sales.

The period for which an advertisement can be sustained on a visual medium like the television is greatly restricted because of the expenses. The process of remembering can also not be relied on because of the limited duration of the commercials. Podcasting for online business is a blessing for advertisers, internet marketers and web masters.

Extended functions for podcasting for online businesses can be applications like employee training, information dissemination, or even product demonstration. Since podcasts can carry audio and picture files, they are remarkable aids for all business purposes and not just marketing alone.

Podcasting for online businesses is relatively much cheaper and most businesses can create in-house podcasts. The only tools needed are a personal computer and some software, most of which can be downloaded free of cost. Novel ideas and gadgets for podcasting are discovered almost daily and the internet serves useful in keeping us updated about these upgrades.

- Develop True One-on-One Relationships: Though traditional advertising owns a very respectable place in the media world, podcasting allows the target client to get an idea about the face, voice and life of the product. If a podcast is developed even moderately well, it gives the company an opportunity for genuine one-on-one face time with new as well as old clients. The only effort is to give that primary amount of time required to develop and release the podcast. Customers become acquainted with the company through that individual and a greater level of trust can be established.

- Create Anticipation for Future Communication: We only need to witness the success of YouTube to understand how much the level of anticipation for more correspondence from the same distributor. Average people are offering numerous opinions on sequential podcasts and videos. Messages that are more creative reach hundreds of people within days because they become popular so fast. This popularity has what is called a "viral impact" that traditional media can only dream of achieving.

- Measurability: depending on which platform you need to host your podcast on, there are many ways of devising the client's behavior in reference to the message displayed. Like HTML email where links can be visited and judged for follow-through to the main offer, podcasts too can be scrutinized statistically to check how many people watched them and at what times. Unlike the TV or radio that has passive recipients for the message, podcasts have an active audience that have voluntarily selected your display and are examining it attentively with genuine interest. Measuring conversion rates for podcasting is relatively easier than for other kinds of mass media.

- Immediate Call to Action: Though statistics case analysis are still being built, many anecdotal cases record a rise in scales, contact from prospects, people sought out for speaking appointments and rising mass media exposure due to podcast communication. The justification for these triumphs is that for the 1-3 minutes that you engage your prospect, you have the chance to generate a compelling message that is not in competition with any other advertising agent.

Therefore, if you're planning to develop your own podcast from the very beginning, the first effort you should make is to browse the internet to attain the latest features that have been added to this wonderful technology. Once you are done with podcasting for online business, be ready for the shower of orders that will start coming in.

Raven Blair Davis
"The Talk Show Maven"
Raven@womenpower-radio.com


http://www.careersfromthekitchentable.com/

~ Notes ~

# About Raven, aka, The Talk Show Maven!

*America's Leading Authority on Leveraging the Power of Your Voice!*

## The Talk Show Maven Looking to the Future

One of the things Raven Blair Davis is not, is a fly by night, one hit wonder! She's got BIG plans for the future. Keep your eye out for all the wonderful things she has planned, some of which include:

**Careers from The Kitchen Table Reality TV Show** - Raven's taking her increasingly popular, Careers from the Kitchen Table Radio show to the streets and teaching men and women all over how to start their own business from home.

The Amazing Women of Power
http://www.AWOPTalk247.com
The World's Leading Positive Programming Network

**Careers from the Kitchen Table**

(www.careersfromthekitchentable.com) Airs live on *the Amazing Women of Power Positive Broadcasting Network* every Thursday and Saturday at 11AM CT, CFKT targets men and women (home based businesses and enthusiasts) who are looking to spend more time at home with their children, perhaps have lost their job or have been forced into early retirement and are looking for ways to create a consistent income all from the comfort of their own home.

**BONUS AUDIO:** Raven interviews Hip Hop & Business Mogul Russell Simmons

http://raven.audioacrobat.com/download/667ca9f5-28e0-3c5f-61ee-55444310ccac.mp3

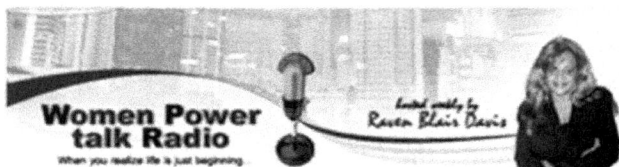

**Women Power Talk Radio** (www.womenpower-radio.com) - Named one of the Best Top 100 Business Podcasts by Anita Campbell's Business Trends two years in a row, Women Power was created to help women of all ages ignite the unstoppable power that lies within them. Sign up for your free newsletter and receive the e-book **"Seven Action Steps on 'How to Ignite Your UnStoppable Power'"** http://www.womenpower-radio.com

**B**ONUS **AUDIO**: Diana Nightingale interviews Raven on her talk show journey

http://raven.audioacrobat.com/download/18fd4ae2-5694-2d07-9695-2d6ddb8023c5.mp3

---

**Mentoring from MLM Divas Live** (www.mentoringfrom-mlmdivaslive.com) - Secret Home-Based Business Ingredients from MLM Women Millionaires Listeners will discover three secret ingredients needed to cook up network marketing success.

**B**ONUS **AUDIO**: Raven and co-host Lisa Kitter

http://raven.audioacrobat.com/download/28211659-6d99-301b-1b59-762c2df4a34d.mp3

---

**Raven's Celebrity Rave** (http://amazingwomenofpower.com/radio/celebrity-raves - Aired on the Amazing Women of Power Positive Broadcasting Network every Tuesday at Noon ET. Raven rolls out the red carpet and celebrates those who give back by spotlighting celebrities all around the world...from ALL walks of life...who are making a difference by paying it forward!

## Check out who's on the red carpet next!

**B**ONUS **AUDIO**: Raven and Grammy Engineer Khaliq Glover interview bobby Brooks Wilson, the son of the late Jackie Wilson.
http://raven.audioacrobat.com/download/fb64e1f3-541e-e652-9e5f-50823049edeb.mp3

# Raven's Books

**Kitchen Table Radio Home Study Course** (www.kitchentableradio.com) -
In this course Raven shares the secrets that made her an award winning
radio show host and teaches her students step-by-step how to produce
and profit from their own radio show.

**Broadcast Your Passion to Profits**
(www.broadcastpassion.com) – In this book, Raven shares how you can
attract more customers to your business with the power of your voice using
radio, Internet radio, and podcasting as your platform.

**How to Turn Your Telephone into a Cash Cow** (www.telephonecashcow.com)
An audio eWorkbook that includes 9
innovative outlets in which Raven
shares once again how effective the
power of your voice can be in
successfully creating or growing your
business. When your potential
clients hear your voice chances are they will connect with you more than through email. 20% of
people remember what they read versus 80% who remember what they hear.

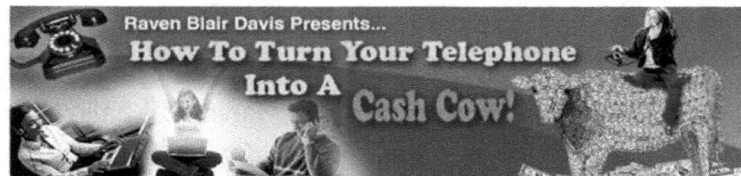

# BONUS AUDIO: Join Raven as she explains the *Insider Secrets to Cold Calling!*

http://www.audioacrobat.com/play/Wn35XKnb

---

Raven is living proof that you CAN make your dreams a reality with a bit of hard
work, dedication and desire. It's up to YOU to make it happen. Every single
person, even you, has the ability within to become UNSTOPPABLE!

Raven says: *"From a seed that was placed in my heart in the hospital ICU Unit
to interviewing famous thought leaders and celebrities – YES dreams do come
true if you follow your passion, be committed to your purpose and NEVER EVER
give up on your dream! If you can dream it….you can achieve it!"*

**Following are pictures of Raven hanging out with mentors and celebrities!**

Raven & Alex Mandossian

Raven & Sherri Shepard

Raven & Lisa Nichols

Raven & Joan Rivers

Raven & Khaliq Glover

Raven & Master P

Raven & Sheryl Lee Roth

Raven & Marla Maples

Raven & Kim Fields

**To hear more heart to heart celebrity interviews, be sure to visit** http://www.womenpower-radio.com **and subscribe to the newsletter too**! Sign up for your free newsletter and receive the free e-book **"Seven Action Steps on 'How to Ignite Your UnStoppable Power'"**

*Interested in booking Raven to speak at your next event!*
You will not have anyone falling asleep!
Email: raven@womenpower-radio.com or call 800-431-0842
See Raven in action http://www.ravenspeaks.com

**Here's a great site for inspirational movie clips:**
http://www.walkthetalk.com/pages/inspirational-movies.htm

# Raven's Recommended Resources

## RAVENS TOP 10 FAVORITE BOOKS!

1. **Instant Income** Janet Switzer
2. **Yes Energy** Loral Langemeier
3. **Unstoppable** Cynthia Kersey
4. **Now What** Lisa Nichols
5. **Think and Grow Rich** Napoleon Hill
6. **The Game Of Life and How to Play It** Florence Scovel Shinn
7. **Change Your Attitude Change Your Life** Denise Brown
8. **Success Principles** Jack Canfield
9. **Think Like A Champion** Donald Trump
10. **The Law of Business Attraction** T Harv Eckard and Adryenn Ashley

## RAVENS TOP 10 FAVORITE AUDIO BOOKS!

1. **The Strangest Secrets** Earl Nightingale
2. **It's Not Over Until You Win** Les Brown & Ona Brown
3. **The Challenge To Succeed** Jim Rhone
4. **The 4 Hour Work Week** Tim Ferris
5. **One Minute Millionaire** Mark Victor Hansen & Robert Allen
6. **The Magic of the Colors** Jerry Clark
7. **Choose To Be Rich** Robert Kiyosaki
8. **Multiple Streams of Internet Income** Robert Allen
9. **Affirmacize** Ona Brown
10. **THE Greatest Networker In The World** John Milton Fogg

## RAVENS TOP 10 INSPIRING VIDEOS/MOVIES

1. **The Secret**
2. **The Social Network**
3. **Rudy**
4. **A Beautiful Mind**
5. **Startup.com**
6. **Pursuit of Happiness**
7. **Facing The Giants**
8. **Pass It On**
9. **Pay It Forward**
10. **The Opus**

# Thanks to the Incredible Team!

*Without your hard work, this book would not be in our hands today!*

**Outstanding Virtual Assistance**

Peggy@outstandingvirtualassistance.com

http://www.outstandingvirtualassistance.com

**Darnell Brown**
Graphic Artist Extraordinaire
http://www.blucanvis.com
Darnell@blucanvis.com

**Jaime Boone Nicholson**
Project Manager

# *Heartfelt THANKS to you all!*

# Thanks to our Sponsors

# CREATING BEING WELL - SASKIA JENNINGS

Holistic Life Coach & Healer, Radio Talk Show Host

FREE BREAKTHROUGH SESSION:
TRANSFORM YOUR MIDLIFE CRISIS INTO MIDLIFE BLISS!

Do you feel like time is slipping by and you're not doing what you are meant to do with your life?
**Congratulations!**
you are one step away from changing your life and

"Transform your Midlife Crisis into Midlife Bliss!"

visit me: http://creatingbeingwell.com

Lola Scarborough
**YOGA LOLA STUDIOS**
A Yoga, Healing & Learning Center

1701 Highway 3 South
League City, Texas 77573
281-684-3168
lola@yogalola.com
www.yogalola.com
www.bodybuddiesyogalola.com

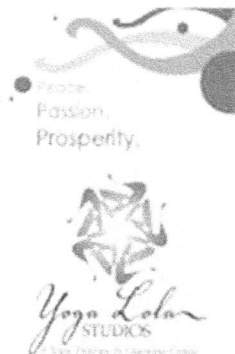

Peace
Passion,
Prosperity.

*Life2x*
The Power of
**Health and Wealth**

Trini Rocha
956-343-8111

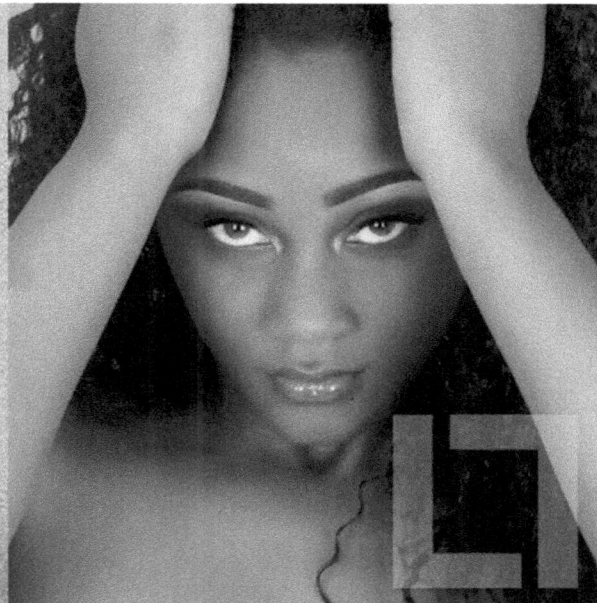

# ~ Notes ~

# Raven's Recommended Businesses

Don't forget to visit for more great audios
http://www.careersfromthekitchentable.com/audiobonus

Business Listings are In Alphabetical Order

A.K. A Coach and Company
**Annie Kirschenmann**
6844 35th St. SE
Windsor, ND 58424
Email:  annie@akacoachandcompany.com
Phone:  701-763-6406
Website:  www.akacoachandcompany.com
Facebook:  www.facebook.com/pages/AK-A-Coach-and-Company/26696788139?sk
LinkedIn:  http://www.linkedin.com/in/anniekirschenmann
Twitter:  www.twitter.com/#!/AnnieKCoach

Visit http://www.CreativityMatrix.com for your free "right brain – left brain" business tips
delivered directly to your email inbox once a month.  Just signup for the newsletter!

---

A Stronger Bond
**LaTricia Smith**
PO Box 48522
Cumberland, NC 28331
Email: info@astrongerbond.com
Phone:  910-816-9270
Toll free: 888-568-9619
Website: www.astrongerbond.com
Facebook: www.facebook.com/astrongerbond
LinkedIn: www.linkedin.com/in/latriciasmith
Twitter: www.twitter.com/LaTriciaSmith

Be sure to get your free resources that will improve your relationships at
http://www.astrongerbond.com/resources

Absolute Numbers
**Carolyn Jones, MA**
Email: Carolyn@absolutenumbers.com
Phone: 510-250-0854
Website: http://www.absolutenumbers.com
Facebook: http://www.facebook.com/absolutenumbers
LinkedIn: http://www.linkedin.com/in/carolynjones1

Are You Lost in Your Financials? Let me be your guide through financial transformation. Visit www.absolutenumbers.com/specialgifts for a FREE webinar on valuable strategies to transform your bottom line immediately. As a BONUS, you'll get my Financial Projections Starter Kit, the opportunity for a Complimentary Strategy Session, and more!

Adonai Business Solutions, LLC
**Kristi Pavlik**
332 Stoll
Lansing, MI 48917
Email: kristi@adonai-llc.com
Phone: 517-507-5939
Website: http://www.adonai-llc.com
Facebook: https://www.facebook.com/#!/TeamAdonai
LinkedIn: http://www.linkedin.com/in/kristipavlik
Twitter: http://twitter.com/KristiPavlik

Do you begin each day overwhelmed and not sure where to start? Do you find yourself over-tasked or forgetting things that need to be done? Download a complimentary copy of How to Find Your Ideal VA System as my gift to you. http://www.adonai-llc.com

Alycia Schlesinger, M.A., MNLP
**Alycia Schlesinger**
Email: amsbreeze@yahoo.com
Website: www.nextgreatetspeaker.com SEARCH #32
FaceBook: http://www.facebook.com/alycia.schlesinger
LinkedIn: http://www.linkedin.com/pub/alycia-schlesinger/4/902/311

Affirmations International Publishing Co
**Dr. Anne Marie Evers**
Email: annemarieevers@shaw.ca
Website: http://www.annemarieevers.com/damevers
FaceBook: http://www.facebook.com#!/pages/Affirmations-DrAnneMarieEvers
Phone: Toll Free Business Number 1-877-923-3476
Websites www.annemarieevers.com    www.annemariesangelchapel.com

Affirmation Coaching I am now taking new clients
My book, Affirmations Your Passport to Happiness 8th edition on www.amazon.com

Please visit www.annemarieevers.com and join up for your Free Daily Affirmation in your inbox.

Also please visit www.annemariesangelchapel.com and listen to the 8 Free Audio short, yet very powerful positive, helpful meditations on the following subjects:
Career; Forgiveness; Health; Money; Relationships; Stop Smoking; Self-Esteem and Weight Reduction and Maintenance absolutely free of cost

The first five people that email me at annemarievers@shaw.ca will be gifted with a copy of my 260 page e-book, Affirmation Toolbox.

---

Ambit Energy
**Ken and Gretchen Umbdenstock**
Email: gretchenumbdenstock@yahoo.com
Phone: 847-417-2229
Website: www.umby.energy526.com
Website: www.umbyljoinambit.com

---

Ameriplan®
**Joelle Niedecken**
Email: jniedecken@ameriplan.net
Website: http://www.deliveringonthepromise.com/dreamsrock

---

Amethyst Wyldfyre Enterprises, LLC
**Amethyst Wyldfyre**
Email: amethyst@theempoweredmessenger.com

Website: http://www.theempoweredmessenger.com
FaceBook: http://www.facebook.com/awyldfyre
LinkedIn: www.linkedin.com/in/amethystwyldfyrehttp
Twitterwww.twitter.com/awyldfyre

---

Annointed Assistant
**Christine Davis**
PO Box 720154
Byram, MS  39272-1054
Email:  Christine@AnnointedAssistant.com
Website:  www.AnnointedAssistant.com
Facebook: http://www.facebook.com/AnnointedAssistant
LinkedIn:  http://www.linkedin.com/in/annointedassistant
Twitter:  http://twitter.com/A2Assist

---

Another 8 Hours, Inc.
**Kelly Poelker**
106A East Fourth St.
O'Fallon, IL  62269
Email:  kp@another8hours.com
Phone: 618-624-3080
Website:  http://www.another8hours.com
Facebook:  http://www.facebook.com/kellypoelker
LinkedIn: http://www.linkedin/in/kellypoelker
Twitter:  http://www.twitter.com/kellypoelker

If you're a business owner who is in complete overwhelm and struggling to get it all done, you need to put Another 8 Hours in your day.  Call me for a free 30-minute consultation.  If you're interested in pursuing a career as a Virtual Assistant, take advantage of our free Virtual Assistant Self-Assessment Tool at

http://www.academyvp.com/virtual-assistant-self-assessment

---

Applied Awareness Systems Institute
**JoAnn Martin**
Email:  wisdomwellnessandwealth@gmail.com
Website:  www.wisdomwellnessandwealth.com

FaceBook: http://www.facebook.com/budhafly@gmail
Twitter http://www.twitter.com/joannmartin12

Providing upliftment and transformation through education, motivation and inspiration to all who desire to experience more happiness, improved health and increased abundance.

---

The Art Song Preservation Society of New York, Inc.
**Blair Boone**
Email: ASPSNY@gmail.com
Website: http://www.ArtSongPreservationSocietyNY.com
Twitter: https://twitter.com/ASPSNY

Private Voice Lessons
Group Voice Lessons
Workshops, Master Classes and Lectures in the area of Art Song
Recitals/Performances
Subscribe to our newsletter!
http://www.artsongpreservationsocietyny.org/subscribe.html

---

Authentic Communications
**Lorrie Crystal Eigles**
Email: Lorrie@myauthenticlifecoaching.com
Website: http://myauthenticlifecoaching.com
LinkedIn: http://www.linkedin.com/in/lorrieeigles
Visit: http://myauthenticlifecoaching.com for my free article: "Life Transitions--What Are They?" We all go through them; you can learn to successfully!

---

Aunt K's Place
**Lea Rutherford-Williams**
Phone: 877-257-3721
Website: www.auntksplace.org
Website: www.auntksplace.com
Website: www.etenterprises.us
Website: www.LeaSpeaks.com

---

Austin Properties Unlimited Multiple Listing Service
**Realtor - Alvernad Austin**
Website: www.har.com/LadyAustin

---

Avalaura's Healing Center
**Avalaura Beharry**
Email: avalaura@avalaura.com
Website: http://www.avalaura.com
FaceBook: www.facebook.com/AvalaurasHealingCenter
LinkedIn: www.linkedin.com/in/avalaura
Twitter: https://twitter.com/HealerAvalaura

Avalaura's clients are professional, educated women who are spiritual, open minded and ready to transform their lives. They may feel lost, stuck, spiritually disconnected, unfulfilled, unbalanced and unsure of who they are or their purpose for being. They come to Avalaura for help in overcoming personal obstacles and transforming their lives. Call or email Avalaura for a FREE consultation. Find out how you can work with her too!

---

**Regina Baker**
Speaker, Consultant and Program Director, AWOP Radio Network
PO Box 24813
Houston, TX  77229-4813
Email: email@reginabaker.com
Phone:  800-294-1461
Website: http://ReginaBaker.com
Please be sure to subscribe to Regina's offer and get your free report "Sales Funnel Marketing" http://reginabaker.com/sales-funnel-process/

---

Bay College Planning Specialist
**Dan Evertsz**
Email: Dan@baycollegeplanners.com
Website: www.thecollegemoneypro.com
FaceBook: http://www.facebook.com/DanEvertsz-collegemoneypro

Parents of college bound high school students are encouraged to visit Dan's website and sign up for a free financial assessment for college funding.  Dan will waive the normal $197.00 assessment fee for readers of this book.

Be A Legacy – Queen of Accountability
**Kimberley Borgens, CBC**
PO Box 8633
Stockton, CA 95208
Email: dreamteam@bealegacy.com
Phone: 209-993-7632
Website: http://www.bealegacy.com
Facebook: http://www.facebook.com/QueenofAccountability
LinkedIn: http://linkedin.com/in/kimberleyborgens
Twitter: http://twitter.com/BeALegacy

When you are tired of doing business alone! Get "20 Ways to Increase Your Confidence" free report and more tools on accountability at www.bealegacy.com. Get the E-book Partner Up for Success and begin creating your ideal accountability partner.

Bless-d
**Joan Day-Gilbert**
6454 Park Central Way #D
Indianapolis, IN 46260
Email: Bless-d1@sbcglobal.net
Phone: 317-989-8601
Website: http://www.bless-d.com

Bonnie Terry Learning
**Bonnie Terry, M. Ed., BCET**
Phone: 530-888-7160
Website: http://www.bonnieterry.com
Twitter: http://twitter.com/#!/bonnieterry_btl
Blog: http://bonnieterry.com/blog

All individuals who want to improve their learning skills for themselves or their children whether they have dyslexia, a learning disability, ADHD, are falling through the cracks, or are even gifted but take too long to do their homework. Get 10 FREE Homework Tips at http://www.BonnieTerryLearning.com

**Beverly Boston**
Master Coach-For BIG Thinkers
Email: info@BeverlyBoston.com
Phone: 604-727-4363
Website: www.BeverlyBoston.com

For the next generation Big Thinkers get 3 FREE reports on client attraction and solid business building principles for your small businesses go here: www.BeverlyBoston.com

Breakthrough Results
**Cathy Hansell**
Email: chansell@breakthroughresults.org
Website: http://www.breakthroughresults.org
FaceBook: http://www.facebook.com/#!/cathy.hansell.5
LinkedIn: http://www.linkedin.com/in/cathyhansell

Breakthrough Results provides world class expertise in implementing superior safety cultures to reduce injuries and improve productivity and morale. Contact Cathy Hansell for a free one-hour consultation.

---

BRECS Corp.
**Carrie Sharpshair**
Email: carrie@brecsmail.com
Website: http://yescarrie.com
FaceBook: https://www.facebook.com/SmallBusinessPlanningExpert
LinkedIn: http://www.linkedin.com/in/carriesharpshair
Twitter: http://www.twitter.com/@TheSharpCookie

Are you a chief "everything" officer in a service profession?  Have you realized you're ready to put your rear in gear to get clear and focused so that you can achieve success on your terms? Check out http://yescarrie.com for a great audio class and the opportunity to chat with me!

---

Bright Futures Consulting
**BETH DENNARD, ED D**
Email: bdennard@brightfuturesllc.com
Phone: 281-486-0023
Website: www.brightfuturesllc.com

---

**Dr. Linne Bourget, MA, MBA Ph.D.**
Website: www.whatyousayiswhatyouget.com

Every woman must know her best to have the most success with the least stress! For help from the national leader in strengths-based business growth, visit www.whatyousayiswhatyouget.com and sign up for our free monthly positive leadership newsletter with practical tips to strengthen your success! Free articles, Dr. Bourget's full bio, and client list, testimonials PLUS 40 products to help you with more gain and less pain! Email us for small business consulting offerings.

---

Breakthrough Results, LLC
**Cathy A. Hansell, CCSR, MS, JD**
Executive Producer and Host, Safety Breakthrough Talk Radio
Email: chansell@breakthroughresults.org
Phone: 888-609-6723; 908-652-1366
Website: www.breakthroughresults.org

---

**Carmen Chandler**
Jewelry Designer
Email: chandler.creations@ymail.com
Phone: 281-380-2022

---

Victory House Publishing, LLC
**Carmen L Cook**
Email: CarmenCookOnline@gmail.com
Website: http://www.Facebook.com/SEODrivenFanPage
Ideal Client - Small to medium size companies.
Freebie - http://www.300Comments.com

---

**Chris Carter – Attorney**
Email: Cris@CrisCarterLaw.com
Website: www.CrisCarterLaw.com
Website: www.CrisCarterMVP.com
The legal and business advice your business needs at a price you can afford. Visit today and receive the audio "Your Guide on Hiring an Attorney"

**Traci Campbell**

Website: http://www.traciscampbell.com

Go to the contact page on www.traciscampbell.com and send us your email address and enter in code RAVEN10 in the subject line to receive a FREE audio and transcript as well as 20% discount on The C.H.A.M.P Within program!! (book and workbook)

**Barclay Fisher**

Email: barclayf527@gmail.com

Website: www.BarclayFisher.com

FaceBook: http://www.facebook.com/Barclayfisher

LinkedIn: http://www.linkedin.com/in/barclayfisher

Barclay Fisher will guide you or your company to the highest goals. You can change direction by deciding to remove the current obstacles in your path of development. Contact at Barclayfisher.com and receive a FREE 30 MINUTE coaching session. Do It Now!!

Creation Consulting Practice

**Dr. Venus Opal Reese**

10220 Nantucket Dr.

Providence, TX  76227

Email: dr.vor@drvenusopalreese.com

Phone: 214-551-9233

Website: http://www.drvenusopalreese.com  or www.defyimpossible.com

Facebook: http://www.facebook.com/drvenusopalreese

LinkedIn: http://www.linkedin.com/in/drvenusoreese

Twitter: www.twitter.com/dr_venusoreese

*For executives, entrepreneurs, CEOs and heart-centered agents of change who want to make BIG money, make a difference, be FULFILLED, and be PROUD of yourself—all at the same time! Visit* http://www.defyimpossible.com

Couch Talk Life Coaching

**Ashley Dais**

326 Kingsport Drive, NE

Concord, NC  28025

Email: couchtalklifecoaching@gmail.com

Phone: 704-619-7028
Website: www.ashleydais.com
Facebook: http://www.facebook.com/#!/CouchTalkLifeCoaching
Twitter: http://twitter.com/#!/AshleyDias

I am a counselor and life coach and I work with men and women who struggle with mental, emotional, and social roadblocks to help them become unstuck and break negative cycles. Do you or someone you know struggles with being stuck? I provide a FREE Planning Guide Session for those who are ready to get started to becoming free of their "stuck Syndrome!" Sign up at http://www.ashleydais.com

---

Confidence Connections
**Kathleen B Schulweis, CPCC, PCC**
Strategic Coaching for Success
Phone: 323-935-6477
Website: http://www.linkedin.com/in/confidenceconnections

Need a Confidence Boost? http://www.confidenceconnections.com for help and support!

---

**Mariana Cooper**
Website: www.trustyourahamoments.com
Website: www.ahamoments.tv
Facebook: www.facebook.com/ahamomentsinc

to get your free gifts to include the full audio of my sold out Teleseminar "GodWon't Deliver a Million Dollars into Chaos" includes a powerful guided meditation and the free transcript plus a subscription to the Aha! Moments Ezine with free tips, articles and info for Enlightened Entrepreneurs go to: www.trustyourahamoments.com

---

Creating Being Well
**Saskia Jennings-de Quaasteniet**
37 Silver Point Drive
Parry Sound, ON, Canada  P2A 2W8
Email: Saskia@creatingbeingwell.com
Phone: 705-773-8411
Website: www.creatingbeingwell.com

Saskia is the one for heart-centered support & guidance when YOU are ready to move forward in life: to feel better, happy, more balanced and open for inspiration, so you can easily manage your life's challenges. We will be Creating Being Well together! www.creatingbeingwell.com

---

**Dr. Sarah David, Ph.D.**
Email: sdavid@consultant.com

Visit www.empoweredwomensinstitute.com for a free report on the 7 Characteristics of Successful Entrepreneurs and an opportunity to take a free personal brand assessment, subscribe to the Empowered Women's Institute Newsletter for exciting upcoming announcements on pre-launch activities, training, networking and an opportunity to be a *Charter Member* as we launch our new online community to help you lead, learn and connect with other empowered women!

---

**Bill Davis**
Lifestyle Coach
Website: www.mydailydirector.com

---

Danise Peña Coaching & Consulting
**Danise Peña**
Email: danise@danisepena.com
Website: www.DanisePena.com
FaceBook: www.facebook.com/danisepenacoaching

Are you afraid to put yourself out there, professionally or in life? If it's too scary to do what you know you need to do to get what you want, or you're tired of having to grit your teeth and gut it out, I can help to ease the fears so you can take action. You might find taking action is fun! Please visit www.DanisePena.com for the opportunity to sign up for a complimentary consultation.

---

Debbie Luxton Coaching
**Debbie Luxton**
Email: dluxton@sbcglobal.net
Website: http://www.debbieluxton.com
FaceBook: http://www.facebook.com/truthforlifesjourney

LinkedIn: http://www.linkedin.com/in/coachdebluxton
Twitter http://www.twitter.com/CoachDebLuxton

Debbie offers a FREE Kit titled: **The Stress to Serenity Breakthrough Kit.**
Are you ready to put forth healthy boundaries, take control of your life, identify and correct self-sabotaging behaviors, eliminate feelings of guilt, shame or self-judgment, develop enriching spiritual practices, have a renewed sense of self-purpose? Then don't delay! Pick up your FREE Kit today.

---

Density Driven Radio
**Lorena Douglas**
Email: Rena@destinydrivenradio.com
Website: www.destinydrivenradio.com
phone # 704-918-5652
FaceBook: http://www.facebook.com/destinydrivenradio
LinkedIn: www.linkedin.com/destinydrivenradio
Twitter: www.twitter.com/destinydrivenradio

Destiny Driven Life Coaching
Discover Your God Given Destiny
Achieve Your Purpose In Life
Step Out On Faith
Find your Purpose + Density   first look inside
Yourself and wake the Sleeping Giant from within

To learn more and receive A Free Report download! Vital Tips in Finding Your Passion Bonus Plus Complementary 20 minutes coaching session visit www.destinydrivenradio.com

---

DGK Unlimited
**Dr. Dorine Kramer**
Email: drdorine@drdorinekramer.com
Website: www.drdorinekramer.com
FaceBook: http://www.facebook.com/Dr.Dorine
LinkedIn: www.linkedin.com/in/dorinekramer

Have you lost yourself in raising your children? Are you feeling alone, confused, irrelevant or useless because your children no longer require your full attention? If this sounds like you or someone you love and you are ready to reach out, please don't wait like I did. I would be honored to help. When you go to www.drdorinekramer.com you can sign up to receive your free Empty Nester Essentials Toolkit and schedule your complimentary **"From Being Mom to Being Me"** strategy session with me personally. I also offer individualized and group coaching programs, as well as VIP days, if I feel they are a good match for your needs.

---

Discover the Amazing YOU! Coaching
**Deb Scott**
PO Box 551
Newburyport, MA 01950
Email: deb@greenskyandbluegrass.com
Phone: 978-462-2215
Website: http://www.greenskyandbluegrass.com
Facebook: http://www.facebook.com/authorandmotivationalspeaker
LinkedIn: http://www.linkedin.com/in/debscottauthorspeaker
Twitter: http://www.twitter.com/@greenskydeb

If you want to be your best in Business or the business of Living - I can help you! Click here to get your FREE GIFT of three 30 minute Coaching sessions
http://www.greenskyandbluegrass.com/free-professional-coaching

---

Dreams Rock
**Joelle Niedecken**
Email: jniedecken@ameriplan.com
Phone: 877-303-4065  432-689-9447
Website: http://www.dreamsrock.com

Visit http://www.deliveringonthepromise.com/dreamsrock TODAY to receive your FREE prescription card valued at $100

---

Edwards & Associates
**Linda Howell Edwards**
PO Box 724051
Atlanta, GA 31139
Email: LEdwards@theedwardsgroup.org
Phone: 678-239-4479
Website: www.theedwardsgroup.org

---

Entrepreneur Success System
**Joseph DiChiara**
Email: Info@joedichiara.biz
Website: www.JoeDichiara.biz
Facebook: http://www.facebook.com/microbusinesspros?v=wall
LinkedIn: http://www.linkedin.com/profile/view?id=10471213&trk=tab_pro
Twitter: https://twitter.com/joedbizsuccess

The starting point to success is A Definite Chief Aim and will serve as the foundation of your business. This 3 part statement is invaluable and required for every one of my students going through my Wize Business Model. If you contact me at info@joedichiara.biz I will provide you with the worksheets and instructions for developing your own Definite Chief Aim. If you register on my site www.joedichiara.biz you can download my free report The Myths about Small Business Failure.

And last-if you act now-I will provide you with a free 45 minute Definite Chief Aim consultation to make sure you are on the road to success.

---

Femme Addiction Studios of Fitness
**Linda Doyle**
Email: femmeaddiction@yahoo.com
Website: www.femmeaddiction.com
FaceBook: http://www.facebook.com/lindadoyle

Linda Doyle, Femme Addiction Studios of Fitness
3405 SW College Road, Ocala, Fl.34474
352-361-0424
www.femmeaddiction.com  femmeaddiction@yahoo.com
Linda coaches women between the ages of 30-65 with virtual classes, group classes and VIP days. She has found this to format generates the most results.  She currently has Travel workouts, Chair Dance routines and Bridal Bootcamp available on her website.

---

Franklin Quest Education and Leadership Foundation, Inc.
**Tyra Franklin, MBA/PA**
*"Your destiny is hidden among your fears"*
Website: http://franklinquest.pbworks.com

---

Fyntoon Solutions
**Sheila McClain**
2000 W. Kettleman Lane Ste 201A
Lodi, CA  95242
Email:  fyntoon@yahoo.com
Phone:  209-712-2073
Website:  www.fyntoonsolutions.com
Facebook:  http://facebook.com/Sheila.McClain.CertifiedLifeCoach

Full Circle Service Center LLC
**Nancy Lee Bentley, Wholistic Health Expert**
Email:  Nancy@TrulyCultured.com
Website:  www.TrulyCultured.com
Pinterest:  http://www.pinterest.com/trulycultured
LinkedIn:  http://www.linkedin.com/profile/view?id=16731452&amp;trk=tab_pro
Twitter:  http://twitter.com/EatWrite4U

Interested in the deeper meanings and significances of the spotlight on 2012
that can help us build a new, healthier world for the future?  Read and watch
Nancy Lee's whole first hand story and share in the priceless  "no woo-woo" gifts,
lessons and insights she received on her unlikely Pilgrimage with the Mayan Elders across
America at 11.11.11 in her new book:  *Serpent Mound to Sedona, The Heart of the Mayan
Elder Crystal Skulls Journey* at www.SerpentMoundtoSedona.com

For a FREE 30-Minute "Full Circle" Coaching Session with Nancy Lee Bentley
please feel free to contact her at  Nancy@TrulyCultured.com
For More Information about our products and services, visit www.TrulyCultured.com

Fuller Life Concepts
**Kim Fuller**
Email:  kim@fullerlifeconcepts.com
Website:  www.fullerlifeconcepts.com
FaceBook:  http://www.facebook.com/pages/Fuller-Life-Concepts/186931154687947?ref=hl
LinkedIn:  www.linkedin.com/pub/kim-fuller/5/a31/291
Twitter:  https://twitter.com/KimFullerlife

Kim is a Life Coach and the owner of Fuller Life Concepts. Fuller Life Concepts provides life
coaching services to professional women who want to live a Fuller Life: Healthy, Focused, and
Fulfilling.  Her ideal client is a professional female who feels overwhelmed and wants to stay on
task, set realistic goals and accepts support with staying accountable.  She is ready to change.
Free CD on her ABCDs to Awareness and Free consultations can be obtained through her
website.

**Claudette Gadsden-Hrobak**
Email: Claudette@CoachClaudette.com
Website: www.CoachClaudette.com
FaceBook: www.facebook.com/Coach-Claudette
LinkedIn: www.linkedin.com/in/CoachClaudette
Twitter: www.twitter.com/CoachClaudette

Coach Claudette helps women and their daughters enjoy a better quality of life by uncovering and changing negative and limiting thoughts and beliefs to positive empowering life experiences. In short they learn to wallow in their beauty and their greatness.
Visit her website to opt in for her mailing list. You will receive periodic tips on being a more amazing you and free guided meditation tracks to help you start and end your day in gratitude.

**Ellen Gaver**
Email: EcoMomTeam@charter.net
Phone: 805.474.822
Website: http://www.EcoMomTeam.com

**Lou Giles**
Phone: 832-513-5916
Website: www.smartchoicelegal.com

Talking Health With Linda
**Linda Giles**
email: talkinghealthwithlinda@gmail.com
Website: www.ardysslife.com/lsgiles
Facebook: www.facebook.com/lindastanleygiles
LinkedIn: www.linkedin.com/in/lsgiles
Twitter:https://twitter.com/pamper1956

I challenge you to make a plan for your health. If you lack energy, need to lose weight, stop unhealthy habits, have any health issues, you owe it to yourself to make some changes to live your BEST life.

My idea client is someone who is looking for a healthy lifestyle. It does not matter the age - we have products for everyone. I offer a line of medical grade reshaping garments that lift, support and reshape the body, nutritional supplements, anti-aging skin care line, green cleaning products, and healthy cappuccinos with Omega 3 (heart/brain health), Collagen (skin/muscle), Weight Loss, Sweet Balance (glucose control), and a weight loss plan - Transform 90.  An appointment with me will change your life.

I provide free consultations, and offer discounts for repeat customers. All senior clients receive a senior discount.

---

Glow Life Coaching
**Anne Gordon**
2521 NW Coe Ct.
Bend, OR 97701
Email:  anne@glowlifecoaching.com
Phone:  541-306-4445
Website:  www.glowlifecoaching.com
Facebook:  www.fcebook.com/annegordonor
LinkedIn:  www.linkedin.com/pub/anne-gordon/23/848/7a5

Visit www.glowlifecoaching.com to sign up for her newsletter and blog.  You will be the first to hear about events, products and free stuff.  Plus, you will receive inspiring stores and tools to help you on your journey.

---

GOVtips.biz

**Doña Storey**
Email:  dona.storey@govtips.biz
Website:  www.govtips.biz
FaceBook: http://www.facebook.com/awyldfyre
LinkedIn: http://www.linkedin.com/profile/view?id=20222402&locale=en_US&trk=tya
Twitter: https://twitter.com/GOVtips

Visit GOVtips.biz for a free gift and information on how to successfully sell to the World's largest customer.

---

Great Small Business Advice
**Allison Babb**
Small Business Coach
Email: info@greatsmallbusinessadvice.com
Phone: 678-401-7948
Website:  www.GreatSmallBusinessAdvice.com

For a 1-hour audio on How to Attract More Clients, you can go to
www.greatsmallbusinessadvice.com/audio

---

Ground Level Consulting
**Christina Suter**
3579 E Foothill Blvd #320
Pasadena, CA  91107
Email:  Christina@groundlevel-consulting.com
Phone: 310-463-5942
Website: www.grourndlevel-consulting.com
LinkedIn: http://www.linkedin.com/in/christinalsmith

Let me help clarify what your business needs in a free initial consultation:  Fill in the Contact form on my website, mention "Kitchen Table" in your message and Opt In for the newsletter and access to the audio archives from Christina talk show "Ask Christina First" on the Amazing Woman of Power Network

---

Hair Dreams By Christal, Inc.
**Christal Mercier**
514 Texas Parkway, Suite A
Missouri City, Texas 77489
Email:  HairDreamsByChristalInc@yahoo.com
Phone: 877-499-9433
Website: www.HairDreamsbyChristal.org
LinkedIn: http://www.linkedin.com/pub/christal-mercier/20/238/8a5
Twitter: http://www.twitter.com/HairDreamsInc
We focus on women and children who suffer from various types of hair loss, due to cancer, alopecia, medication side-effects, etc. For a more detailed list of our services or to inquire about donating to our organization, please visit: http://www.hairdreamsbychristal.org

---

**Monica Hancock**
Window Fashions Designer
Email: mhancock@creationsbymonica.net
Phone: (281) 820-1977
Website: www.creationsbymonica.net

For ideas on window treatment designs, you can go to www.creationsbymonica.net

Harmony Harbor Hypnosis
**Angie Monko**
2476 Pheasant Run Drive
Maryland Heights, MO  63043
Email:  4monko@att.net
Phone:  314-422-6520
Website:  www.harmonyharbor.com
Facebook:  www.facebook.com/HarmonyHarborHypnosis
LinkedIn:  www.linkedin.com/in/harmonyharbor
Twitter:  www.twitter.com/angiemonko4monko@att.net

Visit http://www.harmonyharbor.com and get access to my free newsletter, Create Your Destiny, and free report on how to release weight forever without willpower.  You can also apply for a complementary coaching session!

Motivational Life Coaching
**Roberta Harris**
Motivational Speaking
Email: rdhartist@att.net
Phone: 713-256-9037
Website: www.robertaharris.com

Heir to Life, LLC
**Arris Charles**
11601 Shadow Creek Pkwy #317
Pearland, TX  77584
Email:  Arris@HeirToLife.com
Phone:  832-729-6317
Website:  www.HeirToLife.com
LinkedIn:  http://www.linkedin.com/in/heirtolife
Twitter:  CoachArris

Tired of just going through the motions? Ready to empower your mind, body and spirit to fulfill God's extraordinary calling for your life? Wondering how to balance your life on the inside and out? Visit http://www.InnerLifeFitness.com to download a free report to help you live with Authentic Life Balance.

Help 2 Grow Life Coaching
**MARTHA JOHNSON**
Phone:  678-949-9195
Website:  www.Help2GrowLifeCoaching.com
Help2GrowTalkRadio:  www.help2grow.podomatic.com

**NG KHAI SIUNG**

Email:  khai@aboutkhai.com
Website:  http://www.inspirationdna.com
FaceBook: http://facebook.com/khaisiung
Twitter:  http://www.twitter.com/khaing

Helping Families Improve, Inc
**Kingsley Grant**
Email:  kingsleyogrant@gmail.com
Website:  http://www.helpingothershope.com
FaceBook: https://www.facebook.com/kingsleygrant
LinkedIn: http://www.linkedin.com/in/kingsleygrant
Twitter: www.twitter.com/kinglsleygrant

Kingsley helps people break through those stuck feeling by teaching them how to map their way to a preferred state.

Holistic Wellness Consultant
**Beverly Basila, H.H.C., H.L.C., N.W.E., C.G.P.**
BeverlySmiles@aol.com
www.BeverlysHolisticWellness.com
Miami / Coral Gables, FL  33145
Email: BeverlySmiles@aol.com
Phone:  305- 442- 2987
Website: www.BeverlysHolisticWellness.com

Special Areas of Interest: Gluten Sensitivity, Celiac Disease, Delayed Onset Food Intolerances, GAPS Protocol (Gut & Psychology Syndrome)  Visit Beverly's website www.BeverlysHolisticWellness.com to view an extensive list of Recommended Books and Inspirational Quotes.

---

**Victor Holman**
Business Performance Coach
Email: victor.holman@lifecycle-performance-pros.com
Phone: 202-415-5363
Website: www.Lifecycle-Performance-Pros.com

To get a FREE BUSINESS MANAGEMENT KIT and jumpstart your business, go to www.Lifecycle-Performance-Pros.com

---

**Dr. Renee Hornbuckle**
Email: reneehornbuckle@sbcglobal.net
Website: www.reneehornbuckle.com

If you're already a Coach or you would like to become a client, you can learn more about the benefits of being a Compass Client/Coach. Visit www.mylifecompass.com/womenofinfluence to find out more and join my team as a client or become a Certified Compass Coach!

---

I Love My Life! Coaching
**Alanna Levenson**
13547 Ventura Blvd., #242,
Sherman Oaks, CA 91423
Email: Alanna@i-love-my-life.com
Phone: 213-400-7970
Website: http://i-love-my-life.com
Facebook: https://www.facebook.com/pages/I-Love-My-Life-Coaching/192310894122167
LinkedIn: http://www.linkedin.com/pub/alanna-levenson/0/3a0/7a0

---

Illuminated Life, LLC
**Melanie McGhee**
718 Hickory Lane
Maryville, TN 37801
Email: Melanie@peacefruit.com

Phone: 865-384-4104
Website: http://www.peacefruit.com
Facebook: http://www.facebook.com/peacefruit
Twitter: http://www.twitter.com/melaniemcghee

I provide small group retreats, private retreats, coaching and psychotherapy. Visit my site - http://www.peacefruit.com - when you opt-in, I will send you a free meditation recording along with regular encouragement and insights about how to create a more peace-filled life.

---

Impact Coaching LLC
**Susan Brown, Ed.S.**
Certified Leadership and Success Coach
Email: susanbrown.impactcoaching@gmail.com
Phone: 678-787-2406
Website: www.impactcoach.wordpress.com
Internet Radio Show: http://thewinonline.com/shows/awaken-the-leader

Take the first step in getting your personal leadership development plan by Contacting Susan for a free consultation at 678-787-2406 or log on to her website at www.impactcoach.wordpress.com.

Listen to Susan on *Awaken the Leader Within* found at: http://thewinonline.com/shows/awaken-the-leader

---

Inspired Learning Centers Canada Inc
**Rayna Bergerman**
56 Deermoss Cres. SE
Calgary, AB, Canada T2J 6P4
Email: Rayna@inspiremorestudents.com
Phone: 403-863-1939
Website: www.inspiremorestudents.com
Facebook: www.facebook.com/rayna.bergerman
LinkedIn: http://ca.linkedin.com/pub/rayna-bergerman/30/b7b/965
Twitter: www.twitter.com/raynabergerman

To grow a confident and capable learner download your FREE 7 Part Mini-Course focusing on action steps you can take right now to improve your child's academic and personal growth. Go to www.InspireMoreStudents.com

International Gift Express
**Carol Newman**
A Gift of Excellence
Phone:  415-381-5252
Website:  www.vernoncompany.com/newman.htm

Intuitive Healing
**Kimberly Sherry**
kim@kimberlysherry.com
http://www.hearts-expanding-allow-love.com
FaceBook: https://www.facebook.com/KimberlyCampbellSherry

As an International Energetic Healer, Seer, and Spiritual Advisor, I help conscious women break through their sabotaging thoughts and fears to unleash their entrepreneurial genius to the world and stop wasting their time and money.

To discover how to stop the hemorrhaging of over-giving and open the channels to receiving all you desire, visit my website and opt-in for your free video: "5 Magic Minutes".

IWin, Inc.
**Bonny Valentine**
bonnye@everwinning.org
www.everwinning.org
FaceBook: http://www.facebook.com/everwinning.org
P.O.Box 574
Salisbury,NC 28144
704-754-6690 Business
bonnye@everwinning.org
www.everwinning.org

I offer Life Coaching consulting for those whom are interested in finding out what they are called to do in this world.  Freebie: 30minute consultation with an applicable tool to use to get started.

Liberated Life Coaching
**Criss Ittermann**
Life & Small Business Coach
Email: info@liberatedlifecoaching.com
Phone: 866-993-8932
Website: LiberatedLifeCoaching.com

For an exclusive 60 minute free audio called "SURRENDER™ to Passion" please visit www.revx.me/table

---

JJ the Life Coach
**JJ Frederickson**
PO Box 113
Honey Creek, WI 53138
Email: JJ@JJthelifecoach.com
Phone: 414-732-3320
Website: http://www.jjthelifecoach.com
Facebook: http://www.facebook.com/jjthelifecoach
LinkedIn: http://www.linkedin.com/in/jjthelifecoach
Twitter: http://twitter.com/jjthelifecoach

The first half of life you're on the treadmill, maybe managing a household, forging a career, or both. As a mid-lifer, things should be easier. You worked hard to get where you are, and now you're ready for some fun. But you're still on the treadmill and can't seem to get off. Why? For years, stress and fear did a tango in your brain -- a tango that's created mental patterns and habits that hold you back and keep joy at arm's length. JJ the Life Coach can help you take back your brain and take back your life! JJ takes people from midlife stress to their midlife best. She coaches and teaches mid-lifers how to tackle stress in their jobs, relationships, blended families, finances, and retirement. She is the creator of Live Life Easy Stress Solution DVD and Workbook, and as WTMJ's original Life Coaching Expert, her weekly TV segment gave viewer tips on how to get out of their heads and start living life easy! Want less stress, right now? Sign up for the free 90-Second Trick to Stop Stress in its Tracks at www.JJtheLifeCoach.com

---

**Jean Jones**
2601 Cartwright Rd Suite D259
Missouri City, TX 77459
Email: jaepolk4@aol.com
Phone: 281-702-220

Email Jean for more on free products for you as an Arbonne pamper hostess, free spa day and new consultant training as well as Holiday Specials and free gift wrapping!

---

JSYI a Division of Right On Enterprises
**Deborah Bishop**
414 Munn Rd.
Nashville, TN 37214
Email:  livealimitlesslife@gmail.com
Phone:  615-376-9905  /  800-582-8772
Website:  http://www.deborahbishop.com
Facebook:  http://www.facebook.com/deborahbishop

Your Personal Solution to Professional Success.
Whether you are starting up or starting over, discover how you can stop struggling and start thriving today.  Schedule your FREE one-on-one Consultation now at http://www.deborabishop.com

---

Joy Centered Life
**Gwen Lepard**
gwen@joyfullivingradio.com
www.joyfullivingradio.com
FaceBook: http://www.facebook.com/gwen.lepard
LinkedIn: http://joyfullivingradio.com/linkedIn
Twitter https://twitter.com/gwenlepard

Creator of the "Be the Sun, 3 Keys to Joy" and the Quantum Joy Experience, Gwen Lepard helps divorced women who have been victims of verbal abuse and suffer from anxiety, fear, shame and loss of self-esteem heal, recover and rediscover their joy.

Join Gwen weekly on the Amazing Women of Power Network, Tuesdays at 10 AM Pacific for Joyful Living Radio, Empowering Women Through Joy.

Go to www.joyfullivingradio.com to receive access to no cost Hypnosis mp3s to relieve pain, eliminate anxiety and help you sleep better, so you can live a more joyful life!

---

Kim L. Miles, LLC
**Kim L. Miles**
3931 S Jebel Way
Aurora, CO 80013
Email: kim@kimlmiles.com
Phone: 303-690-7661
Website: http://www.kimlmiles.com
Facebook:http://www.facebook.com/media/set/?set=a.2256864113100.118499.1593278215&saved#!/CoachKimMiles
LinkedIn: Kim Miles (ACC)
Twitter: Kim_Miles

Sign up for my newsletter and a 30 minute complimentary phone coaching session via http://www.kimlmiles.com

---

**Kimber King**
Email: Kimber_king@msn.com
Phone: 801-923-8744
Website: www.kimberking.com

Kimber King is an expert in Social Networking and what it takes to make money from home using the internet. Visit www.kimberking.com for a FREE 30 minute recording that you will learn 4 simple steps you can start using right now to turn your "play-time" on Social Networking sites like FaceBook and Twitter into profits!

---

**Sandhan**
sandhaninc@gmail.com
KISS
www.thrillbootcamp.com
FaceBook: http://http://www.facebook.com/sandhancoaching

---

LDRA Performance Consultants, Inc.
**Linda Adams**
PO Box 12119
Baltimore, MD 21281
Email: linda@letschataboutcredit.com
Phone: 888-592-4512

Website: www.letschataboutcredit.com
Twitter: www.twitter.com/credittweet

Our 52 week online Personal Credit Builder Program is designed to guide you through the conflicting information out there on how to improve your credit. We help you create a strong foundation so that you will be able to build and maintain your good credit. Credit education is for everyone. Because Identity Theft is a rising threat to everyone's good credit you can e-mail me for a free special report on Identity Theft and a short training video on how to get your free credit report from www.AnnualCreditReport.com.

---

**Diane Lampe**
Entrepreneur and mentor, best-selling author
Email: diane@lampeteam.com
Phone: 972-670-7691
Website: www.lampeteam.com

For how to create a business helping protect families or to view our services, you can go to www.lampeteam.com

---

Learning RX
**Clara M. Samuelson**
Phone: 832.886.5878
Website: www.learningrx.com/sugerland

---

**Diamond Leone**
Creative Coach
Email: diamondleone@gmail.com
Phone: 703-209-9012
Website: www.DiamondLeone.com

To get a free guide to help you discover what you're passionate about, go to www.diamondleone.com/passion

---

**Anne-Marie Lerch**
Business Strategist & Mindset Coach
Email: info@CoachMeNow.com
Phone: 1-877-83-SMILE (76453)
Website: www.CoachMeNow.com

for a free Audio Summary of "Think and Grow Rich" go to www.CoachMeNow.com

---

**NG KHAI SIUNG**
khai@aboutkhai.com
http://www.inspirationaldna.com
FaceBook: http://facebook.com/khaisiung
Twitter: http://www.twitter.com/khaing

---

**Honey Leveen, LUTCF, CLTC**
Your LTC Insurance Specialist LLC
Phone: 713-988-4671
Website: www.honeyleveen.com

---

Lesley A. Sive, Tax Consulting
**Leslie Sive**
info@lesleysivetaxconsulting.com
www.lesleysivetaxconsulting.com
FaceBook: https://www.facebook.com/pages/Lesley-A-Sive-Tax-Consulting/180243202054162
LinkedIn: http://www.linkedin.com/profile/view?id=91080392&trk=tab_pro

Through her representation, Lesley takes the pain and weight off individuals and business in dealing with their federal and state tax issues. Her expertise includes protecting her clients from federal and state tax collection action, determining the best resolution of their tax issues, setting up the resolution with the IRS or state, releasing levies and liens, representing clients on appeal and handling audits. She also works on preventing tax problems through education and public speaking.

---

Life Arena Coaching
**Lynn Doxon**
4005 Tara NE
Albuquerque, NM 87111

Email: lynn@lifeareanacoaching.com
Phone: 505-459-3597
Website: www.lifearenacoach.com
Facebook: http://www.facebook.com/home.php#!/pages/Life-Arena-Retirement-Coaching/231602116866331
LinkedIn: https://www.linkedin.com/e/fpf/37456703
Twitter: @lynndoxon

I am eager to work with anyone who is retired or will soon retire to create a vision and plan for the next 5 to 30 years. Bring vision, energy and direction to your retirement years. To discover the best second career to support your retirement goals go to www.lifearenacoach.com

---

Life By Design Coaching/Results Consulting
**Dr. Lisabeth Saunders Medlock**
4420 Mimosa Rd
Columbia, SC 29205
Email: lbdcoaching@aol.com
Phone: 803-960-1844
Website: www.lifebydesigncoaching.org
Facebook: http://www.facebook.com/#!/pages/Life-By-Design-Coaching/181753829028
LinkedIn: http://www.linkedin.com/pub/lisbeth-saunders-medlock/8/bb7/7b6
Twitter: http://twitter.com/#!/lbdcoaching

At Life By Design Coaching I offer individual coaching, workshops, group and individual assessments and a range of consulting services. I focus on personal accountability-the belief that you are in control of your life and the decisions you make that shape your life and create your path. You design your life!

Our coaching company, located in Columbia, SC, focuses on assisting you to redesign, revitalize and redirect your life to achieve your goals and dreams. We address the gap between what is and what can be. Having a life coach is like having a personal trainer to help you reach your life goals.

We specialize in helping clients who seek coaching during a period of transition. You may be feeling stuck, facing difficult decisions, wanting to improve your health and wellness, changing careers, or going through relationship issues.

Life coaching can help you turn life's challenges into a springboard for new beginnings. Instead of just coping and "getting through it", you will begin to see new options and new opportunities to actively live by design, not default. I offer a FREE half hour coaching session and am often running special packages. Check out www.lifebydesigncoaching.org to sign up for a free session and to learn more about the services. The website also includes free life coaching tip of the week videos.

---

Life Career Business Coach
**Dr. Fred (Coach Doc Fred) Simkovsky**
3076 Paige Ave.
Simi Valley, CA 93063
Email: fredsimkovsky@yahoo.com
Phone: 510-506-8281
Website: http://www.lifecareerbusinesscoach.com
Facebook: http://www.facebook.com/fsimkovsky
LinkedIn: http://www.linkedin.com/in/fredsimkovsky

Self-employed people, Under-employed people, Unemployed people who want to become successful in their lives and careers. I provide individualized coaching, simple conversation, an action plan, and support. Group coaching and mentoring. Training and Development. Sign up for my monthly free newsletter for on-going encouragement and advice at my website; http://www.lifecareerbusinesscoach.com

---

Life Coaching World Wide
**Kristen L. Baker**
2 Waterview Circle
Litchfield, NH 03052
Email: lifecoachbaker@aol.com
Phone: 603-204-9728
Website: http://www.lifecoachingworldwide.com
Facebook: http://www.facebook.com/pages/Life-Coaching-World-Wide-Where-Your-Dreams-Become-A-Reality/169934022691

My services include: Life Coaching and Wellness Coaching. I coach in all areas of life, anxiety disorders, fears, phobias, and self-esteem, confidence building, career, chronic pain and WHOLE Life Coaching. Visit www.lifecoachingworldwide.com to opt in to receive 6 modules to unstoppable confidence.

---

Live and Love Richly, LLC
**Leslie Cunningham**

7781 Nez Pierce Drive
Bozeman, MT 59715
Email: leslie@financialdating.com
Phone: 406-586-5561
Website: www.financialdating.com

Visit Leslie's web site, http://www.FinancialDating.com for free articles, free resources and to get her free report, "15 Financial Mistakes Most Couples Make and how YOU can successfully avoid them (written especially for married women entrepreneurs). And take the next steps to create more time and money in your business, marriage and life

---

**Laura Lopez**
Email: Laura@Laura-Lopez.com
Phone: 713.828.8829
Website: http://womenspeakerswhorock.com/
Website: www.Laura-Lopez.com
Twitter: www.twitter.com/connectedleader
Blog: www.LauraLopezBlog.com

Become a better leader and achieve stronger results through others! Download your free e-workbook by Laura Lopez to help you assess and plan your approach to becoming a connected and committed leader. http://www.laura-lopez.com/Assets/Free_CCL_Eworkbook.pdf

---

Lynn Crocker Coaching
**Lynn Crocker**
Lynn@lynncrockercoaching.com
www.lynncrockercoaching.com
FaceBook: www.lynncrockercoaching.com

I assist people with becoming unstuck and introduce them to the tools they need to move forward to create the lives they desire. I provide a safe environment, am a sounding board for new ideas, and assist my clients with finding their direction in times of confusion. I support them with moving beyond the safety of what a they know and expand their thinking process. Visit my website at lynncrockercoaching.com to sign up for a free 30-minute phone consultation.

---

Mable Cannings Intl
**Mable Cannings**

936-652-7801
mable@unleashyourpotentialradio.com
www.unleashyourpotentialradio.com
http://facebook.com/mablecannings
http://linkedin.com/mablecannings
http://twitter.com/mablecannings

Mable Cannings International is a personal development and marketing company providing:

* Personal Individualized Coaching
* Business Startup coaching & consultation
* Business Seminars
* Business marketing Plans and support
* Business branding and image packages, logos, brochures, website content, other presentation and sales materials
* Research and development of funding proposals for nonprofit organizations
* Fundraising support
* Full special events production and promotion company

Aspiring entrepreneurs who have a dream and are motivated to take action; willingness to follow instruction; and are ready to leap into 2013!
Call Mable Cannings @ 1-936-652-7801 for a FREE CONSULTATION

Receive my FREE Report:  20 Soulful Questions Aspiring Entrepreneurs Should Ask Before Venturing into Business. Free at www.unleashyourpoentialradio.com

---

**Deborah Madison**
Phone:  713.208.9622   888.298.1888
Website:  www.prepaidlegal.com/hub/dmadison and www.greatworkplan.com

---

**Marcia Merrill,**
AKA, The Transition Chick
Marketing Coach-Guerrilla Marketing, Career/ Life Transitions Coach
Website:  www.eCareerCorner.com
Please visit my web site & sign up for your FREE Transition Triumph Toolkit! And get my newsletter as a Bonus!  Contains valuable information, resources & special discounts!

---

Make The Impossible Possible
**Faye Kitariev**
coach_faye@me.com
www.fayekitariev.com
FaceBook: http://www.facebook.com/faye.kitariev
LinkedIn: http://www.linkedin.com/profile/view?id=62879867&trk=tab_pro

Faye Kitariev is available for one on one performance or transformation coaching, using unique tools and techniques of performance and spiritual psychology, to bring forward lasting change in all areas of your life. She also conducts workshops, and targeted group seminars. For FREE consultation, or an upcoming high power event, please visit her website at www.fayekitariev.com

---

**Mari Mitchell Porter, CPC**
http://www.lifecoachmari.com
mari@lifecoachmari.com
http://lifecoachmari.com
FaceBook: http://www.facebook.com/mari.mitchellporter?ref=tn_tnmn
Twitter: https://twitter.com/coachmariporter

If you yearn for joyful and fulfilling relationships, if you know it's time to follow your passion. If you're ready for more in your life, contact me for your free, no obligation initial session and find out if I am the right coach for you. lifecoachmari.com  954 243-7297

---

Martha Lask Consulting
**Martha Lask**
120 West Mt. Airy Avenue
Philadelphia, PA  19119
Email:  Martha@marthalask.com
Phone:  215-247-1740
Website:  www.marthalask.com
Blog:  http://www.marthalask-blog.com

Martha Lask Consulting provides customized consulting and coaching services to leaders, sole proprietors, management teams and staff in the non-profit and corporate sectors.  She encourages thoughtful, compassionate communication as she helps her clients shape possibilities and transform challenges into desired outcomes. Click here for free pdf resources about compassionate communication and a story about a "creative journey."
To see Martha's Blog:  http://www.marthalask-blog.com/
To see Martha's Artwork:
http://www.marthalask.com/about/MarthaLask.html#holidaycardarchive

---

Mastro Holistic Consulting
**Louise Mastromarino**
distantholistic@gmail.com
www.distantholistic.com
FaceBook: http://www.facebook.com/#!/louisa.mastromarino
LinkedIn: http://www.linkedin.com/profile/edit?trk=tab_pro

Mastro Holistic Consulting and its divisions offer holistic medicine, career coaching and spiritual development programs, distant services worldwide, resume writing, biofeedback, animal communication and holistic support, intuitive consulting, mediumship programs and training, quantum healing applications, and energy coaching for homes and persons. Stress management, pain management, and relaxation is the primary focus of all sessions. The service's ideal client is one who is courteous and open to new understandings of how health can be influenced by the mind, body, spirit connection. First time clients receive a free 5 X 7 original art design with the purchase of any service. Just mention this publication.

---

"The Millionaire Mentor"
**Paul McCormick**
Phone: 866.333.0852
Website: theauthenticmillionaire.com

---

Michelle DeBerge Life Coach
**Michelle DeBerge**
michelledeberge@me.com
http://www.MichelleDeBerge.com
FaceBook: http://www.Facebook.com/MichelleDeBerge-LifeCoach
LinkedIn: http://www.Linkedin.com/MichelleDeBerge
Twitter http://www.twitter.com/MichelleDeBerge

Contact Michelle now to receive a complimentary Personal Strategy Session. She will assess your current direction in your life or business, identify your obstacles, and present a strategy to clear your blockages and begin moving you forward at an accelerated pace. She'll also provide tips that you can start using right away! Sessions are done via phone or live video chat.

---

Misa Leonessa Life Coaching
**Misa Leonessa Garavaglia**
6350 Wright St.
Felton, CA 95018
Email: inspire@misacoach.com
Phone: 831-335-1265

Website: http://www.misacoach.com
Facebook: http://www.facebook.com/pages/Misa-Leonessa-Life_coaching/196486313059
LinkedIn: http://www.linkedin.com/pub/misa-garavaglia/b/582/259
Twitter: http://twitter.com/#!/misaleonessa

Are you ready to move from survival into a thriving life? Then it could be time to work with Misa to leave that forest of mediocrity and become the person you KNOW you were meant to be. Misa can help you to have healthier, more intimate relationships, live from your authentic self, be inspired by your future instead of driven by your past, and grow a deeper spiritual life. As a Life Coach and Spiritual Director, Misa has superb listening skills, creates a safe environment for honest reflection, offers strong support and encouragement, draws out solutions from her clients, and is a creative option generator. In addition to one on one and group coaching and spiritual direction, Misa also offers classes, workshops, and seminars and is a 5 star rated speaker. Selecting the right coach or spiritual director is important. Sign up for her newsletter and Misa will give you 2 free sessions to jump start your journey into the authentic you and makes a FULL guarantee of her services or your money back! Visit her website to learn more about coaching, spiritual direction, and classes being offered. www.misacoach.com

Motivational Mastermind
**Sherry Prindle**
601 E Highland Ave
St. Joseph, MO 64505
Email: sherry@motivationalmastermind.com
Phone: 817-657-5301
Website: www.motivationalmastermind.com
Facebook: http://www.facebook.com/MotivationalMastermind
LinkedIn: www.linkedin.com/in/SherryPrindle
Twitter: www.twitter.com/sherryprindle

Have you always wanted to help people? Do you have an idea for making the world a better place? What if you could earn a living following your dream changing lives? Go to www.MotivationalMastermind.com and click "How Can I Make Money Changing Lives" for a free profitability analysis and mini-marketing plan with starter steps for your idea.

MONA-VIE
**Ruth Van Buren**
Phone: 702.437.4900  cell 702.354.4900

Website: mymonavie.com/ruth

"Drink it! Feel it! Share it!"

---

My Kick Ass Coach

**Vicki Garcia**

1726 Hogar Dr.

San Jose, CA 95124

Email: Vicki@mykickasscoach.com

Phone: 408-723-5290

Website: http://www.mykickasscoach.com

Facebook: http://www.facebook.com/mykickasscoach

LinkedIn: http://www.linkedin.com/profile/view?id=18437827&trk=tab_pro

Twitter: www.twitter.com/mykickasscoach

If you are a professional who wants to do away with self-sabotaging thoughts and behaviors, download Success Killers, my free e-book or sign up for your Daily Kick in the Ass at http://mykickasscoach.com

---

**Myanda Solutions**

**Shaun Stephenson**

Community Wealth Building

Speaking Engagements

Special Events & Programs

Inspiration and Collaboration

Life/Self-Empowerment Coaching

The Circle of Ten Movement

Email: Shaun6@comcast.net

Phone: 609-560-8370

Website: www.shaunstephenson.com

Website: http://thecircleoften.com

---

My Heart Ties & Apple Creative Group

**Leah Humphries**

Entrepreneur & President

Email: leah@applecreativegroup.com

Phone: 814-833-1950 / 814-746-6325

Website:  www.applecreativegroup.com
Website:  www.myheartties.com

---

Nancy Alert & Associates, LLC
**Nancy Alert**
6226 Old Dominion Dr.
McLean, VA  22101
Email:  nancy@nancyalert.com
Phone:  703-861-7355
Website:  http://www.nancyalert.com
Facebook:  www.facebook.com/AllAboutArlington
LinkedIn:  www.linkedin.com/in/NancyAlert
Twitter:  www.Twitter.com/NancyAlert

Nancy is licensed in Virginia, Washington DC and Maryland in addition to selling new construction nationally and internationally.  Nancy is one of the few agents in the area who literally lists your home in the specific city, state and or countries where the buyers for your home are.  We live and do business in a global economy; it's NOW time for you to hire a global agent with the personal touch, NOT just a local agent!  Nancy teaches classes on how to invest in real estate, how to purchase or sale your home as a short sales, business development and social media.  Nancy has had featured articles in March 2010 issue of Black Enterprise Magazine, July 2010 issue of Commonwealth Magazine (a real estate magazine) and she has written an article for DocuSign.com.

If you are selling your condo or house, downsizing, or looking for a home call Nancy Alert, Nancy specializes in Condos and single family homes in Arlington, Alexandria, McLean, Great Falls, Washington DC, Bethesda, Potomac and National Harbor.  Nancy Alert can get you the condo or home you desire or sell yours fast, Nancy Alert knows how to write a winning contract in the market.  With an Arlington, McLean, Washington DC life style you are close to metro, close to shopping and close to the action call Nancy Alert at 703-861-7355 or visit Nancy online at www.NancyAlert.com because you need a specialist in this Real Estate Market!

All buyers or sellers who register online for my Weekend Events Calendar and enrolled in My Customer Sweepstakes promotion will receive a chance to in a $250.00 Visa Gift Card once a month.  Buyers and sellers who mention Careers from the Kitchen Table and use me as their agent will receive a $1000 credit at settlement towards closing cost and credit.

---

Neu World Designs
**Carol Neu**

carol@neuworlddesigns.com
http://www.neuworlddesigns.com
FaceBook: https://www.facebook.com/CarolLNeu
LinkedIn: http://www.linkedin.com/pub/carol-neu/9/702/383
Twitter https://twitter.com/Emailvideos

Neu World Designs  Your answer to all your graphic needs.  Affordable logos, banners, templates, websites and more.

---

NJ Home Staging and Redesign
**Angela Gagauf**
Email: a@njhomestagingandredesign.com
Phone:  201-317-9072

To learn more about NJ Home Staging and Redesign and to receive our free report, "The Top 10 Mistakes to Avoid When Showing Your Home", visit our website at www.njhomestagingandredesign.com

---

New Paradise Publishing
**Huesan Tran**
Info@HuesanTran.com
www.HuesanTran.com
FaceBook: www.Facebook.com/HuesanTran

1001 Fremont Ave. #633
South Pasadena, CA 91031 USA
888-846-8936

Dr. Huesan Tran integrates spirituality in business, finance and economics and teaches financial healing and energy healing topics.  She offers financial & wealth management services for conscious leaders, business owners and professionals to transform the old paradigm to a New Financial Paradise to live their passion, purpose and mission to make a difference in the world even if they don't like finances.  Her services include:

- Financial & wealth strategies
- IRA/401k & retirement plans
- Business/estate/charitable Planning
- Business and leadership advisory

- Courses and seminars on:
    - o The Meridian Of God™
    - o New Financial Paradigm™ & The New Wealth Model™
    - o Energy healing
    - o Spiritual & economic development
- Speaking & media appearances

Visit www.HuesanTran.com for a Divine Gift and a Free audio on Financial Healing.

---

Numis Network
**Mark Perkett**
Email: marekperk@cox.net
Phone: 949-212-2682
Website: http://www.perksprofits.com

---

**Sheila Pearl**
Life Coach & Speaker
Email: info@LifeCoachSheila.com
Phone: 201-303-5990
Website: www.SheilaPearl.com

For "3 Magic Tips for Feeling Good NOW", go to
www.LifeCoachSheila.com/3tips  For a 30-min. Discovery Conversation, call Sheila

---

**Elizabeth Gilmour**
Master Pilates Practitioner
Email: 281-890-3777
Phone: lissa@pilatesofchampions.com
Website: www.PilatesofChampions.com

Call or write today for an appointment to discuss how the *Pilates of Champions Experience* can work for you.

---

New World Visions International
**Tanya Jones**
5 Ariel Court
Placitas, New Mexico
Email: drtanyaheals@gmail.com
Phone: 404-895-9552 or 505-895-9552
Website: www.tanyajonesmd.com
Facebook: https://www.facebook.com/#!/profile.php?id=690708895
LinkedIn: http://www.linkedin.com/pub/tanya-jones-md/3/114/549
Twitter: www.twitter.com/#!/DrTanya

OnlineBusinessManager.com
**Tina Forsyth**
Box 29016
2515 Highlands Rd W.
Lethbridge, AB, Canada T1J 4Y2
Email: tina@onlinebusinessmanager.com
Phone: 877-576-2229
Website: www.onlinebusinessmanager.com
Facebook: www.facebook.com/tinaobm
LinkedIn: http://www.linkedin.com/in/tinaforsyth
Twitter: www.twitter.com/tinaforsyth

If you are an entrepreneur ready to take your business to the next level I invite you to get your copy of the Free Report: 100+ Ways that an Online Business Manager can Help Boost Business at www.OnlineBusinessManager.com

Outstanding Virtual Assistance
**Peggy Knudson**
Phone: 907-731-5758
Website: http://www.outstandingvirtualassistance.com
Facebook: http://www.facebook.com/#!/ovapeggy
LinkedIn: http://www.linkedin.com/in/ovapeg
Twitter: @ovapeg

Isn't it time you take your business to the next level?
Call for your free, no obligation consultation today!

Oxyfresh Worldwide, Inc.
**Anne M. Duffy**
12233 Pine Valley Club Dr.
Charlotte, NC  28277
Email:  Aduff2@aol.com
Phone:  704-953-0261
Website:  www.oxyfresh.com/anneduffy
Facebook:  Anne Linesch Duffy
LinkedIn:  http://linkdin/AnneDuffy

---

PINGUIORIS AETERNA SOLUTIONS
**El Ha Gahn**
elhagahn@yahoo.com
http://bit.ly/Tlf6hn
FaceBook: https://www.facebook.com/elhagahn

Holistic lifestyle education, life coach, artistic training, personal development strategies
curriculum development, Holistic Program Consultant, workshops, lectures, seminar series

---

Pinnacle Process Solutions, Intl., LLC
**Adil F. Dalal**
www.pinnacleprocess.com
FaceBook: http://facebook.com/Process-Solutions/365122546848539
LinkedIn: http://www.linkedin.com/company/pinnacle-process-solutions-intl-
Twitter: https://twitter.com/#!/PinnacleProcess

---

Practical Assistive Technology Solutions
**Phyl T. Macomber {and Rob}**
Phone:  802.484.3537
Website:  www.practicalatsolutions.com

---

Rimi and Company
**Michelle Peavy**
7251 Topping Rd
Mississauga, Ontario, Canada L4T 2Y6
Email:  michelle@rimipv.com

Phone: 877-643-6254

Website: www.michellepeavy.com

Facebook: http://www.facebook.com/reqs.php?type=1#!/michelle.peavy

LinkedIn: http://www.linkedin.com/pub/michelle-peavy/0/23a/3b4

Twitter: @michellepeavy

---

**Caterina Rando, MA, MCC**

Business strategist, master coach, speaker & publisher

Author of *Learn to Power Think*

Phone: 415 668-4535

Email: cat@attractclientswithease.com

Website: http://www.attractclientswithease.com

Website: http://www.powerdynamicspub.com

Website: http://www.caterinaspeaks.com

Call or email Caterina and mention this book to receive a $200.00 discount on any coaching course or book publication project.

---

**Helen Racz**

Teacher of Vibrational Law, Speaker, Energy Healer and CieAura Founding Master Retailer.

Phone: 281-578-7949

Email: helenracz@comcast.net

Website: www.HelenRacz.com

For free resources to support entrepreneurs with releasing limiting beliefs and energetic blocks to prosperity, go to www.HelenRacz.com/cieaura

---

Rapid Business Building

**Christina Scheiner**, the Massive Income Mentor

Email: info@rapidbusinessbuilding.com

Phone: (415) 897-7001

For the free Ebook, Rapid Building Building NOW !!!, go to:

www.RapidBusinessBuildingNOW.com

---

**Dawn Rickabaugh, Broker**
Owner Financing Coach
Note Queen / Rickabaugh Realty
Phone: 626.292.1875
Fax: 626.451.0454
Website: www.NoteQueen.com
Download your free copy of my book, "Seller Financing on Steroids"

---

**Mary Rives**
Energetics of Health and Wellness
Website: www.energeticsofhealthandwellness.com

---

RM Creations
**Renee and Major Jones**
Phone: 713.443.3748  281.880.8668
Website: www.rmcreations.com

---

**Joe Louis Burroughs**
ROA 4G Business Group, LLC
www.investinyoutalkradio.com

---

**Robert "Rosie" and Vikki "Taylor" Rosenkranz**
Vikki Cummings-Rosenkranz, Internationally Certified Energy Wellness Consultant
Email: Rosenkranz@EarthPatriot.net
Phone: 713.298.5808  281.770.7092
Website: www.EarthPatriot.Net
Website: www.EarthPatriot.Info (catalog and income opportunity page)

---

SBS
**Susan Bock**
8201 Newman Ave. Ste 102
Huntington Beach, CA 92647
Email: susan@susanbock.com
Phone: 714-847-1566

Website: www.susanbock.com
Facebook: http://www.facebook.com/susanbock
LinkedIn: www.linkedin.com/in/susanbockcoachandspeaker
Twitter: www.twitter.com/susanbockspeaks

Susan Bock Transformational Speaker and Coach.   Visit her website and download free resources - such a Learn to Build Your Self-Muscles or Are YOU Stuck in a Rut?

---

SC Health Solutions
**Sharon Cadle,** CEO/Founder
Website: www.LeSharonbeautiboutique.com

---

Second Time Around
**Lorraine Edey, PhD, LCSW, ACC**
PO Box 1779
Jasper, GA  30143
Email: loridey@aol.com
Phone: 678-454-1272
Website: www.secondtimearoundlove.com
Facebook: http://www.facebook.com/lorraine.edey
LinkedIn: http://www.linkedin.com/in/lorraineedey

Second Time Around Love believes that couples who are married for the second time can escape the pain of yet another divorce by learning to thrive and enjoy passionate, intimate, loving lives together.

You bring history, knowledge and the joy of your new love – and we provide guidance, inspiration and passionate recipes for extraordinary relationships and the marriage of your dreams.

Dr. Lorraine Edey is a Certified Imago Therapist and Relationship Coach whose experience in psychology, social work and relationship building spans more than 30 years. Her innovative 10 step process is a full proof method that helped couples in their 40's and 50's attain the next level of marriage mastery and enjoy a new love mindset.

You can contact Dr. Edey for a no cost strategy session. Secxaroundlove@aol.com

---

Strategy Stream
**Ruby Renshaw**
ruby@strategystream.com
https://www.strategystream.com
FaceBook: https://www.facebook.com/StrategyStream

Visit http://strategystream.com to sign up for free transformative business tips and frequent discount codes delivered directly to your email inbox!

---

Synergy Breakthroughs
**Sandra Tucker Jones**
1660 Liege Dr.
Henderson, NV 89012
Email: synergybreakthroughs@gmail.com
Phone: 303-400-8875
Website: www.synergybreakthroughs.com
Facebook: http://www.facebook.com/sandytjones
LinkedIn: http://www.linkedin.com/pubs/sandy-jones/4/231/206

Go to www.SynergyBreakthroughs.com to discover more about life coaching and hypnotherapy, and to receive your free Vision Board Screensaver!

---

The Top Producer Group, LLC
**Carol Mazur**
8722 New Forest Drive
Wilmington, NC 28411
Email: coachcarolmazur@gmail.com
Phone: 910-681-1110
Website: www.thetopprotraining.com
Facebook: http://www.facebook.com/RECoaching
LinkedIn: http://www.linkedin.com/in/carolmazur

The Top Producer Group, LLC offers affordable real estate coaching membership options, giving EVERY agent access to personalized one on one real estate coaching and training. Our Integrity Rule ensures that everything we share has been tested and proven to work by current top producers. Visit http://www.TheTopProducerGroup.com for FREE Coaching Tips.

---

A Southern Voice for Bold Self-Expression
**Tuck Self, The Rebel Belle**
Email: Tuck@TheRebelBelle.com
Phone: (803)736-9240
Website: www.therebelbelle.com
Grab a copy of my free e-guide!
If you are ready to liberate yourself from past conditioning, contact Tuck at (803) 736-9240 or Tuck@therebelbelle.com

---

**Lori Snyder**
Phone: 516-708-9261
Website: www.coachlorisnyder.com

Would you like to get a fresh start towards empowering yourself? During this six week e-course, you will discover, explore and create a whole new outlook to start building your best life. You will also learn powerful new tools that you can use to make the best decisions and choices to become truly happy and successful in every area of your life.
GO to www.Coachlorisnyder.com and go to the products page and sign -up for free e-course.

---

Take Charge! With Dr. Kathryn
**Kathryn Reeves**
102 Lifton Ct.
Roseville, CA  95747
Email: drkathryn@drkathrynonline.com
Phone: 916-663-8266
Website: http://www.drkathrynonline.com
Facebook: http://www.facebook.com/TakeChargeCoach
Twitter: drkathryn1

I provide spiritual guidance to those called to step onto the spiritual path. I require commitment and a willingness to let go of old, negative thought patterns and beliefs and to hold an open mind. Join my list on my website and receive a FREE "Spiritual Journey Starter Kit" as well as an opportunity to schedule a FREE Discovery phone call! Visit http://www.drkathrynonline.com

---

Talking Health with Linda
**Linda Giles**
talkinghealthwithlinda@gmail.com

www.ardysslife.com/lsgiles
FaceBook: http://www.facebook.com/lindastanleygiles
LinkedIn: https://twitter.com/pamper1956

---

**Michelle M. Miller**
Take The Lead Coaching Strategies
Nassau Bahamas
Email: coaching242@yahoo.com
Phone: 242-429-6770
Website: http://taketheleadbook.com
www.ttlcoaching.com

---

TaxMama®
**Eva Rosenberg, MBA, EA**
Phone:  800-594-9829   818-993-1565
Website:  www.TaxMama.com  Where taxes are fun!
Website:  www.TaxMama.com/TaxQuips   And Answers are free
Website:  www.IRSExams.com  Become an Enrolled Agent
Website:  www.MarketWatch.com   the TaxWatch column
Twitter:  www.twitter.com/taxmama

---

The Art Of Teamwork
**Vanora Spreen**
Vanora@TheArtofTeamwork.com
http://www.TheArtofTeamwork.com
FaceBook: http://facebook.com/theartofteamwork

Take the time to assess how your team is performing!  Visit our site
www.theartofteamwork.com and complete our free assessment!

---

The Chief Networking Officer
**Debra Faris**
debra.faris@yahoo.com
FaceBook: http://www.facebook.com/debrafaris
LinkedIn: www.linkedin.com/in/debrafaris
Twitter:  www.twitter.com/Connect2Debra

Coaching programs range from one-on-one, six-month projects & three-day boot camp. Open to out-of-state projects.  Call me for a Free 30 minute consultation at 949-233-1424 or text

---

The Enchanted Self
**Dr. Barbara Becker Holstein, Founder**
Phone:  732.571.1200
Website:  www.enchantedself.com

---

The Healer Within
**Victoria Douskos**
FaceBook: http://www.facebook.com/TheHealerWithinFanPage
LinkedIn: http://www.linkedin.com/profile/edit?trk=hb_tab_pro_top

---

The Natural Executive
**Timi Gleason**
Email:  timi.gleason@gmail.com
Phone:  619-333-6945 (google voice)
Website: www.fatandthirstyradio.com    www.thenaturalexecutive.com

Senior Health & Leadership Coach
"Specializing in quick weight loss & reducing the need for prescription drugs"

Email me with your name and address for my two free articles

---

The Productivity Experts
**Cathy Sexton**
cathy@theproductivityexperts.com
http://www.TheProductivityExperts.com
FaceBook: http://www.facebook.com/cathysextonproductivity
LinkedIn: http://www.linkedin.com/in/cathyasexton
Twitter: http://twitter.com/CathySexton

Ignite Your Performance and receive a free 23 page productivity tip ebook and a productivity assessment go to: http://cathysexton.com/ignite/

---

The Shattered Ceiling Corp
**Yvonne Silver**
24 Evansdale Landing NW
Calgary, Alb, Canada
Email: Yvonne@theshatteredceiling.com
Phone: 403-999-4749
Website: www.theshatteredceiling.com
LinkedIn: http://ca.linkedin.com/in/yvonnesilver
Twitter: www.twitter.com/shatteredsilver

---

Living Royalty Nation – "Coaching for Women that Literally Pays"
**Debora D. Jenkins**
Email: Admin@DeboraDJenkins.com
Phone: 718-644-0951
Website: http://www.deboradjenkins.com
Facebook: http://www.facebook.com/LivingRoyalty

---

The Vision Board Training
**Bonnie Bruderer**
Website: VisionBoardParties.com
Facebook: www.facebook.com/VisionBoards

Will you be the next business to have a Vision Board Kit? We make the product, you make $$$!
$500 of the private label fee www.TheVisionBoardTraining.com

---

The Voice of Thermography
**Dr. Robert L. Kane**
Phone: 650.868.0353
website: www.thermographyexpert.com

---

TheraPure.com Health Essentials
**Jeff Tollefson**
30776 Mirage Circle
Menifee, CA 92584
Email: jeff@therapure.com
Phone: 877-846-8669   951-679-3519

Website: http://www.therapure.com

Facebook: www.facebook.com/therapure

YouTube: www.youtube.com/therapure

---

**Kalin Thomas**

Email: kalinthomas@yahoo.com

Phone: 404-863-8182

Website: www.seetheworldproductions.com

For more on how Kalin got into the TV industry and travel writing, listen to her 1-hour interview with Raven at http://www.womenpower-radio.com/archives.html.

---

**Karen Tompkins**

Classical Feng Shui Consultant

Email: karen@fengshuibeyondthemyth.com

Phone: 214-774-9019

Website: www.FengShuiBeyondtheMyth.com

For *The 8 Myths of Feng Shui* and *From Hitler to Haiti, 56 Years of Feng Shui Influences on Global Events,* go to www.FengShuiBeyondtheMyth.com

---

Unforgettable Brands

**Judy Winslow**

5592 Eastwind Dr

Sarasota, FL 34233

Email: jw@unforgettablebrands.com

Phone: 941-921-7440

Website: http://www.unforgettablebrands.com

Facebook: https://www.facebook.com/judywins

LinkedIn: http://www.linkedin.com/in/judywins

Twitter: http://twitter.com/#!/judywin

We all want to be seen, heard and remembered. A sustainable business can change the lives of many. Touch more people -- Leave a lasting impression. For entrepreneurs and game-changers interested in accelerating results, start with my F.REE gift to you – the 'Being Unforgettable Starter Kit', which can be found at http://www.UnforgettableBrands.com

---

UpYourTeleSales
**Lynn Hidy**
PO Box 42
Paul Smiths, NY 12970
Email: lynn@upyourtelesales.com
Phone: 315-751-0146
Website: http://www.upyourtelesales.com
Facebook: https://www.facebook.com/pages/UpYourTeleSalescom/94567576544
LinkedIn: https://www.linkedin.com/in/lynnhidy
Twitter: http://twitter.com/#!/upyourtelesales

Sign up and receive our easy 3 step objection handling technique, never be surprised by the objections you hear the most again at http://tiny.cc/SignUpYourTeleSales

---

Victory House Publishing
**Carmen Cook**
CarmenCookOnline@Gmail.com
http://www.Make80BucksDaily.com
FaceBook: http://www.Facebook.com/1CarmenCook
LinkedIn: http://www.linkedin.com/in/CarmenLCoo
Twitter http://www.Twitter.com/TwitCarmen

---

Vision In Purpose Coaching and Training
**Anita Kirkman**
254 Wedgewood Terrace Rd,
Madison, AL 35757
Email: anita@visioininpurpose.com
Phone: 256.721.4553
Website: www.visioninpurpose.com
Facebook: http://bit.ly/visioninpurposefb
LinkedIn: http://linkd.in/coachanitak

ENLIGHTEN - EMPOWER – TRANSFORM. We empower home office business women to prosper by transforming their beliefs around time, money, self, and leadership. Get your "Success Building" Virtual Gift Bag including 3 powerful products that will reveal key money making mindsets that empower you to:

Conquer the five common mistakes that kill your revenue and keep you stuck.

Learn all about ideas that sales superstars use to become who they are today and how you can become like them too!

Master the mindsets behind the marketing that help you and your business grow healthily and smoothly.

---

**Dr. Taffy Wagner, D.Min**

Certified Educator in Personal Finances and Consultant www.WifeCFO.com
Email: drtaffy@wifecfo.com
Phone: 303-576-0670

For a no-cost report on how to settle debt, you can go to www.wifecfo.com/products

---

Weingart Book Publishing
**Linda M. Schulman**
weingartbookpublishing@hotmail.com
http://www.talesofwoofie.com
FaceBook: http://www.facebook.com/talesofwoofie
Twitter: http//:www.twitter.com/lindaschulman

Linda M. Schulman is a children's book illustrator and writer. Her publishing company Weingart Book Publishing published Linda's book series Tales of Woofie, and Tales of Woofie Book Two: The Rabbit Chase for 4 to 7 year olds. Visit http://talesofwoofie.com Email weingartbookpublishing@hotmail.com direct for a 40% discount.

---

Wellness Beyond Belief
**Khatira Aboulfatova**
230 Westcott St. Suite 215
Houston, TX  77007
Email: Khatira_a@wellnessbeyondbelief.com
Phone: 832-876-9147
Website: http://www.wellnessbeyondbelief.com
Facebook: http://www.facebook.com/khatira.aboulfatova
LinkedIn: http://www.linkedin.com/pub/khatira-aboulfatova-m-d/1/255/921

Being healthy is a lifestyle by design. Love working with people, who is looking for better ways to transform their health physically, mentally and financially. You can change the way you age naturally from inside and out; you will look and feel 10-20 years younger, vibrant and energetic like you were in your youth.  Visit http://www.wellnessbeyondbelief.com for more information.

---

Westchase Specialty Pharmacy
**Christina Barnett, Pharm.D.**
11301 Richmond Ave, St K-101
Houston, TX  77082
Email:  CBarnett@WestchaseRx.com
Phone:  281-497-5214
Fax:  281-497-5215
Website:  www.WestchaseRx.com
Facebook:  www.Facebook.com/WestchaseRx

People aren't made from cookie cutters; their medicine shouldn't be, either.  Westchase Specialty Pharmacy provides customized medications to match individual patients' needs.  Medicine can be made to address personal medical dilemmas like hormone and thyroid balance and pain management.  Medicine can be made to suit you better by combining multiple meds into fewer (smaller) capsules, making them into liquids or lozenges or lollipops, or making them sustained-release for fewer doses each day.  Medicines that are on back-order or have been discontinued by manufacturers can be provided by our team of specially trained compounders.  Even your pets – from fluffy to furry to feathery – can be medicated more easily and accurately with our help.  Visit the pharmacy for a tour of our amazing facility, to meet our outstanding Patient Care Team, and receive a special "Welcome Gift" of 50% your first Private Consultation or Personalized Nutritional Supplement Regimen.

---

Western & Southern Life
**Craig Anthony Nicholas**
Sales Representative
Phone: 800-289-0849
Website:  www.wslife.com

---

Wings for Women
**Keiko Hsu**
152 Lombard St #704
San Francisco, CA  94111
Email: keiko@wingsforwomen.net
Phone: 415-738-2313

Website: http://www.wingsforwomen.net
Facebook: http://www.facebook.com/pages/Wings-for-women/197249213658076
LinkedIn: http://www.linkedin.com/in/keikohsu
Twitter: http://www.wingsforwomen

Live a Joyful Life After Divorce ... Attain new heights in your life, career, relationships! www.WingsForWomen.net. If you're a busy, career-focused woman who is recently divorced and ready to move on to reinvent your life, visit our website www.WingsForWomen.net and get our free gifts: - A special report "Three Myths that Keep Women Trapped After Divorce ... and How to Break Free"- "Your Passions Discovery Tool" ... A Guide To Identify Your Top 5 Passions

---

Winning at Life International, LLC
LAWRENCE COLE
The Xtreme Marketing Guy
Email: lcole@xtrememarketingguy.com
Phone: 888.474.2161
Website: http://www.xtrememarketingguy.com
Facebook: http://www.facebook.com/xtrememarketingguy

To get your FREE report on "The 7 Deadly Sins of Small Business Marketing", Visit

http://www.xtrememarketingdoneforyou.com

---

Woman's Wellness Center

Terry Tribble, MBA, CMF
Email: info@houstonlacebrow.com
Phone: 713.522.PINK (7465)
Website: www.HoustonLaceBrows.com

---

Women On the Move in Ministry & Business
Elise Thompson
info@wommb.org
www.wommb.org
FaceBook: www.facebook.com/thewommb
Twitter www.twitter.com/wommbmedia

Women On the Move in Ministry & Business offers an international platform where women who are incubating their seeds of purpose can get spiritual and business nourishment to produce fruit that remains as positive forces within their local communities. To get Your Free mp3 download of a recent interview, follow her at www.wommb.org and get connected with Women On The Move In Ministry & Business!

---

WorldSpeak Language Preschools and In-Home Child Care System

**Angelika Putintseva**
Director and Founder
Email: info@WorldSpeakSchool.com
Phone: 310-441-5222
Website: www.WorldSpeakSchool.com

---

Your Angel Guide for Success
**Tami Gulland, ATP, CM**
5133 Caton Lane
Waunakee, WI 53597
Email: tami@angelsforsuccess.com
Phone: 608-850-6437
Website: www.angelsforsuccess.com
Facebook: http://www.facebook.com/tamigulland
LinkedIn: www.linkedin.com/in/tamigulland
Twitter: www.twitter.com/tamigulland

Reduce stress, struggle and overwhelm now! Increase your connection with your Angels and intuition. Get your free report "5 Surefire Steps to Get the Life and Career Answers You Need from Your Angels" at: www.AngelsForSuccess.com

---

Your Everyday Emotional Intelligence Coach
**Patricia Clason, RCC**
2437 N Booth St.
Milwaukee, WI 53212
Email: patricia@patriciaclason.com
Phone: 414-374-5433 / 800-236-4692
Website: http://www.patriciaclason.com
Facebook: www.facebook.com/patricia.clason

Linkedin: http://www.linkedin.com/in/patriciaclason
Twitter: http://twitter.com/EQCoachClason

Emotional Intelligence Coaching is inner strength training for success. Learn more with free resources at www.accountabilitycoachingassociates.comand a free e-book at www.lightly.com/faith. Since you are reading this book, you are my perfect client!!

---

# Dream Big and be Committed to Your Dream…. Make it more than a dream, make it a…reality!

I would like to thank the World's Greatest Mirror Illusionist, Elvis C. Walker, President and Founder of the Angle of Hope Foundation http://www.angleofhopee.com for creating this beautiful glass mural (shown below) and my **Big Dream which I INTEND to make happen – interviewing President Barack & Michelle Obama while they are in office.** While it didn't happen during his first term, I was confident of a second!

Remember, your dream belongs to you and you're responsible for making it happen. Never give up and take the action steps to manifest it, after all, it's your dream and Yes –
*YOU DESERVE IT! Whatever you do – go for your dreams!*

This is my Big Business Dream and I'm going after it…. What's yours?

Email me at raven@careersfromthekitchentable.com and tell me your Biggest Dream that you have for your business and how you intend to manifest it and you'll receive a personal word of encouragement from me (feel free to include your telephone number if you would prefer me to call you with my words of encouragement!)

You will also receive a "free" professionally produced commercial on your new product, service teleseminar, event or book launch. Your commercial will air on my popular www.careersfromthekitchentable.com show (a $197 value – yours free)

All volumes of Careers From the Kitchen Table Home Business Directory are available!

Celebrity and guru interviews, stories of success and inspiration and quick recipes for the busy entrepreneur!

Available via Print, E-Book or Kindle!

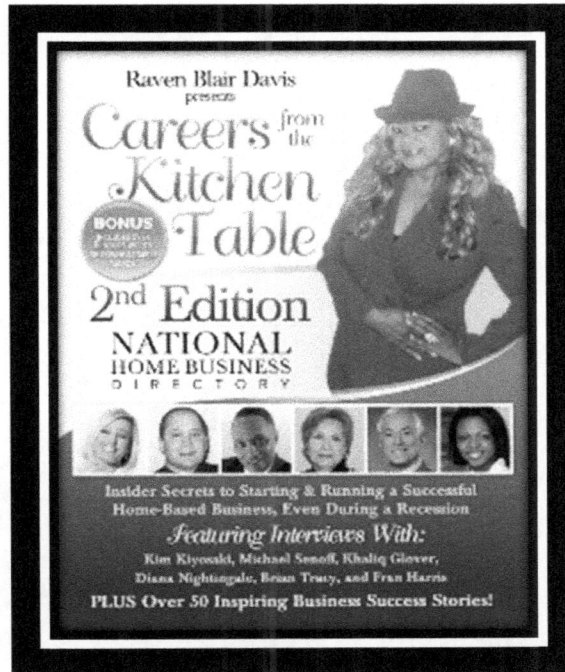

Visit http://www.CareersfromtheKitchenTable.com/Directories for more information and to also find hours of bonus audios too!

www.ingramcontent.com/pod-product-compliance
Lightning Source LLC
Chambersburg PA
CBHW082129210326
41599CB00031B/5915